50% OFF
Online TSI Prep Course!

By Mometrix

Dear Customer,

We consider it an honor and a privilege that you chose our TSI Study Guide. As a way of showing our appreciation and to help us better serve you, we are offering **50% off our online TSI Prep Course**. Many TSI courses are needlessly expensive and don't deliver enough value. With our course, you get access to the best TSI prep material, and **you only pay half price**.

We have structured our online course to perfectly complement your printed study guide. The TSI Prep Course contains **in-depth lessons** that cover all the most important topics, **220+ video reviews** that explain difficult concepts, over **1,150+ practice questions** to ensure you feel prepared, and over **300 digital flashcards**, so you can study while you're on the go.

Online TSI Prep Course

Topics Covered:
- Mathematics
    - *Elementary Algebra and Functions*
    - *Intermediate Algebra and Functions*
    - *Geometry and Measurement*
    - *Data Analysis, Statistics, and Probability*
- Reading
    - *Literary Analysis*
    - *Main Idea and Supporting Details*
    - *Inferences in a Text or Texts*
    - *Author's Use of Language*
- Writing
    - *Foundations of Grammar and Punctuation*
    - *Essay Revision and Sentence Logic*
    - *Agreement and Sentence Structure*

Course Features:
- TSI Study Guide
    - Get content that complements our best-selling study guide.
- 9 Full-Length Practice Tests
    - With over 1050 practice questions, you can test yourself again and again.
- Mobile Friendly
    - If you need to study on the go, the course is easily accessible from your mobile device.
- TSI Flashcards
    - Our course includes a flashcard mode consisting of over 300 content cards to help you study.

To receive this discount, simply head to our website at mometrix.com/university/tsi or simply scan this QR code with your smartphone. At the checkout page, enter the discount code: **tsi50off**

If you have any questions or concerns, please contact us at support@mometrix.com.

Sincerely,

Access Your Online Resources

Don't miss out on the Online Resources included with your purchase!

Your purchase of this product unlocks access to our Online Resources page. Elevate your study experience with our **interactive practice test interface**, along with all of the additional resources that we couldn't include in this book.

Flip to the Online Resources section at the end of this book to find the link and a QR code to get started!

TSI Math

Study Guide 2025-2026

Prep Secrets for the Texas Success Initiative Assessment

5 Full-Length Practice Tests

100+ Online Video Tutorials

3rd Edition Book

Copyright © 2025 by Mometrix Media LLC

All rights reserved. This product, or parts thereof, may not be reproduced, stored in a retrieval system, or transmitted in any form or by any means—electronic, mechanical, photocopy, recording, scanning, or other—except for brief quotations in critical reviews or articles, without the prior written permission of the publisher.

Written and edited by Matthew Bowling

Printed in the United States of America

This paper meets the requirements of ANSI/NISO Z39.48-1992 (Permanence of Paper).

Mometrix offers volume discount pricing to institutions. For more information or a price quote, please contact our sales department at sales@mometrix.com or 888-248-1219.

Mometrix Media LLC is not affiliated with or endorsed by any official testing organization. All organizational and test names are trademarks of their respective owners.

Paperback
ISBN 13: 978-1-5167-2734-6
ISBN 10: 1-5167-2734-7

Dear Future Exam Success Story

First of all, **THANK YOU** for purchasing Mometrix study materials!

Second, congratulations! You are one of the few determined test-takers who are committed to doing whatever it takes to excel on your exam. **You have come to the right place.** We developed these study materials with one goal in mind: to deliver you the information you need in a format that's concise and easy to use.

In addition to optimizing your guide for the content of the test, we've outlined our recommended steps for breaking down the preparation process into small, attainable goals so you can make sure you stay on track.

We've also analyzed the entire test-taking process, identifying the most common pitfalls and showing how you can overcome them and be ready for any curveball the test throws you.

Standardized testing is one of the biggest obstacles on your road to success, which only increases the importance of doing well in the high-pressure, high-stakes environment of test day. Your results on this test could have a significant impact on your future, and this guide provides the information and practical advice to help you achieve your full potential on test day.

Your success is our success

We would love to hear from you! If you would like to share the story of your exam success or if you have any questions or comments in regard to our products, please contact us at **800-673-8175** or **support@mometrix.com**.

Thanks again for your business and we wish you continued success!

Sincerely,
The Mometrix Test Preparation Team

Need more help? Check out our flashcards at:
http://MometrixFlashcards.com/TSI

TABLE OF CONTENTS

INTRODUCTION	1
SECRET KEY #1 – PLAN BIG, STUDY SMALL	2
SECRET KEY #2 – MAKE YOUR STUDYING COUNT	3
SECRET KEY #3 – PRACTICE THE RIGHT WAY	4
SECRET KEY #4 – HAVE A PLAN FOR GUESSING	5
TEST-TAKING STRATEGIES	8
QUANTITATIVE REASONING	**13**
OPERATIONS	13
SUBTRACTION WITH REGROUPING	15
ORDER OF OPERATIONS	16
PROPERTIES OF OPERATIONS	17
PROPERTIES OF EXPONENTS	18
FRACTIONS	19
DECIMALS	22
PERCENTAGES	24
CONVERTING BETWEEN PERCENTAGES, FRACTIONS, AND DECIMALS	25
RATIONAL AND IRRATIONAL NUMBERS	26
PROPORTIONS AND RATIOS	27
CROSS MULTIPLICATION	28
LINEAR EXPRESSIONS	29
SLOPE	29
ALGEBRAIC REASONING	**31**
LINEAR EQUATIONS	31
SOLVING EQUATIONS	32
GRAPHING EQUATIONS	37
INEQUALITIES	39
SOLVING INEQUALITIES	39
GRAPHING INEQUALITIES	41
SYSTEMS OF EQUATIONS	44
POLYNOMIALS	47
RATIONAL AND IRRATIONAL EXPRESSIONS	50
QUADRATICS	52
BASICS OF FUNCTIONS	55
COMMON FUNCTIONS	60
GEOMETRIC AND SPATIAL REASONING	**68**
METRIC AND CUSTOMARY MEASUREMENTS	68
POLYGONS	70
APOTHEM AND RADIUS	71
CONGRUENCE AND SIMILARITY	71
LINE OF SYMMETRY	73
TRIANGLES	73

- Triangle Properties — 74
- Quadrilaterals — 76
- Circles — 81
- 3D Shapes — 82
- Pythagorean Theorem — 85
- Trigonometric Formulas — 85

Probabilistic and Statistical Reasoning — 87
- Probability — 87
- Two-Way Frequency Tables — 91
- Data Analysis — 91
- Measures of Central Tendency — 95
- Displaying Information — 97
- Scatter Plots — 103

TSI Math Practice Test #1 — 105
Answer Key and Explanations for Test #1 — 110
TSI Math Practice Test #2 — 114
Answer Key and Explanations for Test #2 — 118
TSI Math Practice Test #3 — 122
Answer Key and Explanations for Test #3 — 128
TSI Math Practice Test #4 — 132
Answer Key and Explanations for Test #4 — 139
TSI Math Practice Test #5 — 142
- Mathematics — 142
Answer Key and Explanations for Test #5 — 148
- Mathematics — 148
TSI Math Practice Test #6 — 151
Answer Key and Explanations for Test #6 — 156
TSI Math Practice Test #7 — 161
- Mathematics — 161
Answer Key and Explanations for Test #7 — 168
- Mathematics — 168
TSI Math Practice Test #8 — 171
- Mathematics — 171
Answer Key and Explanations for Test #8 — 178
- Mathematics — 178
TSI Math Practice Test #9 — 181
- Mathematics — 181
Answer Key and Explanations for Test #9 — 187
- Mathematics — 187

TSI Math Practice Test #10 _____ **190**
   MATHEMATICS _____ 190
ANSWER KEY AND EXPLANATIONS FOR TEST #1 _____ **195**
   MATHEMATICS _____ 195
HOW TO OVERCOME TEST ANXIETY _____ **200**
ONLINE RESOURCES _____ **206**

Introduction

Thank you for purchasing this resource! You have made the choice to prepare yourself for a test that could have a huge impact on your future, and this guide is designed to help you be fully ready for test day. Obviously, it's important to have a solid understanding of the test material, but you also need to be prepared for the unique environment and stressors of the test, so that you can perform to the best of your abilities.

For this purpose, the first section that appears in this guide is the **Secret Keys**. We've devoted countless hours to meticulously researching what works and what doesn't, and we've boiled down our findings to the four most impactful steps you can take to improve your performance on the test. We start at the beginning with study planning and move through the preparation process, all the way to the testing strategies that will help you get the most out of what you know when you're finally sitting in front of the test.

We recommend that you start preparing for your test as far in advance as possible. However, if you've bought this guide as a last-minute study resource and only have a few days before your test, we recommend that you skip over the first two Secret Keys since they address a long-term study plan.

If you struggle with **test anxiety**, we strongly encourage you to check out our recommendations for how you can overcome it. Test anxiety is a formidable foe, but it can be beaten, and we want to make sure you have the tools you need to defeat it.

Secret Key #1 – Plan Big, Study Small

There's a lot riding on your performance. If you want to ace this test, you're going to need to keep your skills sharp and the material fresh in your mind. You need a plan that lets you review everything you need to know while still fitting in your schedule. We'll break this strategy down into three categories.

Information Organization

Start with the information you already have: the official test outline. From this, you can make a complete list of all the concepts you need to cover before the test. Organize these concepts into groups that can be studied together, and create a list of any related vocabulary you need to learn so you can brush up on any difficult terms. You'll want to keep this vocabulary list handy once you actually start studying since you may need to add to it along the way.

Time Management

Once you have your set of study concepts, decide how to spread them out over the time you have left before the test. Break your study plan into small, clear goals so you have a manageable task for each day and know exactly what you're doing. Then just focus on one small step at a time. When you manage your time this way, you don't need to spend hours at a time studying. Studying a small block of content for a short period each day helps you retain information better and avoid stressing over how much you have left to do. You can relax knowing that you have a plan to cover everything in time. In order for this strategy to be effective though, you have to start studying early and stick to your schedule. Avoid the exhaustion and futility that comes from last-minute cramming!

Study Environment

The environment you study in has a big impact on your learning. Studying in a coffee shop, while probably more enjoyable, is not likely to be as fruitful as studying in a quiet room. It's important to keep distractions to a minimum. You're only planning to study for a short block of time, so make the most of it. Don't pause to check your phone or get up to find a snack. It's also important to **avoid multitasking**. Research has consistently shown that multitasking will make your studying dramatically less effective. Your study area should also be comfortable and well-lit so you don't have the distraction of straining your eyes or sitting on an uncomfortable chair.

The time of day you study is also important. You want to be rested and alert. Don't wait until just before bedtime. Study when you'll be most likely to comprehend and remember. Even better, if you know what time of day your test will be, set that time aside for study. That way your brain will be used to working on that subject at that specific time and you'll have a better chance of recalling information.

Finally, it can be helpful to team up with others who are studying for the same test. Your actual studying should be done in as isolated an environment as possible, but the work of organizing the information and setting up the study plan can be divided up. In between study sessions, you can discuss with your teammates the concepts that you're all studying and quiz each other on the details. Just be sure that your teammates are as serious about the test as you are. If you find that your study time is being replaced with social time, you might need to find a new team.

Secret Key #2 – Make Your Studying Count

You're devoting a lot of time and effort to preparing for this test, so you want to be absolutely certain it will pay off. This means doing more than just reading the content and hoping you can remember it on test day. It's important to make every minute of study count. There are two main areas you can focus on to make your studying count.

Retention

It doesn't matter how much time you study if you can't remember the material. You need to make sure you are retaining the concepts. To check your retention of the information you're learning, try recalling it at later times with minimal prompting. Try carrying around flashcards and glance at one or two from time to time or ask a friend who's also studying for the test to quiz you.

To enhance your retention, look for ways to put the information into practice so that you can apply it rather than simply recalling it. If you're using the information in practical ways, it will be much easier to remember. Similarly, it helps to solidify a concept in your mind if you're not only reading it to yourself but also explaining it to someone else. Ask a friend to let you teach them about a concept you're a little shaky on (or speak aloud to an imaginary audience if necessary). As you try to summarize, define, give examples, and answer your friend's questions, you'll understand the concepts better and they will stay with you longer. Finally, step back for a big picture view and ask yourself how each piece of information fits with the whole subject. When you link the different concepts together and see them working together as a whole, it's easier to remember the individual components.

Finally, practice showing your work on any multi-step problems, even if you're just studying. Writing out each step you take to solve a problem will help solidify the process in your mind, and you'll be more likely to remember it during the test.

Modality

Modality simply refers to the means or method by which you study. Choosing a study modality that fits your own individual learning style is crucial. No two people learn best in exactly the same way, so it's important to know your strengths and use them to your advantage.

For example, if you learn best by visualization, focus on visualizing a concept in your mind and draw an image or a diagram. Try color-coding your notes, illustrating them, or creating symbols that will trigger your mind to recall a learned concept. If you learn best by hearing or discussing information, find a study partner who learns the same way or read aloud to yourself. Think about how to put the information in your own words. Imagine that you are giving a lecture on the topic and record yourself so you can listen to it later.

For any learning style, flashcards can be helpful. Organize the information so you can take advantage of spare moments to review. Underline key words or phrases. Use different colors for different categories. Mnemonic devices (such as creating a short list in which every item starts with the same letter) can also help with retention. Find what works best for you and use it to store the information in your mind most effectively and easily.

Secret Key #3 – Practice the Right Way

Your success on test day depends not only on how many hours you put into preparing, but also on whether you prepared the right way. It's good to check along the way to see if your studying is paying off. One of the most effective ways to do this is by taking practice tests to evaluate your progress. Practice tests are useful because they show exactly where you need to improve. Every time you take a practice test, pay special attention to these three groups of questions:

- The questions you got wrong
- The questions you had to guess on, even if you guessed right
- The questions you found difficult or slow to work through

This will show you exactly what your weak areas are, and where you need to devote more study time. Ask yourself why each of these questions gave you trouble. Was it because you didn't understand the material? Was it because you didn't remember the vocabulary? Do you need more repetitions on this type of question to build speed and confidence? Dig into those questions and figure out how you can strengthen your weak areas as you go back to review the material.

Additionally, many practice tests have a section explaining the answer choices. It can be tempting to read the explanation and think that you now have a good understanding of the concept. However, an explanation likely only covers part of the question's broader context. Even if the explanation makes perfect sense, **go back and investigate** every concept related to the question until you're positive you have a thorough understanding.

As you go along, keep in mind that the practice test is just that: practice. Memorizing these questions and answers will not be very helpful on the actual test because it is unlikely to have any of the same exact questions. If you only know the right answers to the sample questions, you won't be prepared for the real thing. **Study the concepts** until you understand them fully, and then you'll be able to answer any question that shows up on the test.

It's important to wait on the practice tests until you're ready. If you take a test on your first day of study, you may be overwhelmed by the amount of material covered and how much you need to learn. Work up to it gradually.

On test day, you'll need to be prepared for answering questions, managing your time, and using the test-taking strategies you've learned. It's a lot to balance, like a mental marathon that will have a big impact on your future. Like training for a marathon, you'll need to start slowly and work your way up. When test day arrives, you'll be ready.

Start with the strategies you've read in the first two Secret Keys—plan your course and study in the way that works best for you. If you have time, consider using multiple study resources to get different approaches to the same concepts. It can be helpful to see difficult concepts from more than one angle. Then find a good source for practice tests. Many times, the test website will suggest potential study resources or provide sample tests.

Secret Key #4 – Have a Plan for Guessing

When you're taking the test, you may find yourself stuck on a question. Some of the answer choices seem better than others, but you don't see the one answer choice that is obviously correct. What do you do?

The scenario described above is very common, yet most test takers have not effectively prepared for it. Developing and practicing a plan for guessing may be one of the single most effective uses of your time as you get ready for the exam.

In developing your plan for guessing, there are three questions to address:

- When should you start the guessing process?
- How should you narrow down the choices?
- Which answer should you choose?

When to Start the Guessing Process

Unless your plan for guessing is to select C every time (which, despite its merits, is not what we recommend), you need to leave yourself enough time to apply your answer elimination strategies. Since you have a limited amount of time for each question, that means that if you're going to give yourself the best shot at guessing correctly, you have to decide quickly whether or not you will guess.

Of course, the best-case scenario is that you don't have to guess at all, so first, see if you can answer the question based on your knowledge of the subject and basic reasoning skills. Focus on the key words in the question and try to jog your memory of related topics. Give yourself a chance to bring the knowledge to mind, but once you realize that you don't have (or you can't access) the knowledge you need to answer the question, it's time to start the guessing process.

It's almost always better to start the guessing process too early than too late. It only takes a few seconds to remember something and answer the question from knowledge. Carefully eliminating wrong answer choices takes longer. Plus, going through the process of eliminating answer choices can actually help jog your memory.

Summary: Start the guessing process as soon as you decide that you can't answer the question based on your knowledge.

How to Narrow Down the Choices

The next chapter in this book (**Test-Taking Strategies**) includes a wide range of strategies for how to approach questions and how to look for answer choices to eliminate. You will definitely want to read those carefully, practice them, and figure out which ones work best for you. Here though, we're going to address a mindset rather than a particular strategy.

Your odds of guessing an answer correctly depend on how many options you are choosing from.

Number of options left	5	4	3	2	1
Odds of guessing correctly	20%	25%	33%	50%	100%

You can see from this chart just how valuable it is to be able to eliminate incorrect answers and make an educated guess, but there are two things that many test takers do that cause them to miss out on the benefits of guessing:

- Accidentally eliminating the correct answer
- Selecting an answer based on an impression

We'll look at the first one here, and the second one in the next section.

To avoid accidentally eliminating the correct answer, we recommend a thought exercise called **the $5 challenge**. In this challenge, you only eliminate an answer choice from contention if you are willing to bet $5 on it being wrong. Why $5? Five dollars is a small but not insignificant amount of money. It's an amount you could afford to lose but wouldn't want to throw away. And while losing $5 once might not hurt too much, doing it twenty times will set you back $100. In the same way, each small decision you make—eliminating a choice here, guessing on a question there—won't by itself impact your score very much, but when you put them all together, they can make a big difference. By holding each answer choice elimination decision to a higher standard, you can reduce the risk of accidentally eliminating the correct answer.

The $5 challenge can also be applied in a positive sense: If you are willing to bet $5 that an answer choice *is* correct, go ahead and mark it as correct.

Summary: Only eliminate an answer choice if you are willing to bet $5 that it is wrong.

Which Answer to Choose

You're taking the test. You've run into a hard question and decided you'll have to guess. You've eliminated all the answer choices you're willing to bet $5 on. Now you have to pick an answer. Why do we even need to talk about this? Why can't you just pick whichever one you feel like when the time comes?

The answer to these questions is that if you don't come into the test with a plan, you'll rely on your impression to select an answer choice, and if you do that, you risk falling into a trap. The test writers know that everyone who takes their test will be guessing on some of the questions, so they intentionally write wrong answer choices to seem plausible. You still have to pick an answer though, and if the wrong answer choices are designed to look right, how can you ever be sure that you're not falling for their trap? The best solution we've found to this dilemma is to take the decision out of your hands entirely. Here is the process we recommend:

Once you've eliminated any choices that you are confident (willing to bet $5) are wrong, select the first remaining choice as your answer.

Whether you choose to select the first remaining choice, the second, or the last, the important thing is that you use some preselected standard. Using this approach guarantees that you will not be enticed into selecting an answer choice that looks right, because you are not basing your decision on how the answer choices look.

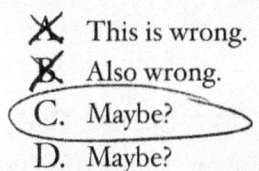

This is not meant to make you question your knowledge. Instead, it is to help you recognize the difference between your knowledge and your impressions. There's a huge difference between thinking an answer is right because of what you know, and thinking an answer is right because it looks or sounds like it should be right.

Summary: To ensure that your selection is appropriately random, make a predetermined selection from among all answer choices you have not eliminated.

Test-Taking Strategies

This section contains a list of test-taking strategies that you may find helpful as you work through the test. By taking what you know and applying logical thought, you can maximize your chances of answering any question correctly!

It is very important to realize that every question is different and every person is different: no single strategy will work on every question, and no single strategy will work for every person. That's why we've included all of them here, so you can try them out and determine which ones work best for different types of questions and which ones work best for you.

Question Strategies

⊘ READ CAREFULLY

Read the question and the answer choices carefully. Don't miss the question because you misread the terms. You have plenty of time to read each question thoroughly and make sure you understand what is being asked. Yet a happy medium must be attained, so don't waste too much time. You must read carefully and efficiently.

⊘ CONTEXTUAL CLUES

Look for contextual clues. If the question includes a word you are not familiar with, look at the immediate context for some indication of what the word might mean. Contextual clues can often give you all the information you need to decipher the meaning of an unfamiliar word. Even if you can't determine the meaning, you may be able to narrow down the possibilities enough to make a solid guess at the answer to the question.

⊘ PREFIXES

If you're having trouble with a word in the question or answer choices, try dissecting it. Take advantage of every clue that the word might include. Prefixes can be a huge help. Usually, they allow you to determine a basic meaning. *Pre-* means before, *post-* means after, *pro-* is positive, *de-* is negative. From prefixes, you can get an idea of the general meaning of the word and try to put it into context.

⊘ HEDGE WORDS

Watch out for critical hedge words, such as *likely, may, can, sometimes, often, almost, mostly, usually, generally, rarely,* and *sometimes.* Question writers insert these hedge phrases to cover every possibility. Often an answer choice will be wrong simply because it leaves no room for exception. Be on guard for answer choices that have definitive words such as *exactly* and *always.*

⊘ SWITCHBACK WORDS

Stay alert for *switchbacks.* These are the words and phrases frequently used to alert you to shifts in thought. The most common switchback words are *but, although,* and *however.* Others include *nevertheless, on the other hand, even though, while, in spite of, despite,* and *regardless of.* Switchback words are important to catch because they can change the direction of the question or an answer choice.

⊘ Face Value

When in doubt, use common sense. Accept the situation in the problem at face value. Don't read too much into it. These problems will not require you to make wild assumptions. If you have to go beyond creativity and warp time or space in order to have an answer choice fit the question, then you should move on and consider the other answer choices. These are normal problems rooted in reality. The applicable relationship or explanation may not be readily apparent, but it is there for you to figure out. Use your common sense to interpret anything that isn't clear.

Answer Choice Strategies

⊘ Answer Selection

The most thorough way to pick an answer choice is to identify and eliminate wrong answers until only one is left, then confirm it is the correct answer. Sometimes an answer choice may immediately seem right, but be careful. The test writers will usually put more than one reasonable answer choice on each question, so take a second to read all of them and make sure that the other choices are not equally obvious. As long as you have time left, it is better to read every answer choice than to pick the first one that looks right without checking the others.

⊘ Answer Choice Families

An answer choice family consists of two (in rare cases, three) answer choices that are very similar in construction and cannot all be true at the same time. If you see two answer choices that are direct opposites or parallels, one of them is usually the correct answer. For instance, if one answer choice says that quantity x increases and another either says that quantity x decreases (opposite) or says that quantity y increases (parallel), then those answer choices would fall into the same family. An answer choice that doesn't match the construction of the answer choice family is more likely to be incorrect. Most questions will not have answer choice families, but when they do appear, you should be prepared to recognize them.

⊘ Eliminate Answers

Eliminate answer choices as soon as you realize they are wrong, but make sure you consider all possibilities. If you are eliminating answer choices and realize that the last one you are left with is also wrong, don't panic. Start over and consider each choice again. There may be something you missed the first time that you will realize on the second pass.

⊘ Avoid Fact Traps

Don't be distracted by an answer choice that is factually true but doesn't answer the question. You are looking for the choice that answers the question. Stay focused on what the question is asking for so you don't accidentally pick an answer that is true but incorrect. Always go back to the question and make sure the answer choice you've selected actually answers the question and is not merely a true statement.

⊘ Extreme Statements

In general, you should avoid answers that put forth extreme actions as standard practice or proclaim controversial ideas as established fact. An answer choice that states the "process should be used in certain situations, if…" is much more likely to be correct than one that states the "process should be discontinued completely." The first is a calm rational statement and doesn't even make a definitive, uncompromising stance, using a hedge word *if* to provide wiggle room, whereas the second choice is far more extreme.

✓ BENCHMARK

As you read through the answer choices and you come across one that seems to answer the question well, mentally select that answer choice. This is not your final answer, but it's the one that will help you evaluate the other answer choices. The one that you selected is your benchmark or standard for judging each of the other answer choices. Every other answer choice must be compared to your benchmark. That choice is correct until proven otherwise by another answer choice beating it. If you find a better answer, then that one becomes your new benchmark. Once you've decided that no other choice answers the question as well as your benchmark, you have your final answer.

✓ PREDICT THE ANSWER

Before you even start looking at the answer choices, it is often best to try to predict the answer. When you come up with the answer on your own, it is easier to avoid distractions and traps because you will know exactly what to look for. The right answer choice is unlikely to be word-for-word what you came up with, but it should be a close match. Even if you are confident that you have the right answer, you should still take the time to read each option before moving on.

General Strategies

✓ TOUGH QUESTIONS

If you are stumped on a problem or it appears too hard or too difficult, don't waste time. Move on! Remember though, if you can quickly check for obviously incorrect answer choices, your chances of guessing correctly are greatly improved. Before you completely give up, at least try to knock out a couple of possible answers. Eliminate what you can and then guess at the remaining answer choices before moving on.

✓ CHECK YOUR WORK

Since you will probably not know every term listed and the answer to every question, it is important that you get credit for the ones that you do know. Don't miss any questions through careless mistakes. If at all possible, try to take a second to look back over your answer selection and make sure you've selected the correct answer choice and haven't made a costly careless mistake (such as marking an answer choice that you didn't mean to mark). This quick double check should more than pay for itself in caught mistakes for the time it costs.

✓ DON'T RUSH

It is very easy to make errors when you are in a hurry. Maintaining a fast pace in answering questions is pointless if it makes you miss questions that you would have gotten right otherwise. Test writers like to include distracting information and wrong answers that seem right. Taking a little extra time to avoid careless mistakes can make all the difference in your test score. Find a pace that allows you to be confident in the answers that you select.

✓ KEEP MOVING

Panicking will not help you pass the test, so do your best to stay calm and keep moving. Taking deep breaths and going through the answer elimination steps you practiced can help to break through a stress barrier and keep your pace.

Final Notes

The combination of a solid foundation of content knowledge and the confidence that comes from practicing your plan for applying that knowledge is the key to maximizing your performance on test day. As your foundation of content knowledge is built up and strengthened, you'll find that the strategies included in this chapter become more and more effective in helping you quickly sift through the distractions and traps of the test to isolate the correct answer.

Now that you're preparing to move forward into the test content chapters of this book, be sure to keep your goal in mind. As you read, think about how you will be able to apply this information on the test. If you've already seen sample questions for the test and you have an idea of the question format and style, try to come up with questions of your own that you can answer based on what you're reading. This will give you valuable practice applying your knowledge in the same ways you can expect to on test day.

Good luck and good studying!

Quantitative Reasoning

Operations

An **operation** is simply a mathematical process that takes some value(s) as input(s) and produces an output. Elementary operations are often written in the following form: *value operation value*. For instance, in the expression $1 + 2$ the values are 1 and 2 and the operation is addition. Performing the operation gives the output of 3. In this way we can say that $1 + 2$ and 3 are equal, or $1 + 2 = 3$.

ADDITION

Addition increases the value of one quantity by the value of another quantity (both called **addends**). Example: $2 + 4 = 6$ or $8 + 9 = 17$. The result is called the **sum**. With addition, the order does not matter, $4 + 2 = 2 + 4$.

When adding signed numbers, if the signs are the same simply add the absolute values of the addends and apply the original sign to the sum. For example, $(+4) + (+8) = +12$ and $(-4) + (-8) = -12$. When the original signs are different, take the absolute values of the addends and subtract the smaller value from the larger value, then apply the original sign of the larger value to the difference. Example: $(+4) + (-8) = -4$ and $(-4) + (+8) = +4$.

SUBTRACTION

Subtraction is the opposite operation to addition; it decreases the value of one quantity (the **minuend**) by the value of another quantity (the **subtrahend**). For example, $6 - 4 = 2$ or $17 - 8 = 9$. The result is called the **difference**. Note that with subtraction, the order does matter, $6 - 4 \neq 4 - 6$.

For subtracting signed numbers, change the sign of the subtrahend and then follow the same rules used for addition. Example: $(+4) - (+8) = (+4) + (-8) = -4$

MULTIPLICATION

Multiplication can be thought of as repeated addition. One number (the **multiplier**) indicates how many times to add the other number (the **multiplicand**) to itself. Example: $3 \times 2 = 2 + 2 + 2 = 6$. With multiplication, the order does not matter, $2 \times 3 = 3 \times 2$ or $3 + 3 = 2 + 2 + 2$, either way the result (the **product**) is the same.

If the signs are the same, the product is positive when multiplying signed numbers. Example: $(+4) \times (+8) = +32$ and $(-4) \times (-8) = +32$. If the signs are opposite, the product is negative. Example: $(+4) \times (-8) = -32$ and $(-4) \times (+8) = -32$. When more than two factors are multiplied together, the sign of the product is determined by how many negative factors are present. If there are an odd number of negative factors then the product is negative, whereas an even number of negative factors indicates a positive product. Example: $(+4) \times (-8) \times (-2) = +64$ and $(-4) \times (-8) \times (-2) = -64$.

DIVISION

Division is the opposite operation to multiplication; one number (the **divisor**) tells us how many parts to divide the other number (the **dividend**) into. The result of division is called the **quotient**. Example: $20 \div 4 = 5$. If 20 is split into 4 equal parts, each part is 5. With division, the order of the numbers does matter, $20 \div 4 \neq 4 \div 20$.

The rules for dividing signed numbers are similar to multiplying signed numbers. If the dividend and divisor have the same sign, the quotient is positive. If the dividend and divisor have opposite signs, the quotient is negative. Example: $(-4) \div (+8) = -0.5$.

> **Review Video: Mathematical Operations**
> Visit mometrix.com/academy and enter code: 208095

PARENTHESES

Parentheses are used to designate which operations should be done first when there are multiple operations. Example: $4 - (2 + 1) = 1$; the parentheses tell us that we must add 2 and 1, and then subtract the sum from 4, rather than subtracting 2 from 4 and then adding 1 (this would give us an answer of 3).

> **Review Video: Mathematical Parentheses**
> Visit mometrix.com/academy and enter code: 978600

EXPONENTS

An **exponent** is a superscript number placed next to another number at the top right. It indicates how many times the base number is to be multiplied by itself. Exponents provide a shorthand way to write what would be a longer mathematical expression, Example: $2^4 = 2 \times 2 \times 2 \times 2$. A number with an exponent of 2 is said to be "squared," while a number with an exponent of 3 is said to be "cubed." The value of a number raised to an exponent is called its power. So 8^4 is read as "8 to the 4th power," or "8 raised to the power of 4."

> **Review Video: Exponents**
> Visit mometrix.com/academy and enter code: 600998

ROOTS

A **root**, such as a square root, is another way of writing a fractional exponent. Instead of using a superscript, roots use the radical symbol ($\sqrt{}$) to indicate the operation. A radical will have a number underneath the bar, and may sometimes have a number in the upper left: $\sqrt[n]{a}$, read as "the nth root of a." The relationship between radical notation and exponent notation can be described by this equation:

$$\sqrt[n]{a} = a^{\frac{1}{n}}$$

The two special cases of $n = 2$ and $n = 3$ are called square roots and cube roots. If there is no number to the upper left, the radical is understood to be a square root ($n = 2$). Nearly all of the roots you encounter will be square roots. A square root is the same as a number raised to the one-half power. When we say that a is the square root of b ($a = \sqrt{b}$), we mean that a multiplied by itself equals b: ($a \times a = b$).

A **perfect square** is a number that has an integer for its square root. There are 10 perfect squares from 1 to 100: 1, 4, 9, 16, 25, 36, 49, 64, 81, 100 (the squares of integers 1 through 10).

> **Review Video: Roots**
> Visit mometrix.com/academy and enter code: 795655
>
> **Review Video: Perfect Squares and Square Roots**
> Visit mometrix.com/academy and enter code: 648063

WORD PROBLEMS AND MATHEMATICAL SYMBOLS

When working on word problems, you must be able to translate verbal expressions or "math words" into math symbols. This chart contains several "math words" and their appropriate symbols:

Phrase	Symbol
equal, is, was, will be, has, costs, gets to, is the same as, becomes	=
times, of, multiplied by, product of, twice, doubles, halves, triples	×
divided by, per, ratio of/to, out of	÷
plus, added to, sum, combined, and, more than, totals of	+
subtracted from, less than, decreased by, minus, difference between	−
what, how much, original value, how many, a number, a variable	x, n, etc.

Review Video: Understanding Word Problems
Visit mometrix.com/academy and enter code: 499199

EXAMPLES OF TRANSLATED MATHEMATICAL PHRASES

- The phrase four more than twice a number can be written algebraically as $2x + 4$.
- The phrase half a number decreased by six can be written algebraically as $\frac{1}{2}x - 6$.
- The phrase the sum of a number and the product of five and that number can be written algebraically as $x + 5x$.
- You may see a test question that says, "Olivia is constructing a bookcase from seven boards. Two of them are for vertical supports and five are for shelves. The height of the bookcase is twice the width of the bookcase. If the seven boards total 36 feet in length, what will be the height of Olivia's bookcase?" You would need to make a sketch and then create the equation to determine the width of the shelves. The height can be represented as double the width. (If x represents the width of the shelves in feet, then the height of the bookcase is $2x$. Since the seven boards total 36 feet, $2x + 2x + x + x + x + x + x = 36$ or $9x = 36$; $x = 4$. The height is twice the width, or 8 feet.)

Subtraction with Regrouping

A great way to make use of some of the features built into the decimal system would be regrouping when attempting longform subtraction operations. When subtracting within a place value, sometimes the minuend is smaller than the subtrahend, **regrouping** enables you to 'borrow' a unit from a place value to the left in order to get a positive difference. For example, consider subtracting 189 from 525 with regrouping.

First, set up the subtraction problem in vertical form:

```
  525
− 189
```

Notice that the numbers in the ones and tens columns of 525 are smaller than the numbers in the ones and tens columns of 189. This means you will need to use regrouping to perform subtraction:

```
   5  2  5
−  1  8  9
```

To subtract 9 from 5 in the ones column you will need to borrow from the 2 in the tens columns:

```
    5   1   15
-   1   8    9
            6
```

Next, to subtract 8 from 1 in the tens column you will need to borrow from the 5 in the hundreds column:

```
    4   11  15
-   1    8   9
         3   6
```

Last, subtract the 1 from the 4 in the hundreds column:

```
    4   11  15
-   1    8   9
    3    3   6
```

Review Video: **Subtracting Large Numbers**
Visit mometrix.com/academy and enter code: 603350

Order of Operations

The **order of operations** is a set of rules that dictates the order in which we must perform each operation in an expression so that we will evaluate it accurately. If we have an expression that includes multiple different operations, the order of operations tells us which operations to do first. The most common mnemonic for the order of operations is **PEMDAS**, or "Please Excuse My Dear Aunt Sally." PEMDAS stands for parentheses, exponents, multiplication, division, addition, and subtraction. It is important to understand that multiplication and division have equal precedence, as do addition and subtraction, so those pairs of operations are simply worked from left to right in order.

For example, evaluating the expression $5 + 20 \div 4 \times (2 + 3)^2 - 6$ using the correct order of operations would be done like this:

- **P:** Perform the operations inside the parentheses: $(2 + 3) = 5$
- **E:** Simplify the exponents: $(5)^2 = 5 \times 5 = 25$
  - The expression now looks like this: $5 + 20 \div 4 \times 25 - 6$
- **MD:** Perform multiplication and division from left to right: $20 \div 4 = 5$; then $5 \times 25 = 125$
  - The expression now looks like this: $5 + 125 - 6$
- **AS:** Perform addition and subtraction from left to right: $5 + 125 = 130$; then $130 - 6 = 124$

Review Video: **Order of Operations**
Visit mometrix.com/academy and enter code: 259675

Properties of Operations

THE COMMUTATIVE PROPERTY

The commutative property applies to addition and multiplication and states that these operations can be completed in any order. The **commutative property of addition** states that numbers and terms can be added together in any order to still get the same value. For example, $3 + 4 = 7$ and $4 + 3 = 7$. Also, we can use the commutative property of addition to show that $3x + 4 + 2^2$ is equivalent to $4 + 3x + 2^2$ and $2^2 + 4 + 3x$. When adding terms, you can add in any order and get the same value.

The **commutative property of multiplication** states that numbers and terms can be multiplied in any order to get the same value. For example, 12×3 is equivalent to 3×12. Additionally, we can use the commutative property of multiplication to assume that $(5 + 3) \times (36 - 6)$ is equivalent to $(36 - 6) \times (5 + 3)$. You can multiply terms in any order and still get the same value.

THE ASSOCIATIVE PROPERTY

The **associative property of addition** states that if three or more terms are being added together, the value is the same regardless of the groupings.

For example, given the expression $3 + 4 + 6$, these terms can be grouped and added in any form. $3 + 4 + 6$ is equivalent to $(3 + 4) + 6$ and is also equivalent to $3 + (4 + 6)$. This can be applied to write equivalent expressions in a variety of ways.

For example, suppose we are given the expression $5 + (y + 2) + 4$. We can generate equivalent expressions knowing the associative property. Knowing that when three or more terms are added, the grouping is irrelevant, we can say that this expression is equivalent to $5 + y + (2 + 4)$, and it is equivalent to $(5 + y) + (2 + 4)$. It is even equivalent to $5 + y + 2 + 4$.

The **associative property of multiplication** states that if three or more terms are being multiplied together, the value is the same regardless of the grouping. We can use this property to identify and generate equivalent expressions.

For example, given the expression $2 \times 7 \times 3$, these terms can be grouped in any way and still get the same value. $2 \times 7 \times 3$ is equivalent to $(2 \times 7) \times 3$ or $2 \times (7 \times 3)$.

THE IDENTITY PROPERTY

The **identity property of multiplication** states that when a number is multiplied by 1, you get the same number. That is, anything multiplied by 1 is itself. For example, $2 \times 1 = 2$, or $1 \times -36 = -36$. Using the identity property of multiplication, we can identify and generate equivalent expressions. Let's say that we are given the expression $15 - (3 \times 4)$. We can generate equivalent expressions using the identity property. One equivalent expression example would be $(15 \times 1) - (3 \times 4)$. Another example would be $15 - (1 \times 3 \times 4)$. We can say these expressions are equivalent because the identity property of multiplication states that we can multiply any portion of an expression by 1 to get the same value.

The **identity property of addition** states that when 0 is added to a number, you get the same number. For example, $2 + 0 = 2$, or $0 + -3 = -3$. We can also use this property to identify and generate equivalent expressions. For example, if we are given the expression $2 \times (1 + 2)$, we could write the equivalent expressions $2 \times (0 + 1 + 2)$ or $(2 + 0) \times (1 + 2)$.

THE INVERSE PROPERTY

The **inverse property of addition** states that the sum of a number and its opposite is always equal to 0. Remember, the opposite of a number is a number that is opposite on the number line from zero, or the same number with the opposite sign. For example, −4 is opposite to 4, and 1,726.9 is opposite to −1,726.9. So, the inverse property of addition states that if you add opposite numbers, their sum is zero. For example, $5 + (-5) = 0$ and $-5 + 5 = 0$.

The **inverse property of multiplication** states that a number multiplied by its reciprocal is always equal to 1. The **reciprocal** of a number is its "flipped" fraction. For example, the reciprocal of 5 is $\frac{1}{5}$, or the reciprocal of $\frac{2}{3}$ is $\frac{3}{2}$. The inverse property of multiplication can be applied for these values, $5 \times \frac{1}{5} = 1$ and $\frac{2}{3} \times \frac{3}{2} = 1$. This is because when you multiply across, you get a fraction that is equal to 1.

$$\frac{2}{3} \times \frac{3}{2} = \frac{6}{6} = 1$$

THE DISTRIBUTIVE PROPERTY

The **distributive property** explains how multiplication and addition interact. It says that when multiplying one number by the sum of two other numbers, the same result can also be obtained by multiplying the one number by each of the numbers individually and then adding the products. For example, to multiply 2 by the sum of 7 and 3, the direct approach says, "the sum of 7 and 3 is 10, and 2 times 10 is 20." This would be expressed as $2 \times (7 + 3) = 2 \times 10 = 20$. On the other hand, the distributive property states that the same answer can be achieved by multiplying each number inside the parentheses and adding the products. That is, "the product of 2 and 7 is 14, the product of 2 and 3 is 6, and the sum of 14 and 6 is 20." This would be expressed as $2 \times (7 + 3) = 2 \times 7 + 2 \times 3 = 14 + 6 = 20$, and it is demonstrated below.

$$2 \times (7 + 3) = 2 \times 7 + 2 \times 3$$

This same concept can be used when multiplying a number by the difference of two numbers. For example, $5 \times (10 - 4) = 5 \times 10 - 5 \times 4$. Since $5 \times 10 = 50$ and $5 \times 4 = 20$, the result is $50 - 20 = 30$. This answer can be checked by subtracting inside the parentheses first and then multiplying: $5 \times (10 - 4) = 5 \times 6 = 30$.

> **Review Video: Commutative, Associative, and Distributive Properties**
> Visit mometrix.com/academy and enter code: 483176

Properties of Exponents

The properties of exponents are as follows:

Property	Description
$a^1 = a$	Any number to the power of 1 is equal to itself
$1^n = 1$	The number 1 raised to any power is equal to 1
$a^0 = 1$	Any number raised to the power of 0 is equal to 1

Property	Description
$a^n \times a^m = a^{n+m}$	Add exponents to multiply powers of the same base number
$a^n \div a^m = a^{n-m}$	Subtract exponents to divide powers of the same base number
$(a^n)^m = a^{n \times m}$	When a power is raised to a power, the exponents are multiplied
$(a \times b)^n = a^n \times b^n$ $(a \div b)^n = a^n \div b^n$	Multiplication and division operations inside parentheses can be raised to a power. This is the same as each term being raised to that power.
$a^{-n} = \dfrac{1}{a^n}$	A negative exponent is the same as the reciprocal of a positive exponent

Note that exponents do not have to be integers. Fractional or decimal exponents follow all the rules above as well. Example: $5^{\frac{1}{4}} \times 5^{\frac{3}{4}} = 5^{\frac{1}{4}+\frac{3}{4}} = 5^1 = 5$.

> **Review Video: Properties of Exponents**
> Visit mometrix.com/academy and enter code: 532558

Fractions

A **fraction** is a number that is expressed as one integer written above another integer, with a dividing line between them $\left(\dfrac{x}{y}\right)$. It represents the **quotient** of the two numbers "x divided by y." It can also be thought of as x out of y equal parts.

The top number of a fraction is called the **numerator**, and it represents the number of parts under consideration. The 1 in $\frac{1}{4}$ means that 1 part out of the whole is being considered in the calculation. The bottom number of a fraction is called the **denominator**, and it represents the total number of equal parts. The 4 in $\frac{1}{4}$ means that the whole consists of 4 equal parts. A fraction cannot have a denominator of zero; this is referred to as "*undefined*."

Fractions can be manipulated, without changing the value of the fraction, by multiplying or dividing (but not adding or subtracting) both the numerator and denominator by the same number. If you divide both numbers by a common factor, you are **reducing** or simplifying the fraction. Two fractions that have the same value but are expressed differently are known as **equivalent fractions**. For example, $\frac{2}{10}, \frac{3}{15}, \frac{4}{20},$ and $\frac{5}{25}$ are all equivalent fractions. They can also all be reduced or simplified to $\frac{1}{5}$.

When two fractions are manipulated so that they have the same denominator, this is known as finding a **common denominator**. The number chosen to be that common denominator should be the least common multiple of the two original denominators. Example: $\frac{3}{4}$ and $\frac{5}{6}$; the least common multiple of 4 and 6 is 12. Manipulating to achieve the common denominator: $\frac{3}{4} = \frac{9}{12}; \frac{5}{6} = \frac{10}{12}$.

> **Review Video: Overview of Fractions**
> Visit mometrix.com/academy and enter code: 262335

PROPER FRACTIONS AND MIXED NUMBERS

A fraction whose denominator is greater than its numerator is known as a **proper fraction**, while a fraction whose numerator is greater than its denominator is known as an **improper fraction**. Proper fractions have values *less than one* and improper fractions have values *greater than one*.

A **mixed number** is a number that contains both an integer and a fraction. Any improper fraction can be rewritten as a mixed number. Example: $\frac{8}{3} = \frac{6}{3} + \frac{2}{3} = 2 + \frac{2}{3} = 2\frac{2}{3}$. Similarly, any mixed number can be rewritten as an improper fraction. Example: $1\frac{3}{5} = 1 + \frac{3}{5} = \frac{5}{5} + \frac{3}{5} = \frac{8}{5}$.

> **Review Video: Proper and Improper Fractions and Mixed Numbers**
> Visit mometrix.com/academy and enter code: 211077

ADDING AND SUBTRACTING FRACTIONS

If two fractions have a common denominator, they can be added or subtracted simply by adding or subtracting the two numerators and retaining the same denominator. If the two fractions do not already have the same denominator, one or both of them must be manipulated to achieve a common denominator before they can be added or subtracted. Example: $\frac{1}{2} + \frac{1}{4} = \frac{2}{4} + \frac{1}{4} = \frac{3}{4}$.

> **Review Video: Adding and Subtracting Fractions**
> Visit mometrix.com/academy and enter code: 378080

MULTIPLYING FRACTIONS

Two fractions can be multiplied by multiplying the two numerators to find the new numerator and the two denominators to find the new denominator. Example: $\frac{1}{3} \times \frac{2}{3} = \frac{1 \times 2}{3 \times 3} = \frac{2}{9}$.

DIVIDING FRACTIONS

Two fractions can be divided by flipping the numerator and denominator of the second fraction and then proceeding as though it were a multiplication problem. Example: $\frac{2}{3} \div \frac{3}{4} = \frac{2}{3} \times \frac{4}{3} = \frac{8}{9}$.

> **Review Video: Multiplying and Dividing Fractions**
> Visit mometrix.com/academy and enter code: 473632

MULTIPLYING A MIXED NUMBER BY A WHOLE NUMBER OR A DECIMAL

When multiplying a mixed number by something, it is usually best to convert it to an improper fraction first. Additionally, if the multiplicand is a decimal, it is most often simplest to convert it to a fraction. For instance, to multiply $4\frac{3}{8}$ by 3.5, begin by rewriting each quantity as a whole number plus a proper fraction. Remember, a mixed number is a fraction added to a whole number and a decimal is a representation of the sum of fractions, specifically tenths, hundredths, thousandths, and so on:

$$4\frac{3}{8} \times 3.5 = \left(4 + \frac{3}{8}\right) \times \left(3 + \frac{1}{2}\right)$$

Next, the quantities being added need to be expressed with the same denominator. This is achieved by multiplying and dividing the whole number by the denominator of the fraction. Recall that a whole number is equivalent to that number divided by 1:

$$= \left(\frac{4}{1} \times \frac{8}{8} + \frac{3}{8}\right) \times \left(\frac{3}{1} \times \frac{2}{2} + \frac{1}{2}\right)$$

When multiplying fractions, remember to multiply the numerators and denominators separately:

$$= \left(\frac{4 \times 8}{1 \times 8} + \frac{3}{8}\right) \times \left(\frac{3 \times 2}{1 \times 2} + \frac{1}{2}\right)$$
$$= \left(\frac{32}{8} + \frac{3}{8}\right) \times \left(\frac{6}{2} + \frac{1}{2}\right)$$

Now that the fractions have the same denominators, they can be added:

$$= \frac{35}{8} \times \frac{7}{2}$$

Finally, perform the last multiplication and then simplify:

$$= \frac{35 \times 7}{8 \times 2} = \frac{245}{16} = \frac{240}{16} + \frac{5}{16} = 15\frac{5}{16}$$

COMPARING FRACTIONS

It is important to master the ability to compare and order fractions. This skill is relevant to many real-world scenarios. For example, carpenters often compare fractional construction nail lengths when preparing for a project, and bakers often compare fractional measurements to have the correct ratio of ingredients. There are three commonly used strategies when comparing fractions. These strategies are referred to as the common denominator approach, the decimal approach, and the cross-multiplication approach.

USING A COMMON DENOMINATOR TO COMPARE FRACTIONS

The fractions $\frac{2}{3}$ and $\frac{4}{7}$ have different denominators. $\frac{2}{3}$ has a denominator of 3, and $\frac{4}{7}$ has a denominator of 7. In order to precisely compare these two fractions, it is necessary to use a common denominator. A common denominator is a common multiple that is shared by both denominators. In this case, the denominators 3 and 7 share a multiple of 21. In general, it is most efficient to select the least common multiple for the two denominators.

Rewrite each fraction with the common denominator of 21. Then, calculate the new numerators as illustrated below.

$$\frac{2}{3} = \frac{14}{21} \qquad \frac{4}{7} = \frac{12}{21}$$

(×7 to numerator and denominator; ×3 to numerator and denominator)

For $\frac{2}{3}$, multiply the numerator and denominator by 7. The result is $\frac{14}{21}$.

For $\frac{4}{7}$, multiply the numerator and denominator by 3. The result is $\frac{12}{21}$.

Now that both fractions have a denominator of 21, the fractions can accurately be compared by comparing the numerators. Since 14 is greater than 12, the fraction $\frac{14}{21}$ is greater than $\frac{12}{21}$. This means that $\frac{2}{3}$ is greater than $\frac{4}{7}$.

USING DECIMALS TO COMPARE FRACTIONS

Sometimes decimal values are easier to compare than fraction values. For example, $\frac{5}{8}$ is equivalent to 0.625 and $\frac{3}{5}$ is equivalent to 0.6. This means that the comparison of $\frac{5}{8}$ and $\frac{3}{5}$ can be determined by comparing the decimals 0.625 and 0.6. When both decimal values are extended to the thousandths place, they become 0.625 and 0.600, respectively. It becomes clear that 0.625 is greater than 0.600 because 625 thousandths is greater than 600 thousandths. In other words, $\frac{5}{8}$ is greater than $\frac{3}{5}$ because 0.625 is greater than 0.6.

USING CROSS-MULTIPLICATION TO COMPARE FRACTIONS

Cross-multiplication is an efficient strategy for comparing fractions. This is a shortcut for the common denominator strategy. Start by writing each fraction next to one another. Multiply the numerator of the fraction on the left by the denominator of the fraction on the right. Write down the result next to the fraction on the left. Now multiply the numerator of the fraction on the right by the denominator of the fraction on the left. Write down the result next to the fraction on the right. Compare both products. The fraction with the larger result is the larger fraction.

Consider the fractions $\frac{4}{7}$ and $\frac{5}{9}$.

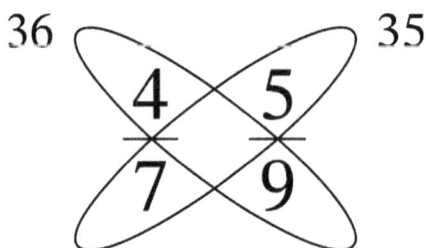

36 is greater than 35. Therefore, $\frac{4}{7}$ is greater than $\frac{5}{9}$.

Decimals

Decimals are one way to represent parts of a whole. Using the place value system, each digit to the right of a decimal point denotes the number of units of a corresponding *negative* power of ten. For example, consider the decimal 0.24. We can use a model to represent the decimal. Since a dime is worth one-tenth of a dollar and a penny is worth one-hundredth of a dollar, one possible model to represent this fraction is to have 2 dimes representing the 2 in the tenths place and 4 pennies representing the 4 in the hundredths place:

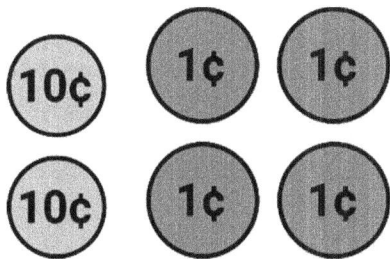

To write the decimal as a fraction, put the decimal in the numerator with 1 in the denominator. Multiply the numerator and denominator by tens until there are no more decimal places. Then simplify the fraction to lowest terms. For example, converting 0.24 to a fraction:

$$0.24 = \frac{0.24}{1} = \frac{0.24 \times 100}{1 \times 100} = \frac{24}{100} = \frac{6}{25}$$

> **Review Video: Decimals**
> Visit mometrix.com/academy and enter code: 837268

OPERATIONS WITH DECIMALS
ADDING AND SUBTRACTING DECIMALS

When adding and subtracting decimals, the decimal points must always be aligned. Adding decimals is just like adding regular whole numbers. Example: $4.5 + 2.0 = 6.5$.

If the problem-solver does not properly align the decimal points, an incorrect answer of 4.7 may result. An easy way to add decimals is to align all of the decimal points in a vertical column visually. This will allow you to see exactly where the decimal should be placed in the final answer. Begin adding from right to left. Add each column in turn, making sure to carry the number to the left if a column adds up to more than 9. The same rules apply to the subtraction of decimals.

> **Review Video: Adding and Subtracting Decimals**
> Visit mometrix.com/academy and enter code: 381101

MULTIPLYING DECIMALS

A simple multiplication problem has two components: a **multiplicand** and a **multiplier**. When multiplying decimals, work as though the numbers were whole rather than decimals. Once the final product is calculated, count the number of places to the right of the decimal in both the multiplicand and the multiplier. Then, count that number of places from the right of the product and place the decimal in that position.

For example, 12.3×2.56 has a total of three places to the right of the respective decimals. Multiply 123×256 to get 31,488. Now, beginning on the right, count three places to the left and insert the decimal. The final product will be 31.488.

> **Review Video: How to Multiply Decimals**
> Visit mometrix.com/academy and enter code: 731574

DIVIDING DECIMALS

Every division problem has a **divisor** and a **dividend**. The dividend is the number that is being divided. In the problem 14 ÷ 7, 14 is the dividend and 7 is the divisor. In a division problem with decimals, the divisor must be converted into a whole number. Begin by moving the decimal in the divisor to the right until a whole number is created. Next, move the decimal in the dividend the same number of spaces to the right. For example, 4.9 into 24.5 would become 49 into 245. The decimal was moved one space to the right to create a whole number in the divisor, and then the same was done for the dividend. Once the whole numbers are created, the problem is carried out normally: 245 ÷ 49 = 5.

> **Review Video: Dividing Decimals**
> Visit mometrix.com/academy and enter code: 560690
>
> **Review Video: Dividing Decimals by Whole Numbers**
> Visit mometrix.com/academy and enter code: 535669

Percentages

Percentages can be thought of as fractions that are based on a whole of 100; that is, one whole is equal to 100%. The word **percent** means "per hundred." Percentage problems are often presented in three main ways:

- Find what percentage of some number another number is.
    - Example: What percentage of 40 is 8?
- Find what number is some percentage of a given number.
    - Example: What number is 20% of 40?
- Find what number another number is a given percentage of.
    - Example: What number is 8 20% of?

There are three components in each of these cases: a **whole** (W), a **part** (P), and a **percentage** (%). These are related by the equation: $P = W \times \%$. This can easily be rearranged into other forms that may suit different questions better: $\% = \frac{P}{W}$ and $W = \frac{P}{\%}$. Percentage problems are often also word problems. As such, a large part of solving them is figuring out which quantities are what. For example, consider the following word problem:

In a school cafeteria, 7 students choose pizza, 9 choose hamburgers, and 4 choose tacos. What percentage of student choose tacos?

To find the whole, you must first add all of the parts: $7 + 9 + 4 = 20$. The percentage can then be found by dividing the part by the whole $\left(\% = \frac{P}{W}\right): \frac{4}{20} = \frac{20}{100} = 20\%$.

> **Review Video: Computation with Percentages**
> Visit mometrix.com/academy and enter code: 693099

CALCULATING PERCENT CHANGE

Suppose a quantity has a particular value (the *old value*) and then we add something (the *change*) to it to get another value (the *new value*). We can describe this process by the simple equation (old value) + change = (new value). If we know the old and new values, we can rearrange this equation to find the change, getting change = (new value) − (old value). For instance, if a store's price for a box of computer paper goes from $20 last week to $25 this week, this is a change of (new value) − (old value) = $25 − $20 = $5. Or, if the size of the freshman class at a college goes from 500 students one year to 440 students the next year, this is a change of (new value) − (old value) = 440 − 500 = −60 students. So, we see that change can be positive or negative.

Instead of the word *change*, we sometimes use the words *increase* or *decrease* to specify whether the value goes up or down, respectively. In the examples above, the price of computer paper increases by $5 and the freshman class decreases by 60 students. Note that the decrease is 60 students and not –60 because the word *decrease* already means that the value goes down. So, *increase* is the same as positive change and *decrease* is the opposite or negative change.

If the changing quantity represents an amount (how much of something there is), we can also calculate the **percent change**. This is the change expressed as a percentage of the old amount. To calculate this, we divide the change by the old amount and express the quotient as a percent. That is, we use the formula percent change $= \frac{\text{change}}{\text{old value}}$, converting the resulting decimal answer to a percent. In the examples above, the price of a box of computer paper has a percent change of $\frac{\text{change in price}}{\text{old price}} = \frac{\$5}{\$20} = 0.25 = 25\%$, and the size of the freshman class at the college has a percent change of $\frac{\text{change in enrollment}}{\text{old enrollment}} = \frac{-60}{500} = -0.12 = -12\%$. We can also use the terms *percent increase* and *percent decrease*, saying that the price of computer paper increases by 25% and the size of the freshman class decreases by 12%. Note that the denominator is always the old amount, never the new amount.

Example: Your landlord raises your rent from $1,500 to $1,700 per month. To find the percent change in your rent (rounded to the nearest tenth of a percent), you calculate as follows.

$$\text{percent change in rent} = \frac{\text{change in rent}}{\text{old rent}} = \frac{(\text{new rent}) - (\text{old rent})}{\text{old rent}}$$
$$= \frac{\$1{,}700 - \$1{,}500}{\$1{,}500} = \frac{\$200}{\$1{,}500} = 0.1333\ldots \approx 13.3\%$$

Therefore, the percent change in your rent is approximately 13.3%.

> **Review Video: Percent Change**
> Visit mometrix.com/academy and enter code: 907890

Converting Between Percentages, Fractions, and Decimals

Converting decimals to percentages and percentages to decimals is as simple as moving the decimal point. To *convert from a decimal to a percentage*, move the decimal point **two places to the right**. To *convert from a percentage to a decimal*, move it **two places to the left**. It may be helpful to remember that the percentage number will always be larger than the equivalent decimal number. Example:

$$0.23 = 23\% \quad 5.34 = 534\% \quad 0.007 = 0.7\%$$
$$700\% = 7.00 \quad 86\% = 0.86 \quad 0.15\% = 0.0015$$

To convert a fraction to a decimal, simply divide the numerator by the denominator in the fraction. To convert a decimal to a fraction, put the decimal in the numerator with 1 in the denominator. Multiply the numerator and denominator by tens until there are no more decimal places. Then simplify the fraction to lowest terms. For example, converting 0.24 to a fraction:

$$0.24 = \frac{0.24}{1} = \frac{0.24 \times 100}{1 \times 100} = \frac{24}{100} = \frac{6}{25}$$

Fractions can be converted to a percentage by finding equivalent fractions with a denominator of 100. Example:

$$\frac{7}{10} = \frac{70}{100} = 70\% \quad \frac{1}{4} = \frac{25}{100} = 25\%$$

To convert a percentage to a fraction, divide the percentage number by 100 and reduce the fraction to its simplest possible terms. Example:

$$60\% = \frac{60}{100} = \frac{3}{5} \quad 96\% = \frac{96}{100} = \frac{24}{25}$$

> **Review Video: Converting Fractions to Percentages and Decimals**
> Visit mometrix.com/academy and enter code: 306233
>
> **Review Video: Converting Percentages to Decimals and Fractions**
> Visit mometrix.com/academy and enter code: 287297
>
> **Review Video: Converting Decimals to Fractions and Percentages**
> Visit mometrix.com/academy and enter code: 986765
>
> **Review Video: Converting Decimals, Improper Fractions, and Mixed Numbers**
> Visit mometrix.com/academy and enter code: 696924

Rational and Irrational Numbers

The term **rational** means that the number can be expressed as a ratio or fraction. That is, a number, r, is rational if and only if it can be represented by a fraction $\frac{a}{b}$ where a and b are integers and b does not equal 0. The set of rational numbers includes integers and decimals. If there is no finite way to represent a value with a fraction of integers, then the number is **irrational**. Common irrational numbers are π and the square roots of whole numbers that are not perfect squares (e.g.,

$\sqrt{5}$ or $\sqrt{21}$). The sum or product of an integer and an irrational number is always irrational (e.g., 3π or $7 + \sqrt{6}$).

> **Review Video: Rational and Irrational Numbers**
> Visit mometrix.com/academy and enter code: 280645
>
> **Review Video: Ordering Rational Numbers**
> Visit mometrix.com/academy and enter code: 419578
>
> **Review Video: Irrational Numbers on a Number Line**
> Visit mometrix.com/academy and enter code: 433866

Proportions and Ratios

PROPORTIONS

There is a **proportion** between two variable quantities if there is a constant relationship between their products or quotients, a relationship that does not change as the quantities themselves change.

Given variable quantities x and y, we say that they are **directly proportional** (or that y **varies directly with** x) if their quotient or *ratio* is constant—that is, if there is a constant k such that $\frac{y}{x} = k$ is always true. Another way of saying this is that y is a constant multiple of x, so that $y = kx$ is always true. We call the number k the **constant of proportionality**. For example, if you drive at a constant 50 miles per hour, then the distance, y, that you travel in miles is 50 times the number of hours, x, that you drive. In symbols, $y = 50x$ miles (or $\frac{y}{x} = 50$ mph). So, the distance you travel, y, is directly proportional to (or varies directly with) the time you travel, x, with constant of proportionality $k = 50$ mph.

The quantities x and y are **inversely proportional** (or y varies inversely with x) if their product is constant—that is, if there is a constant k such that $xy = k$ is always true. Another way of saying this is to say that y is a constant multiple of the reciprocal of x so that $y = \frac{k}{x}$ is always true. For instance, suppose you drive at speed (rate) y mph for x hours, going a total of 120 miles. Since rate × time = distance, we get $xy = 120$ miles (or $y = \frac{120}{x}$ miles per hour). Thus, your driving speed, y, is inversely proportional to (or varies inversely with) your drive time, x, with constant of proportionality $k = 120$ miles.

> **Review Video: Proportions**
> Visit mometrix.com/academy and enter code: 505355

RATIOS

A **ratio** expresses the sizes of two quantities relative to each other. For instance, suppose we have 3 copies of sheet music to share among 6 singers. We can divide the singers into groups of 2 and give each group 1 copy of the music. Thus, there is 1 copy of the music for every 2 singers, and we say that the **ratio** of sheet music to singers is 1 to 2, which we write either as a fraction $\frac{1}{2}$ or using a colon 1 : 2. Of course, it is also true there are 3 copies for every 6 singers so that the ratio of sheet music to singers is also 3 to 6, which we write as $\frac{3}{6}$ or 3 : 6. So, the ratios $\frac{1}{2}$ and $\frac{3}{6}$ express the same relative quantities of music and singers. We say that these ratios are equal or **equivalent**, and we note that ratios are equal precisely when their fractions are equal (so, in this case, $\frac{1}{2} = \frac{3}{6}$ as fractions). We can also express the quantities in the other order and say that the ratio of singers to music is $\frac{2}{1}$ or $2:1$ (or $\frac{6}{3}$ or $6:3$).

> **Review Video: Ratios**
> Visit mometrix.com/academy and enter code: 996914

CONSTANT OF PROPORTIONALITY

If variable quantities x and y are proportional and we know a pair of corresponding values for them, then we can find their constant of proportionality. If they are directly proportional, we use the formula $\frac{y}{x} = k$. If they are inversely proportional, we use the formula $xy = k$

Example: The cost in dollars, y, of buying fence posts is directly proportional to the number, x, that you buy. If it costs $51 to buy 17 fence posts, what is the constant of proportionality? Because of direct proportionality, we know that $\frac{y}{x} = k$. Since this works for every pair of corresponding x- and y-values, it also works for $x = 17$ and $y = 51$. This gives us $\frac{51}{17} = k$, which simplifies to $k = 3$. Note also that this is the unit price, namely $3 per fence post.

WORK/UNIT RATE

Unit rate expresses a quantity of one thing in terms of one unit of another. For example, if you travel 30 miles every two hours, a unit rate expresses this comparison in terms of one hour: in one hour you travel 15 miles, so your unit rate is 15 miles per hour. Other examples are how much one ounce of food costs (price per ounce) or figuring out how much one egg costs out of the dozen (price per 1 egg, instead of price per 12 eggs). The denominator of a unit rate is always 1. Unit rates are used to compare different situations to solve problems. For example, to make sure you get the best deal when deciding which kind of soda to buy, you can find the unit rate of each. If soda #1 costs $1.50 for a 1-liter bottle, and soda #2 costs $2.75 for a 2-liter bottle, it would be a better deal to buy soda #2, because its unit rate is only $1.375 per 1-liter, which is cheaper than soda #1. Unit rates can also help determine the length of time a given event will take. For example, if you can paint 2 rooms in 4.5 hours, you can determine how long it will take you to paint 5 rooms by solving for the unit rate per room and then multiplying that by 5.

> **Review Video: Rates and Unit Rates**
> Visit mometrix.com/academy and enter code: 185363

Cross Multiplication

FINDING AN UNKNOWN IN EQUIVALENT EXPRESSIONS

It is often necessary to apply information given about a rate or proportion to a new scenario. For example, if you know that Jedha can run a marathon (26.2 miles) in 3 hours, how long would it take her to run 10 miles at the same pace? Start by setting up equivalent expressions:

$$\frac{26.2 \text{ mi}}{3 \text{ hr}} = \frac{10 \text{ mi}}{x \text{ hr}}$$

Now, cross multiply and solve for x:

$$26.2x = 30$$
$$x = \frac{30}{26.2} = \frac{15}{13.1}$$
$$x \approx 1.15 \text{ hrs } or \text{ 1 hr 9 min}$$

So, at this pace, Jedha could run 10 miles in about 1.15 hours or about 1 hour and 9 minutes.

> **Review Video: Cross Multiplying Fractions**
> Visit mometrix.com/academy and enter code: 893904

Linear Expressions

TERMS AND COEFFICIENTS

Mathematical expressions consist of a combination of one or more values arranged in terms that are added together. As such, an expression could be just a single number, including zero. A **variable term** is the product of a real number, also called a **coefficient**, and one or more variables, each of which may be raised to an exponent. Expressions may also include numbers without a variable, called **constants** or **constant terms**. The expression $6s^2$, for example, is a single term where the coefficient is the real number 6 and the variable term is s^2. Note that if a term is written as simply a variable to some exponent, like t^2, then the coefficient is 1, because $t^2 = 1t^2$.

LINEAR EXPRESSIONS

A **single variable linear expression** is the sum of a single variable term, where the variable has no exponent, and a constant, which may be zero. For instance, the expression $2w + 7$ has $2w$ as the variable term and 7 as the constant term. It is important to realize that terms are separated by addition or subtraction. Since an expression is a sum of terms, expressions such as $5x - 3$ can be written as $5x + (-3)$ to emphasize that the constant term is negative. A real-world example of a single variable linear expression is the perimeter of a square, four times the side length, often expressed: $4s$.

In general, a **linear expression** is the sum of any number of variable terms so long as none of the variables have an exponent and none of the terms have two variables multiplied together. For example, $3m + 8n - \frac{1}{4}p + 5.5q - 1$ is a linear expression, but $3y^3$ and $5xy$ are not. In the same way, the expression for the perimeter of a general triangle $(a + b + c)$ is linear, but the expression for the area of a square (s^2) is not.

Slope

FINDING SLOPE GIVEN GRAPH OR TABLE

On a graph with two points, (x_1, y_1) and (x_2, y_2), the **slope** is found with the formula $m = \frac{y_2 - y_1}{x_2 - x_1}$; where $x_1 \neq x_2$ and m stands for slope. If the value of the slope is **positive**, the line has an *upward direction* from left to right. If the value of the slope is **negative**, the line has a *downward direction* from left to right. Consider the following example:

A new book goes on sale in bookstores and online stores. In the first month, 5,000 copies of the book are sold. Over time, the book continues to grow in popularity. The data for the number of copies sold is in the table below.

# of Months on Sale	1	2	3	4	5
# of Copies Sold (In Thousands)	5	10	15	20	25

So, the number of copies that are sold and the time that the book is on sale is a proportional relationship. In this example, an equation can be used to show the data: $y = 5x$, where x is the number of months that the book is on sale. Also, y is the number of copies sold. So, the slope of the corresponding line is $\frac{\text{rise}}{\text{run}} = \frac{5}{1} = 5$.

FINDING SLOPE GIVEN AN EQUATION

When given an equation of a line, it is necessary to solve for y to determine the slope of the line. Given the equation $6x + 2y = 8$, find the slope. First, subtract $6x$ from both sides of the equation, resulting in $2y = -6x + 8$. Then divide both sides of the equation by 2, resulting in $y = -3x + 4$. This then allows us to conclude that the slope of the line is $m = -3$, the coefficient of x. Once an equation is in the form $y = mx + b$, the slope and y-intercept can easily be determined. For this reason, we refer to the equation $y = mx + b$ as "slope-intercept form" of the equation of a line.

> **Review Video: Finding the Slope of a Line**
> Visit mometrix.com/academy and enter code: 766664

Algebraic Reasoning

Linear Equations

Equations like $5x = 100$ and $8x - 120 = 200$ and $6x + 4y = 240$ are **linear equations**. Linear equations are named based off the number of distinct variables they include. For example, the equation $3x + 30 = 8x$ is a **one-variable linear equation** because it involves only the single variable x. It does not matter that x appears more than once. Any equations that can be written as $ax + b = 0$, where $a \neq 0$, falls into this category. Furthermore, the equation $3x - 5y = 14 + 9y$ is a **two-variable linear equation** because it involves the two variables x and y. The equation $7x + 8y - 12z + 14w = 56$ is a linear equation in four variables.

SATISFYING THE EQUATION

When given a one-variable linear equation, the goal is typically to solve it. This means that we want to find the number that makes the equation true if we substitute it for the variable. That number is the **solution,** or root, of the equation. For instance, the equation $5x = 10$ has the solution $x = 2$. This is true because when 2 is substituted for x, the result is $5 \cdot 2 = 10$, which is true. On the other hand, $x = 6$ can not be a solution because $5 \cdot 6 \neq 10$, so it is false. Two equations with the same solution are **equivalent equations**. For example, the equations $5x = 10$ and $5x + 3 = 13$ are equivalent because both have the same solution of $x = 2$.

DETERMINING A SOLUTION SET

The **solution set** is the set of all solutions of an equation. In the previous example, the solution set would be 2. Solutions to a linear equation in two variables consist of pairs of numbers. For instance, the equation $6x + 4y = 240$ has the solution $x = 20$ and $y = 30$ since $6 \cdot 20 + 4 \cdot 30 = 240$ is true. We can write this solution as the ordered pair (20,30) and plot it as a point on the coordinate plane. Such equations usually have infinitely many solutions; and if we plot the points for all these solutions we get a line, which is a picture of all the solutions. We call this **graphing the equation**. When an equation has no true solutions, it is referred to as an **empty set**.

LINEAR EQUATION FORMS

Linear equations can be written many ways. Below is a list of some forms linear equations can take:

- **Standard Form**: $Ax + By = C$; the slope is $\frac{-A}{B}$ and the y-intercept is $\frac{C}{B}$
- **Slope Intercept Form**: $y = mx + b$, where m is the slope and b is the y-intercept
- **Point-Slope Form**: $y - y_1 = m(x - x_1)$, where m is the slope and (x_1, y_1) is a point on the line

- **Two-Point Form**: $\frac{y-y_1}{x-x_1} = \frac{y_2-y_1}{x_2-x_1}$, where (x_1, y_1) and (x_2, y_2) are two points on the given line
- **Intercept Form**: $\frac{x}{x_1} + \frac{y}{y_1} = 1$, where $(x_1, 0)$ is the point at which a line intersects the x-axis, and $(0, y_1)$ is the point at which the same line intersects the y-axis

> **Review Video: Slope-Intercept and Point-Slope Forms**
> Visit mometrix.com/academy and enter code: 113216
>
> **Review Video: Converting Between Standard and Slope-Intercept Forms**
> Visit mometrix.com/academy and enter code: 982828
>
> **Review Video: Linear Equations Basics**
> Visit mometrix.com/academy and enter code: 793005

Solving Equations

MANIPULATING EQUATIONS

LIKE TERMS

Like terms are terms in an equation that have the same variable, regardless of whether they also have the same coefficient. This includes terms that *lack* a variable; all constants (i.e., numbers without variables) are considered like terms. If the equation involves terms with a variable raised to different powers, the like terms are those that have the variable raised to the same power.

For example, consider the equation $x^2 + 3x + 2 = 2x^2 + x - 7 + 2x$. In this equation, 2 and –7 are like terms; they are both constants. The terms $3x$, x, and $2x$ are like terms, they all include the variable x raised to the first power. The terms x^2 and $2x^2$ are like terms, they both include the variable x, raised to the second power. The terms $2x$ and $2x^2$ are not like terms; although they both involve the variable x, the variable is not raised to the same power in both terms. The fact that they have the same coefficient, 2, is not relevant.

> **Review Video: Rules for Manipulating Equations**
> Visit mometrix.com/academy and enter code: 838871

CARRYING OUT THE SAME OPERATION ON BOTH SIDES OF AN EQUATION

When solving an equation, the general procedure is to carry out a series of operations on both sides of an equation, choosing operations that simplify the equation when doing so. The reason why the same operation must be carried out on both sides of the equation is because that leaves the meaning of the equation unchanged, and yields a result that is equivalent to the original equation. This would not be the case if we carried out an operation on one side of an equation and not the other. Consider what an equation means: it is a statement that two values or expressions are equal. If we carry out the same operation on both sides of the equation—add 3 to both sides, for example—then the two sides of the equation are changed in the same way, and so remain equal. If we do that to only one side of the equation—add 3 to one side but not the other—then that wouldn't be true; if we change one side of the equation but not the other then the two sides are no longer equal.

COMBINING LIKE TERMS

Combining like terms refers to adding or subtracting like terms—terms with the same variable—and therefore reducing sets of like terms to a single term. The main advantage of doing this is that it simplifies the equation. Often, combining like terms can be done as the first step in solving an equation, though it can also be done later, such as after distributing terms in a product.

For example, consider the equation $2(x + 3) + 3(2 + x + 3) = -4$. The 2 and the 3 in the second set of parentheses are like terms, and we can combine them, yielding $2(x + 3) + 3(x + 5) = -4$. Now we can carry out the multiplications implied by the parentheses, distributing the outer 2 and 3 accordingly: $2x + 6 + 3x + 15 = -4$. The $2x$ and the $3x$ are like terms, and we can add them together: $5x + 6 + 15 = -4$. Now, the constants 6, 15, and -4 are also like terms, and we can combine them as well: subtracting 6 and 15 from both sides of the equation, we get $5x = -4 - 6 - 15$, or $5x = -25$, which simplifies further to $x = -5$.

> **Review Video: Solving Equations by Combining Like Terms**
> Visit mometrix.com/academy and enter code: 668506

CANCELING TERMS ON OPPOSITE SIDES OF AN EQUATION

Two terms on opposite sides of an equation can be canceled if and only if they *exactly* match each other. They must have the same variable raised to the same power and the same coefficient. For example, in the equation $3x + 2x^2 + 6 = 2x^2 - 6$, $2x^2$ appears on both sides of the equation and can be canceled, leaving $3x + 6 = -6$. The 6 on each side of the equation *cannot* be canceled, because it is added on one side of the equation and subtracted on the other. While they cannot be canceled, however, the 6 and -6 are like terms and can be combined, yielding $3x = -12$, which simplifies further to $x = -4$.

It's also important to note that the terms to be canceled must be independent terms and cannot be part of a larger term. For example, consider the equation $2(x + 6) = 3(x + 4) + 1$. We cannot cancel the x's, because even though they match each other they are part of the larger terms $2(x + 6)$ and $3(x + 4)$. We must first distribute the 2 and 3, yielding $2x + 12 = 3x + 12 + 1$. Now we see that the terms with the x's do not match, but the 12s do, and can be canceled, leaving $2x = 3x + 1$, which simplifies to $x = -1$.

ISOLATING VARIABLES

To isolate a variable means to manipulate the equation so that the variable appears by itself on one side of the equation, and does not appear at all on the other side. Generally, an equation or inequality is considered to be solved once the variable is isolated and the other side of the equation or inequality is simplified as much as possible. In the case of a two-variable equation or inequality, only one variable needs to be isolated; it will not usually be possible to simultaneously isolate both variables.

For a linear equation—an equation in which the variable only appears raised to the first power—isolating a variable can be done by first moving all the terms with the variable to one side of the equation and all other terms to the other side. (*Moving* a term really means adding the inverse of the term to both sides; when a term is *moved* to the other side of the equation its sign is flipped.)

Then combine like terms on each side. Finally, divide both sides by the coefficient of the variable, if applicable. The steps need not necessarily be done in this order, but this order will always work.

> **Review Video: Solving Equations for Specific Variables**
> Visit mometrix.com/academy and enter code: 130695
>
> **Review Video: Solving Equations Involving Algebraic Fractions**
> Visit mometrix.com/academy and enter code: 237770
>
> **Review Video: Solving One-Step Equations**
> Visit mometrix.com/academy and enter code: 777004

SOLVING ONE-VARIABLE LINEAR EQUATIONS
EQUATIONS WITH ONE SOLUTION (THE USUAL CASE)

To solve a one-variable linear equation, we use the techniques above to isolate the variable.

1. If any coefficients or constants are fractions, it is often helpful first to multiply both sides of the equation by the least common denominator (of all fractions) to clear the fractions.
2. Simplify both sides of the equation by combining any like terms.
3. Put all terms with the variable on one side of the equation and all constant terms on the other side, by adding or subtracting the same terms on both sides of the equation.
4. Divide both sides by the coefficient of the variable (or multiply both sides by its reciprocal).
5. When we have a value for the variable, we can check it by substituting the value into the original equation to make sure it produces a true result.

Consider the following example for solving the equation $\frac{2}{3}x + 8 = 14$:

$3 \cdot \left(\frac{2}{3}x + 8\right) = 3 \cdot 14$	Clear fractions by multiplying both sides by 3.
$2x + 24 = 42$	Simplify, remembering to apply the distributive property.
$2x + 24 - 24 = 42 - 24$	Subtract 24 from both sides to isolate $2x$.
$2x = 18$	Simplify by combining like terms.
$\frac{2x}{2} = \frac{18}{2}$	Divide both sides by 2 to isolate x.
$x = 9$	Simplify

Finally, we check this answer by substituting $x = 9$ into the original equation to make sure we get a true result.

$$\frac{2}{3}x + 8 = \frac{2}{3}(9) + 8 = 6 + 8 = 14$$

This is correct, so the value of x is 9.

> **Review Video: Solving Equations Using the Distributive Property**
> Visit mometrix.com/academy and enter code: 765499

EQUATIONS WITH MORE THAN ONE SOLUTION

Some types of non-linear equations, such as equations involving squares of variables, may have more than one solution. For example, the equation $x^2 = 4$ has two solutions: 2 and −2. Equations with absolute values can also have multiple solutions: $|x| = 1$ has the solutions $x = 1$ and $x = -1$.

It is possible for a linear equation to have more than one solution but only if the equation is true regardless of the value of the variable. We call such an equation an **identity**. In this case, the equation has infinitely many solutions, because every possible value of the variable is a solution. We discover that a linear equation is an identity when our attempts to isolate the variable cause the variable to disappear, leaving a *true* equation involving only constants. For example, consider the equation $2(3x + 5) = x + 5(x + 2)$. Distributing, we get $6x + 10 = x + 5x + 10$; combining like terms gives $6x + 10 = 6x + 10$, and the $6x$-terms cancel to leave $10 = 10$. This is clearly true, so the original equation is an identity. We could also cancel the 10's leaving $0 = 0$, which is also is clearly true—in general if both sides of the equation can be reduced to match one another exactly, the original equation is an identity.

EQUATIONS WITH NO SOLUTION

Some types of non-linear equations, such as equations involving squares of variables, may have no solution. For example, the equation $x^2 = -2$ has no solutions in the real numbers because the square of a real number must be positive. Similarly, $|x| = -1$ has no solution because the absolute value of a number is always positive.

It is also possible for a linear equation to have no solution. We call such an equation a **contradiction**. We discover that a linear equation is a contradiction when our attempts to isolate the variable cause the variable to disappear, leaving a *false* equation involving only constants. For example, the equation $2(x + 3) + x = 3x$ has no solution. We can see this by trying to solve it: first we distribute, leaving $2x + 6 + x = 3x$. Combining like terms gives us $3x + 6 = 3x$, and cancelling the term $3x$ on both sides leaves us with $6 = 0$. This is clearly false, so the original equation is a contradiction, having no solutions.

FEATURES OF EQUATIONS THAT REQUIRE SPECIAL TREATMENT

A linear equation is an equation in which variables only appear by themselves: not multiplied together, not with exponents other than one, and not inside absolute value signs or any other functions. For example, the equation $x + 1 - 3x = 5 - x$ is a linear equation; while x appears multiple times, it never appears with an exponent other than one, or inside any function. The two-variable equation $2x - 3y = 5 + 2x$ is also a linear equation. In contrast, the equation $x^2 - 5 = 3x$ is *not* a linear equation, because it involves the term x^2. The equation $\sqrt{x} = 5$ is not linear, because it involves a square root. The equation $(x - 1)^2 = 4$ is not linear because even though there's no exponent on the x directly, it appears as part of an expression that is squared. The two-variable equation $x + xy - y = 5$ is not linear because it includes the term xy, where two variables are multiplied together.

As we see above, linear equations can always be solved (or shown to have no solution) by combining like terms and performing simple operations on both sides of the equation. Some non-linear equations can be solved by similar methods, but others may require more advanced methods of solution, if they can be solved analytically at all.

SOLVING EQUATIONS INVOLVING ROOTS

In an equation involving roots, the first step is to isolate the term with the root, if possible, and then raise both sides of the equation to the appropriate power to eliminate it. Consider an example equation, $2\sqrt{x+1} - 1 = 3$. In this case, begin by adding 1 to both sides, yielding $2\sqrt{x+1} = 4$, and then dividing both sides by 2, yielding $\sqrt{x+1} = 2$. Now square both sides, yielding $x + 1 = 4$. Finally, subtracting 1 from both sides yields $x = 3$.

Squaring both sides of an equation (or raising both sides to any *even* power) may, however, yield a spurious solution—a solution to the squared equation that is *not* a solution of the original equation. It's therefore necessary to plug the solution back into the original equation to make sure it works. In this case, it does: $2\sqrt{3+1} - 1 = 2\sqrt{4} - 1 = 2(2) - 1 = 4 - 1 = 3$.

The same procedure applies for other roots as well. For example, given the equation $3 + \sqrt[3]{2x} = 5$, we can first subtract 3 from both sides, yielding $\sqrt[3]{2x} = 2$ and isolating the root. Raising both sides to the third power yields $2x = 2^3$; i.e., $2x = 8$. We can now divide both sides by 2 to get $x = 4$.

> **Review Video: Solving Equations Involving Roots**
> Visit mometrix.com/academy and enter code: 297670

SOLVING EQUATIONS WITH EXPONENTS

In solving an equation with powers of a variable, sometimes it is possible to eliminate all but one term involving the variable. In that case, we can isolate the power of the variable and then take the appropriate root of both sides to eliminate the exponent. For instance, for the equation $2x^3 + 17 = 5x^3 - 7$, we can subtract $5x^3$ from both sides to get $-3x^3 + 17 = -7$, and then subtract 17 from both sides to get $-3x^3 = -24$. Finally, we can divide both sides by –3 to get $x^3 = 8$. Since this isolates the cube of the variable, we can take the cube root of both sides to get $x = \sqrt[3]{8} = 2$.

One important but often overlooked point is that equations with an exponent greater than 1 may have more than one answer. The solution to $x^2 = 9$ isn't simply $x = 3$; it's $x = \pm 3$ (that is, $x = 3$ or $x = -3$). For a slightly more complicated example, consider the equation $(x-1)^2 - 1 = 3$. Adding 1 to both sides yields $(x-1)^2 = 4$; taking the square root of both sides yields $x - 1 = 2$. We can then add 1 to both sides to get $x = 3$. However, there's a second solution. We also have the possibility that $x - 1 = -2$, in which case $x = -1$. Both $x = 3$ and $x = -1$ are valid solutions, as can be verified by substituting them both into the original equation.

> **Review Video: Solving Equations with Exponents**
> Visit mometrix.com/academy and enter code: 514557
>
> **Review Video: Adding and Subtracting with Exponents**
> Visit mometrix.com/academy and enter code: 875756

SOLVING EQUATIONS WITH ABSOLUTE VALUES

When solving an equation with an absolute value, the first step is to isolate the absolute value term. We then consider two possibilities: when the expression inside the absolute value is positive or when it is negative. In the former case, the expression in the absolute value equals the expression on the other side of the equation; in the latter, it equals the additive inverse of that expression—the expression times negative one. We consider each case separately and finally check for spurious solutions.

For instance, consider solving $|2x - 1| + x = 5$ for x. We can first isolate the absolute value by moving the x to the other side: $|2x - 1| = -x + 5$. Now, we have two possibilities. First, that $2x - 1$ is positive, and hence $2x - 1 = -x + 5$. Rearranging and combining like terms yields $3x = 6$, and hence $x = 2$. The other possibility is that $2x - 1$ is negative, and hence $2x - 1 = -(-x + 5) = x -$

5. In this case, rearranging and combining like terms yields $x = -4$. Substituting $x = 2$ and $x = -4$ back into the original equation, we see that they are both valid solutions.

Note that the absolute value of a sum or difference applies to the sum or difference as a whole, not to the individual terms; in general, $|2x - 1|$ is not equal to $|2x + 1|$ or to $|2x| - 1$.

> **Review Video: Solving Absolute Value Equations**
> Visit mometrix.com/academy and enter code: 501208

EXTRANEOUS SOLUTIONS

An **extraneous solution** may arise when we square both sides of an equation (or raise both sides to an even power) as a step in solving it or under certain other operations on the equation. It is a solution to the squared or otherwise modified equation that is *not* a solution of the original equation. To identify an extraneous solution, it's useful when you solve an equation involving roots or absolute values to plug the solution back into the original equation to make sure it's valid.

TWO-VARIABLE EQUATIONS

Similar to methods for a one-variable equation, solving a two-variable equation involves isolating a variable: manipulating the equation so that a variable appears by itself on one side of the equation, and not at all on the other side. However, in a two-variable equation, you will usually only be able to isolate one of the variables; the other variable may appear on the other side along with constant terms, or with exponents or other functions. If an equation has multiple variables, the problem should tell you which variable to isolate.

> **Review Video: Solving Equations with Variables on Both Sides**
> Visit mometrix.com/academy and enter code: 402497

Graphing Equations

GRAPHICAL SOLUTIONS TO EQUATIONS

When equations are shown graphically, they are usually shown on a **Cartesian coordinate plane**. The Cartesian coordinate plane consists of two number lines placed perpendicular to each other and intersecting at the zero point, also known as the origin. The horizontal number line is known as the x-axis, with positive values to the right of the origin, and negative values to the left of the origin. The vertical number line is known as the y-axis, with positive values above the origin, and negative values below the origin. Any point on the plane can be identified by an ordered pair in the form (x, y), called coordinates. The x-value of the coordinate is called the abscissa, and the y-value of the coordinate is called the ordinate. The two number lines divide the plane into **four quadrants**: I, II, III, and IV.

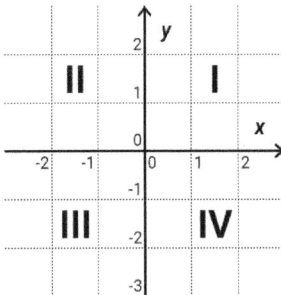

Note that in quadrant I $x > 0$ and $y > 0$, in quadrant II $x < 0$ and $y > 0$, in quadrant III $x < 0$ and $y < 0$, and in quadrant IV $x > 0$ and $y < 0$.

Recall that if the value of the slope of a line is positive, the line slopes upward from left to right. If the value of the slope is negative, the line slopes downward from left to right. If the y-coordinates are the same for two points on a line, the slope is 0 and the line is a **horizontal line**. If the x-coordinates are the same for two points on a line, there is no slope and the line is a **vertical line**. Two or more lines that have equivalent slopes are **parallel lines**. **Perpendicular lines** have slopes that are negative reciprocals of each other, such as $\frac{a}{b}$ and $\frac{-b}{a}$.

> **Review Video: Cartesian Coordinate Plane and Graphing**
> Visit mometrix.com/academy and enter code: 115173

GRAPHING EQUATIONS IN TWO VARIABLES

One way of graphing an equation in two variables is to plot enough points to get an idea for its shape and then draw the appropriate curve through those points. A point can be plotted by substituting in a value for one variable and solving for the other. If the equation is linear, we only need two points and can then draw a straight line between them.

For example, consider the equation $y = 2x - 1$. This is a linear equation—both variables only appear raised to the first power—so we only need two points. When $x = 0$, $y = 2(0) - 1 = -1$. When $x = 2$, $y = 2(2) - 1 = 3$. We can therefore choose the points $(0, -1)$ and $(2, 3)$, and draw a line between them:

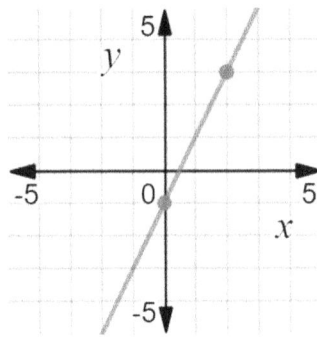

Inequalities

Commonly in algebra and other upper-level fields of math you find yourself working with mathematical expressions that do not equal each other. The statement comparing such expressions with symbols such as < (less than) or > (greater than) is called an *inequality*. An example of an inequality is $7x > 5$. To solve for x, simply divide both sides by 7 and the solution is shown to be $x > \frac{5}{7}$. Graphs of the solution set of inequalities are represented on a number line. Open circles are used to show that an expression approaches a number but is never quite equal to that number.

> **Review Video: Solving One-Step Inequalities**
> Visit mometrix.com/academy and enter code: 229684
>
> **Review Video: Solving Multi-Step Inequalities**
> Visit mometrix.com/academy and enter code: 347842
>
> **Review Video: Solving Inequalities Using All 4 Basic Operations**
> Visit mometrix.com/academy and enter code: 401111

TYPES OF INEQUALITIES

Conditional inequalities are those with certain values for the variable that will make the condition true and other values for the variable where the condition will be false. **Absolute inequalities** can have any real number as the value for the variable to make the condition true, while there is no real number value for the variable that will make the condition false. Solving inequalities is done by following the same rules for solving equations with the exception that when multiplying or dividing by a negative number the direction of the inequality sign must be flipped or reversed. **Double inequalities** are situations where two inequality statements apply to the same variable expression. Example: $-c < ax + b < c$.

> **Review Video: Conditional and Absolute Inequalities**
> Visit mometrix.com/academy and enter code: 980164

Solving Inequalities

DETERMINING SOLUTIONS TO INEQUALITIES

To determine whether a coordinate is a solution of an inequality, you can substitute the values of the coordinate into the inequality, simplify, and check whether the resulting statement holds true. For instance, to determine whether $(-2,4)$ is a solution of the inequality $y \geq -2x + 3$, substitute the values into the inequality, $4 \geq -2(-2) + 3$. Simplify the right side of the inequality and the result is $4 \geq 7$, which is a false statement. Therefore, the coordinate is not a solution of the inequality. You can also use this method to determine which part of the graph of an inequality is shaded. The graph of $y \geq -2x + 3$ includes the solid line $y = -2x + 3$ and, since it excludes the point $(-2,4)$ to the left of the line, it is shaded to the right of the line.

> **Review Video: Graphing Linear Inequalities**
> Visit mometrix.com/academy and enter code: 439421

FLIPPING INEQUALITY SIGNS

When given an inequality, we can always turn the entire inequality around, swapping the two sides of the inequality and changing the inequality sign. For instance, $x + 2 > 2x - 3$ is equivalent to $2x - 3 < x + 2$. Aside from that, normally the inequality does not change if we carry out the same operation on both sides of the inequality. There is, however, one principal exception: if we *multiply* or *divide* both sides of the inequality by a *negative number*, the inequality is flipped. For example, if we take the inequality $-2x < 6$ and divide both sides by –2, the inequality flips and we are left with $x > -3$. This *only* applies to multiplication and division, and only with negative numbers. Multiplying or dividing both sides by a positive number, or adding or subtracting any number regardless of sign, does not flip the inequality. Another special case that flips the inequality sign is when reciprocals are used. For instance, $3 > 2$ but the relation of the reciprocals is $\frac{1}{3} < \frac{1}{2}$.

COMPOUND INEQUALITIES

A **compound inequality** is an equality that consists of two inequalities combined with *and* or *or*. The two components of a proper compound inequality must be of opposite type: that is, one must be greater than (or greater than or equal to), the other less than (or less than or equal to). For instance, "$x + 1 < 2$ or $x + 1 > 3$" is a compound inequality, as is "$2x \geq 4$ and $2x \leq 6$." An *and* inequality can be written more compactly by having one inequality on each side of the common part: "$2x \geq 1$ and $2x \leq 6$," can also be written as $1 \leq 2x \leq 6$.

In order for the compound inequality to be meaningful, the two parts of an *and* inequality must overlap; otherwise, no numbers satisfy the inequality. On the other hand, if the two parts of an *or* inequality overlap, then *all* numbers satisfy the inequality and as such the inequality is usually not meaningful.

Solving a compound inequality requires solving each part separately. For example, given the compound inequality "$x + 1 < 2$ or $x + 1 > 3$," the first inequality, $x + 1 < 2$, reduces to $x < 1$, and the second part, $x + 1 > 3$, reduces to $x > 2$, so the whole compound inequality can be written as "$x < 1$ or $x > 2$." Similarly, $1 \leq 2x \leq 6$ can be solved by dividing each term by 2, yielding $\frac{1}{2} \leq x \leq 3$.

> **Review Video: Compound Inequalities**
> Visit mometrix.com/academy and enter code: 786318

SOLVING INEQUALITIES INVOLVING ABSOLUTE VALUES

To solve an inequality involving an absolute value, first isolate the term with the absolute value. Then proceed to treat the two cases separately as with an absolute value equation, but flipping the inequality in the case where the expression in the absolute value is negative (since that essentially involves multiplying both sides by –1.) The two cases are then combined into a compound inequality; if the absolute value is on the greater side of the inequality, then it is an *or* compound inequality, if on the lesser side, then it's an *and*.

Consider the inequality $2 + |x - 1| \geq 3$. We can isolate the absolute value term by subtracting 2 from both sides: $|x - 1| \geq 1$. Now, we're left with the two cases $x - 1 \geq 1$ or $x - 1 \leq -1$: note that in the latter, negative case, the inequality is flipped. $x - 1 \geq 1$ reduces to $x \geq 2$, and $x - 1 \leq -1$ reduces to $x \leq 0$. Since in the inequality $|x - 1| \geq 1$ the absolute value is on the greater side, the two cases combine into an *or* compound inequality, so the final, solved inequality is "$x \leq 0$ or $x \geq 2$."

> **Review Video: Solving Absolute Value Inequalities**
> Visit mometrix.com/academy and enter code: 997008

SOLVING INEQUALITIES INVOLVING SQUARE ROOTS

Solving an inequality with a square root involves two parts. First, we solve the inequality as if it were an equation, isolating the square root and then squaring both sides of the equation. Second, we restrict the solution to the set of values of x for which the value inside the square root sign is non-negative.

For example, in the inequality, $\sqrt{x-2} + 1 < 5$, we can isolate the square root by subtracting 1 from both sides, yielding $\sqrt{x-2} < 4$. Squaring both sides of the inequality yields $x - 2 < 16$, so $x < 18$. Since we can't take the square root of a negative number, we also require the part inside the square root to be non-negative. In this case, that means $x - 2 \geq 0$. Adding 2 to both sides of the inequality yields $x \geq 2$. Our final answer is a compound inequality combining the two simple inequalities: $x \geq 2$ and $x < 18$, or $2 \leq x < 18$.

Note that we only get a compound inequality if the two simple inequalities are in opposite directions; otherwise, we take the one that is more restrictive.

The same technique can be used for other even roots, such as fourth roots. It is *not*, however, used for cube roots or other odd roots—negative numbers *do* have cube roots, so the condition that the quantity inside the root sign cannot be negative does not apply.

> **Review Video: Solving Inequalities Involving Square Roots**
> Visit mometrix.com/academy and enter code: 800288

SPECIAL CIRCUMSTANCES

Sometimes an inequality involving an absolute value or an even exponent is true for all values of x, and we don't need to do any further work to solve it. This is true if the inequality, once the absolute value or exponent term is isolated, says that term is greater than a negative number (or greater than or equal to zero). Since an absolute value or a number raised to an even exponent is *always* non-negative, this inequality is always true.

Graphing Inequalities

GRAPHING SIMPLE INEQUALITIES

To graph a simple inequality, we first mark on the number line the value that signifies the end point of the inequality. If the inequality is strict (involves a less than or greater than), we use a hollow circle; if it is not strict (less than or equal to or greater than or equal to), we use a solid circle. We then fill in the part of the number line that satisfies the inequality: to the left of the marked point for less than (or less than or equal to), to the right for greater than (or greater than or equal to).

For example, we would graph the inequality $x < 5$ by putting a hollow circle at 5 and filling in the part of the line to the left:

GRAPHING COMPOUND INEQUALITIES

To graph a compound inequality, we fill in both parts of the inequality for an *or* inequality, or the overlap between them for an *and* inequality. More specifically, we start by plotting the endpoints of each inequality on the number line. For an *or* inequality, we then fill in the appropriate side of the line for each inequality. Typically, the two component inequalities do not overlap, which means the shaded part is *outside* the two points. For an *and* inequality, we instead fill in the part of the line that meets both inequalities.

For the inequality "$x \leq -3$ or $x > 4$," we first put a solid circle at –3 and a hollow circle at 4. We then fill the parts of the line *outside* these circles:

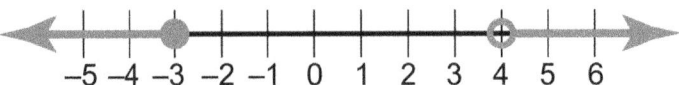

GRAPHING INEQUALITIES INCLUDING ABSOLUTE VALUES

An inequality with an absolute value can be converted to a compound inequality. To graph the inequality, first convert it to a compound inequality, and then graph that normally. If the absolute value is on the greater side of the inequality, we end up with an *or* inequality; we plot the endpoints of the inequality on the number line and fill in the part of the line *outside* those points. If the absolute value is on the smaller side of the inequality, we end up with an *and* inequality; we plot the endpoints of the inequality on the number line and fill in the part of the line *between* those points.

For example, the inequality $|x + 1| \geq 4$ can be rewritten as $x \geq 3$ or $x \leq -5$. We place solid circles at the points 3 and –5 and fill in the part of the line *outside* them:

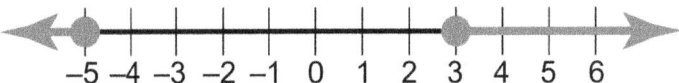

GRAPHING INEQUALITIES IN TWO VARIABLES

To graph an inequality in two variables, we first graph the border of the inequality. This means graphing the equation that we get if we replace the inequality sign with an equals sign. If the inequality is strict ($>$ or $<$), we graph the border with a dashed or dotted line; if it is not strict ($\geq$ or $\leq$), we use a solid line. We can then test any point not on the border to see if it satisfies the inequality. If it does, we shade in that side of the border; if not, we shade in the other side. As an example, consider $y > 2x + 2$. To graph this inequality, we first graph the border, $y = 2x + 2$. Since it is a strict inequality, we use a dashed line. Then, we choose a test point. This can be any point not on the border; in this case, we will choose the origin, (0,0). (This makes the calculation easy and is generally a good choice unless the border passes through the origin.) Putting this into the original inequality, we get $0 > 2(0) + 2$, i.e., $0 > 2$. This is *not* true, so we shade in the side of the border that does *not* include the point (0,0):

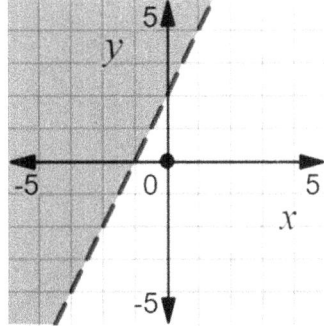

GRAPHING COMPOUND INEQUALITIES IN TWO VARIABLES

One way to graph a compound inequality in two variables is to first graph each of the component inequalities. For an *and* inequality, we then shade in only the parts where the two graphs overlap; for an *or* inequality, we shade in any region that pertains to either of the individual inequalities.

Consider the graph of "$y \geq x - 1$ and $y \leq -x$":

We first shade in the individual inequalities:

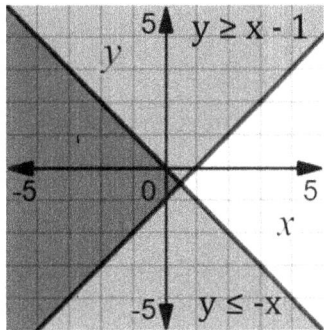

Now, since the compound inequality has an *and*, we only leave shaded the overlap—the part that pertains to *both* inequalities:

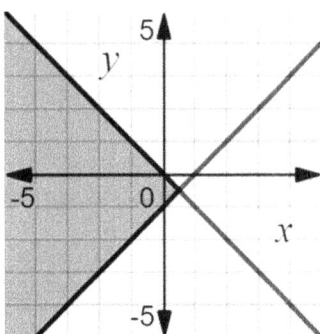

If instead the inequality had been "$y \geq x - 1$ or $y \leq -x$," our final graph would involve the *total* shaded area:

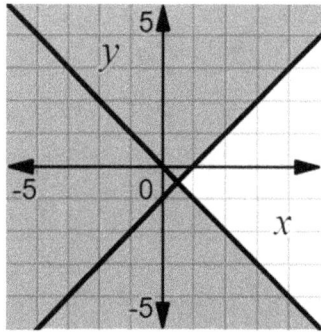

> **Review Video: Graphing Solutions to Inequalities**
> Visit mometrix.com/academy and enter code: 391281

Systems of Equations

SOLVING SYSTEMS OF EQUATIONS

A **system of equations** is a set of simultaneous equations that all use the same variables. A solution to a system of equations must be true for each equation in the system. **Consistent systems** are those with at least one solution. **Inconsistent systems** are systems of equations that have no solution.

> **Review Video: Solving Systems of Linear Equations**
> Visit mometrix.com/academy and enter code: 746745

SUBSTITUTION

To solve a system of linear equations by **substitution**, start with the easier equation and solve for one of the variables. Express this variable in terms of the other variable. Substitute this expression in the other equation and solve for the other variable. The solution should be expressed in the form (x, y). Substitute the values into both of the original equations to check your answer. Consider the following system of equations:

$$x + 6y = 15$$
$$3x - 12y = 18$$

Solving the first equation for x: $x = 15 - 6y$

Substitute this value in place of x in the second equation, and solve for y:

$$3(15 - 6y) - 12y = 18$$
$$45 - 18y - 12y = 18$$
$$30y = 27$$
$$y = \frac{27}{30} = \frac{9}{10} = 0.9$$

Plug this value for y back into the first equation to solve for x:

$$x = 15 - 6(0.9) = 15 - 5.4 = 9.6$$

Check both equations if you have time:

$$9.6 + 6(0.9) = 15 \qquad 3(9.6) - 12(0.9) = 18$$
$$9.6 + 5.4 = 15 \qquad 28.8 - 10.8 = 18$$
$$15 = 15 \qquad 18 = 18$$

Therefore, the solution is (9.6, 0.9).

> **Review Video: The Substitution Method**
> Visit mometrix.com/academy and enter code: 565151
>
> **Review Video: Substitution and Elimination**
> Visit mometrix.com/academy and enter code: 958611

ELIMINATION

To solve a system of equations using **elimination**, begin by rewriting both equations in standard form $Ax + By = C$. Check to see if the coefficients of one pair of like variables add to zero. If not, multiply one or both of the equations by a non-zero number to make one set of like variables add to zero. Add the two equations to solve for one of the variables. Substitute this value into one of the original equations to solve for the other variable. Check your work by substituting into the other equation. Now, let's look at solving the following system using the elimination method:

$$5x + 6y = 4$$
$$x + 2y = 4$$

If we multiply the second equation by -3, we can eliminate the y-terms:

$$5x + 6y = 4$$
$$-3x - 6y = -12$$

Add the equations together and solve for x:

$$2x = -8$$
$$x = \frac{-8}{2} = -4$$

Plug the value for x back in to either of the original equations and solve for y:

$$-4 + 2y = 4$$
$$y = \frac{4 + 4}{2} = 4$$

Check both equations if you have time:

$$5(-4) + 6(4) = 4 \qquad -4 + 2(4) = 4$$
$$-20 + 24 = 4 \qquad -4 + 8 = 4$$
$$4 = 4 \qquad 4 = 4$$

Therefore, the solution is (−4,4).

> **Review Video: The Elimination Method**
> Visit mometrix.com/academy and enter code: 449121

GRAPHICALLY

To solve a system of linear equations **graphically**, plot both equations on the same graph. The solution of the equations is the point where both lines cross. If the lines do not cross (are parallel), then there is **no solution**.

For example, consider the following system of equations:

$$y = 2x + 7$$
$$y = -x + 1$$

Since these equations are given in slope-intercept form, they are easy to graph; the y-intercepts of the lines are (0,7) and (0,1). The respective slopes are 2 and −1, thus the graphs look like this:

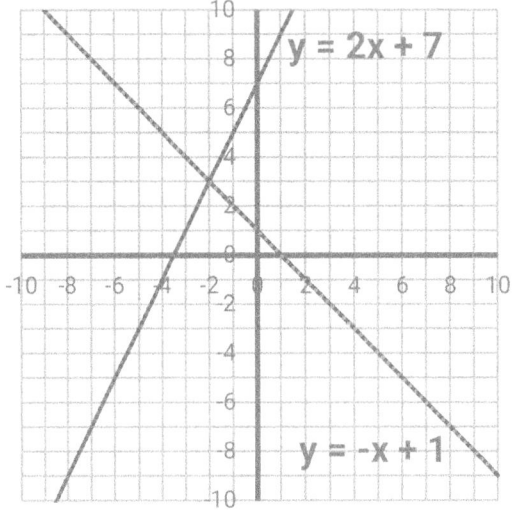

The two lines intersect at the point (−2,3), thus this is the solution to the system of equations.

Solving a system graphically is generally only practical if both coordinates of the solution are integers; otherwise the intersection will lie between gridlines on the graph and the coordinates will be difficult or impossible to determine exactly. It also helps if, as in this example, the equations are in slope-intercept form or some other form that makes them easy to graph. Otherwise, another method of solution (by substitution or elimination) is likely to be more useful.

> **Review Video: Solving Systems by Graphing**
> Visit mometrix.com/academy and enter code: 634812

SOLVING SYSTEMS OF EQUATIONS USING THE TRACE FEATURE

Using the trace feature on a calculator requires that you rewrite each equation, isolating the y-variable on one side of the equal sign. Enter both equations in the graphing calculator and plot the graphs simultaneously. Use the trace cursor to find where the two lines cross. Use the zoom feature if necessary to obtain more accurate results. Always check your answer by substituting into the original equations. The trace method is likely to be less accurate than other methods due to the resolution of graphing calculators but is a useful tool to provide an approximate answer.

Polynomials

MONOMIALS AND POLYNOMIALS

A **monomial** is a single constant, variable, or product of constants and variables, such as 7, x, $2x$, or $x^3 y$. There will never be addition or subtraction symbols in a monomial. Like monomials have like variables, but they may have different coefficients. A **polynomial** is a monomial or the result of combining two or more monomials by sums or differences. In a polynomial we call each monomial a **term**. Two terms make a **binomial** (e.g., $2x + 3y$), three terms make a **trinomial** (e.g., $5x^2 - 4x + 9$). The **degree of a monomial** is the sum of the exponents of the variables. The **degree of a polynomial** is the highest degree of any individual term.

> **Review Video: Polynomials**
> Visit mometrix.com/academy and enter code: 305005

SIMPLIFYING POLYNOMIALS

Simplifying polynomials requires combining like terms. The like terms in a polynomial expression are those that have the same variables raised to the same powers. It is often helpful to connect the like terms with arrows or lines in order to separate them from the other monomials. Once you have determined the like terms, you can rearrange the polynomial by placing them together. Remember to include the sign that is in front of each term. Once the like terms are placed together, you can apply each operation and simplify. When adding and subtracting polynomials, only add and subtract the **coefficients**, or the number part; the variable and exponent stay the same.

ADDING POLYNOMIALS

To add polynomials, you need to add like terms. These terms have the same variable part. For example, the terms $4x^2$ and $3x^2$ both include x^2 terms. To find the sum of like terms, find the sum of the coefficients. Then, keep the same variable part. You can use the distributive property to distribute the plus sign to each term of the polynomial. For example:

$(4x^2 - 5x + 7) + (3x^2 + 2x + 1) =$
$(4x^2 - 5x + 7) + 3x^2 + 2x + 1 =$
$(4x^2 + 3x^2) + (-5x + 2x) + (7 + 1) =$
$7x^2 - 3x + 8$

SUBTRACTING POLYNOMIALS

To subtract polynomials, you need to subtract like terms. To find the difference of like terms, find the difference of the coefficients. Then, keep the same variable part. You can use the distributive property to distribute the minus sign to each term of the polynomial. For example:

$(-2x^2 - x + 5) - (3x^2 - 4x + 1) =$
$(-2x^2 - x + 5) - 3x^2 + 4x - 1 =$
$(-2x^2 - 3x^2) + (-x + 4x) + (5 - 1) =$
$-5x^2 + 3x + 4$

> **Review Video: Adding and Subtracting Polynomials**
> Visit mometrix.com/academy and enter code: 124088

Multiplying Polynomials

In general, multiplying polynomials is done by multiplying each term in one polynomial by each term in the other and adding the results. In the specific case for multiplying binomials, there is a useful acronym, FOIL, that can help you make sure to cover each combination of terms. The **FOIL method** for $(Ax + By)(Cx + Dy)$ would be:

F	Multiply the *first* terms of each binomial	$(\overbrace{Ax}^{first} + By)(\overbrace{Cx}^{first} + Dy)$	ACx^2
O	Multiply the *outer* terms	$(\overbrace{Ax}^{outer} + By)(Cx + \overbrace{Dy}^{outer})$	$ADxy$
I	Multiply the *inner* terms	$(Ax + \overbrace{By}^{inner})(\overbrace{Cx}^{inner} + Dy)$	$BCxy$
L	Multiply the *last* terms of each binomial	$(Ax + \overbrace{By}^{last})(Cx + \overbrace{Dy}^{last})$	BDy^2

Then, add up the result of each and combine like terms: $ACx^2 + (AD + BC)xy + BDy^2$.

For example, using the FOIL method on binomials $(x + 2)$ and $(x - 3)$:

First: $(\boxed{x} + 2)(\boxed{x} + (-3)) \rightarrow (x)(x) = x^2$
Outer: $(\boxed{x} + 2)(x + \boxed{(-3)}) \rightarrow (x)(-3) = -3x$
Inner: $(x + \boxed{2})(\boxed{x} + (-3)) \rightarrow (2)(x) = 2x$
Last: $(x + \boxed{2})(x + \boxed{(-3)}) \rightarrow (2)(-3) = -6$

This results in: $(x^2) + (-3x) + (2x) + (-6)$

Combine like terms: $x^2 + (-3 + 2)x + (-6) = x^2 - x - 6$

> **Review Video: Multiplying Polynomials**
> Visit mometrix.com/academy and enter code: 598293
>
> **Review Video: Multiplying Terms Using the FOIL Method**
> Visit mometrix.com/academy and enter code: 854792

Dividing Polynomials

Use long division to divide a polynomial by either a monomial or another polynomial of equal or lesser degree.

When **dividing by a monomial**, divide each term of the polynomial by the monomial.

> **Review Video: Dividing Monomials**
> Visit mometrix.com/academy and enter code: 584409

When **dividing by a polynomial**, begin by arranging the terms of each polynomial in order of one variable. You may arrange in ascending or descending order, but be consistent with both polynomials. To get the first term of the quotient, divide the first term of the dividend by the first term of the divisor. Multiply the first term of the quotient by the entire divisor and subtract that product from the dividend. Repeat for the second and successive terms until you either get a remainder of zero or a remainder whose degree is less than the degree of the divisor. If the quotient has a remainder, write the answer as a mixed expression in the form:

$$\text{quotient} + \frac{\text{remainder}}{\text{divisor}}$$

For example, we can evaluate the following expression in the same way as long division:

$$\frac{x^3 - 3x^2 - 2x + 5}{x - 5}$$

$$\begin{array}{r}
x^2 + 2x + 8 \\
x - 5 \overline{)\, x^3 - 3x^2 - 2x + 5 } \\
\underline{-(x^3 - 5x^2)} \\
2x^2 - 2x \\
\underline{-(2x^2 - 10x)} \\
8x + 5 \\
\underline{-(8x - 40)} \\
45
\end{array}$$

$$\frac{x^3 - 3x^2 - 2x + 5}{x - 5} = x^2 + 2x + 8 + \frac{45}{x - 5}$$

> **Review Video: Dividing Polynomials by Monomials**
> Visit mometrix.com/academy and enter code: 253551
>
> **Review Video: Dividing Trinomials by Binomials**
> Visit mometrix.com/academy and enter code: 651465

When **factoring** a polynomial, first see whether you can factor out a nontrivial greatest common factor (GCF). For example, the trinomial $3x^5 - 18x^4 + 15x^3$ has a GCF of $3x^3$ since the GCF of 3, 18, and 15 is 3 and the GCF of x^5, x^4, and x^3 is x^3. Factoring out the GCF simplifies the expression to $3x^3(x^2 - 6x + 5)$.

To factor a quadratic trinomial (this comes up frequently), first check whether it is a perfect square trinomial (see bulleted list below). If not, see if you can factor it by trial and error by making clever choices of values for a and b (or a, b, c, and d) in the formulas below (this amounts to trying to use the FOIL mnemonic backwards):

$$x^2 + (a + b)x + ab = (x + a)(x + b)$$
$$(ac)x^2 + (ad + bc)x + bd = (ax + b)(cx + d)$$

For instance, you would try to factor the trinomial $x^2 - 6x + 5$ using the equation $x^2 + (a + b)x + ab = (x + a)(x + b)$. This means that you need to find integers a and b such that $a + b = -6$ and $ab = 5$. Starting with $ab = 5$, you can see that the only ways to write 5 as a product of integers are $(1)(5) = 5$ and $(-1)(-5) = 5$. So, it is easy to see that you want $a = -1$ and $b = -5$ since $a + b = -1 + (-5) = -6$ and $ab = (-1)(-5) = 5$. This tells you that $x^2 - 6x + 5 = (x - 1)(x - 5)$.

For polynomials with four terms (usually a cubic polynomial), sometimes factoring by grouping works: You group the two higher-power terms and the two lower-power terms, factor the GCF out of each group, and then factor out the resulting common binomial factor, if there is one. For example, $x^3 + 5x^2 + 3x + 15 = (x^3 + 5x^2) + (3x + 15) = x^2(x + 5) + 3(x + 5) = (x^2 + 3)(x + 5)$.

Once you have found the factors, write the original polynomial as the product of all the factors. Make sure all of the factors are either monomials, or else linear or irreducible quadratic polynomials (*irreducible* means they have no real zeros, which is easy to check with the quadratic formula). Check your work by multiplying the factors to make sure you get the original polynomial.

> **Review Video: Factoring Out Common Monomial Factors**
> Visit mometrix.com/academy and enter code: 398578
>
> **Review Video: Factoring Trinomials of the Form x^2+bx+c**
> Visit mometrix.com/academy and enter code: 270556

Below are patterns of some special products to remember to help make factoring easier:

- Perfect square trinomials: $x^2 + 2xy + y^2 = (x + y)^2$ or $x^2 - 2xy + y^2 = (x - y)^2$. For example, $x^2 + 10x + 25 = (x + 5)^2$.
- Difference between two squares: $x^2 - y^2 = (x + y)(x - y)$. For example, $x^2 - 9 = (x + 3)(x - 3)$.
- Sum of two cubes: $x^3 + y^3 = (x + y)(x^2 - xy + y^2)$. For example, $x^3 + 27 = (x + 3)(x^2 - 3x + 9)$.
    - Note: the second factor is *not* the same as a perfect square trinomial, so do not try to factor it further.
- Difference between two cubes: $x^3 - y^3 = (x - y)(x^2 + xy + y^2)$. For example, $x^3 - 1000 = (x - 10)(x^2 + 10x + 100)$.
    - Again, the second factor is *not* the same as a perfect square trinomial.
- Perfect cubes: $x^3 + 3x^2y + 3xy^2 + y^3 = (x + y)^3$ and $x^3 - 3x^2y + 3xy^2 - y^3 = (x - y)^3$

> **Review Video: Factoring the Difference of Two Squares**
> Visit mometrix.com/academy and enter code: 128954

Rational and Irrational Expressions

RATIONAL EXPRESSIONS

Rational expressions are fractions with polynomials in both the numerator and the denominator; the value of the polynomial in the denominator cannot be equal to zero. Be sure to keep track of values that make the denominator of the original expression zero as the final result inherits the same restrictions. For example, a denominator of $x - 3$ indicates that the expression is not defined when $x = 3$ and, as such, regardless of any operations done to the expression, it remains undefined there.

To **add or subtract** rational expressions, first find the common denominator, then rewrite each fraction as an equivalent fraction with the common denominator. Finally, add or subtract the numerators to get the numerator of the answer, and keep the common denominator as the denominator of the answer.

When **multiplying** rational expressions, factor each polynomial and cancel like factors (a factor which appears in both the numerator and the denominator). Then, multiply all remaining factors in the numerator to get the numerator of the product, and multiply the remaining factors in the denominator to get the denominator of the product. Remember: cancel entire factors, not individual terms.

To **divide** rational expressions, take the reciprocal of the divisor (the rational expression you are dividing by) and multiply by the dividend.

> **Review Video: Rational Expressions**
> Visit mometrix.com/academy and enter code: 415183

SIMPLIFYING RATIONAL EXPRESSIONS

To simplify a rational expression, factor the numerator and denominator completely. Factors that are the same and appear in the numerator and denominator have a ratio of 1. For example, look at the following expression:

$$\frac{x-1}{1-x^2}$$

The denominator, $(1 - x^2)$, is a difference of squares. It can be factored as $(1 - x)(1 + x)$. The factor $1 - x$ and the numerator $x - 1$ are opposites and have a ratio of –1. Rewrite the numerator as $-1(1 - x)$. So, the rational expression can be simplified as follows:

$$\frac{x-1}{1-x^2} = \frac{-1(1-x)}{(1-x)(1+x)} = \frac{-1}{1+x}$$

Note that since the original expression is only defined for $x \neq \{-1, 1\}$, the simplified expression has the same restrictions.

> **Review Video: Reducing Rational Expressions**
> Visit mometrix.com/academy and enter code: 788868
>
> **Review Video: Simplifying Algebraic Expressions with Parentheses**
> Visit mometrix.com/academy and enter code: 850843

IRRATIONAL EXPRESSIONS

Irrational expressions are mathematical expressions that contain an irrational number and cannot be simplified into a rational form. Usually, this includes expressions that contain radicals or constants such as π. Most commonly, you will encounter these in the forms of expressions containing roots of non-perfect squares.

BASIC OPERATIONS ON RADICAL EXPRESSIONS

To add or subtract radical numbers, the numbers within the radicals must match, similar to finding a common denominator in fractions:

$$a\sqrt{x} + b\sqrt{x} = (a+b)\sqrt{x}$$
$$a\sqrt{x} - b\sqrt{x} = (a-b)\sqrt{x}$$

To multiply radicals, the numbers outside the radical are multiplied together and the numbers inside the radical are multiplied together:

$$a\sqrt{x} \times b\sqrt{y} = ab\sqrt{xy}$$

To divide radicals, the radical must be eliminated from the denominator by multiplying both numerator and denominator by a value that will make the denominator a rational number:

$$\frac{a\sqrt{x}}{b\sqrt{y}} = \frac{a\sqrt{x}\sqrt{y}}{b\sqrt{y}\sqrt{y}} = \frac{a\sqrt{xy}}{by}$$

> **Review Video: Adding and Subtracting Radical Expressions**
> Visit mometrix.com/academy and enter code: 752176

EXAMPLE

To solve $\frac{(3\sqrt{6})(2\sqrt{3})}{4\sqrt{5}}$, we first multiply the numerator, inside the radical and out: $3 \times 2\sqrt{6 \times 3} = 6\sqrt{18} = 18\sqrt{2}$. To divide, we multiply both numerator and denominator by a value that will eliminate the radical:

$$\frac{18\sqrt{2} \times \sqrt{5}}{4\sqrt{5} \times \sqrt{5}} = \frac{18\sqrt{10}}{4 \times 5} = \frac{18\sqrt{10}}{20} = \frac{9\sqrt{10}}{10}$$

Quadratics

SOLVING QUADRATIC EQUATIONS

A quadratic equation is an equation that can be written (possibly after simplification) in the form $ax^2 + bx + c = 0$. Thus, the **solutions** of this equation are precisely the **zeros** of the quadratic polynomial $P(x) = ax^2 + bx + c$. On the graph of this polynomial the zeros, if any, appear as x-intercepts. There are several ways to find these solutions including the quadratic formula, factoring, completing the square, and graphing the function.

> **Review Video: Quadratic Equations Overview**
> Visit mometrix.com/academy and enter code: 476276
>
> **Review Video: Solutions of a Quadratic Equation on a Graph**
> Visit mometrix.com/academy and enter code: 328231

QUADRATIC FORMULA

The **quadratic formula** gives the zeros of a quadratic polynomial. It always works, but it is sometimes a little harder to use than other methods. To use it to solve a quadratic equation, rewrite the equation in the form $ax^2 + bx + c = 0$, where a, b, and c are coefficients. Now, as explained above, the solutions of the equation are the zeros of the quadratic polynomial $P(x) = ax^2 + bx + c$. To find them, substitute the values of a, b, and c into the Quadratic Formula:

$$x = \frac{-b \pm \sqrt{b^2 - 4ac}}{2a}$$

After simplification this formula produces two, one, or zero real solutions, depending on whether the **discriminant** (the number $b^2 - 4ac$ under the radical) is positive, zero, or negative. It is a good practice to check each solution by substituting it into the original equation. Incidentally, if the discriminant is negative, then the equation does have two complex solutions, but you often ignore these as meaningless in real-world settings.

> **Review Video: Using the Quadratic Formula**
> Visit mometrix.com/academy and enter code: 163102

FACTORING

To solve a quadratic equation by factoring, begin by rewriting the equation in the standard form, $ax^2 + bx + c = 0$. In the important special case that $a = 1$, the goal of factoring is to find numbers f and g such that $x^2 + bx + c = (x + f)(x + g) = x^2 + (f + g)x + fg$. In other words, you want to choose f and g to make $fg = c$ and $f + g = b$. To do this, find pairs of numbers (factors) whose product is c and look for a pair whose sum is b.

For example, suppose you want to find the solutions of the equation $x^2 + 6x - 16 = 0$ by factoring. Here $b = 6$ and $c = -16$. First, you find the pairs of numbers whose product is -16. These are -4 and 4, -8 and 2, -2 and 8, -1 and 16, and 1 and -16. The pair -2 and 8 has a sum of 6. This means $f = -2$ and $g = 8$. So, the factorization is $x^2 + 6x - 16 = (x + f)(x + g) = (x - 2)(x + 8)$, allowing you to rewrite the original equation as $(x - 2)(x + 8) = 0$. The only way for a product to equal zero is for one of the factors to equal zero; so, either $x - 2 = 0$ (in which case $x = 2$) or $x + 8 = 0$ (in which case $x = -8$). Thus, the equation has the solution $x = 2$ or $x = -8$.

In the case that $a \neq 1$, you can attempt to factor the quadratic polynomial $ax^2 + bx + c$ in the form $(mx + f)(nx + g)$ by a similar trial-and-error procedure, but the work tends to be much harder.

> **Review Video: Factoring Quadratic Equations**
> Visit mometrix.com/academy and enter code: 336566

COMPLETING THE SQUARE

The technique of completing the square comes from a simple observation: Suppose you have the expression $x^2 + bx$. If you take half the linear coefficient, b, square it, and add the result to the expression, the result is always a perfect square trinomial:

$$x^2 + bx + \left(\frac{b}{2}\right)^2 = \left(x + \frac{b}{2}\right)^2$$

For example, if you begin with $x^2 + 6x$ and add the square of half of 6 (half of 6 is 3, and $3^2 = 9$), then you get a perfect square trinomial:

$$x^2 + 6x + 9 = (x + 3)^2$$

This also works if b is negative. For instance, if you begin with the expression $x^2 - 10x$ and complete the square by adding 25 (half of -10 is -5, and $(-5)^2 = 25$), then you get another perfect square trinomial:

$$x^2 - 10x + 25 = (x - 5)^2$$

Now, suppose you want to solve the equation $x^2 + bx + c = 0$. Subtract c from both sides, to get the equation $x^2 + bx = -c$. Complete the square on the left side by adding $(b/2)^2$, but also add this same term to the right side so that the new equation is equivalent to the old one:

$$x^2 + bx + \left(\frac{b}{2}\right)^2 = -c + \left(\frac{b}{2}\right)^2$$

$$\left(x + \frac{b}{2}\right)^2 = -c - \left(\frac{b}{2}\right)^2$$

Take square roots of both sides:

$$x + \frac{b}{2} = \pm\sqrt{-c + \left(\frac{b}{2}\right)^2}$$

Remember to include $\pm$ since every positive number has both a positive and a negative square root. Subtract $b/2$ from both sides to isolate the variable x to finish the problem:

$$x = -\frac{b}{2} \pm \sqrt{-c + \left(\frac{b}{2}\right)^2}$$

This may sound complicated, but in practice it is not hard. For example, suppose you want to solve the equation $x^2 + 6x - 16 = 0$ by completing the square. First, add 16 to both sides:

$$x^2 + 6x = 16$$

Half of 6 is 3 and $3^2 = 9$, so complete the square by adding 9 to both sides of the equation:

$$x^2 + 6x + 9 = 16 + 9$$
$$(x + 3)^2 = 25$$

Now take square root of both sides, remembering to include the $\pm$:

$$\sqrt{(x+3)^2} = \pm\sqrt{25}$$
$$x + 3 = \pm 5$$
$$x = -3 \pm 5$$

So we see that the two solutions to the equation are $x = 2$ and $x = -8$.

> **Review Video: Completing the Square**
> Visit mometrix.com/academy and enter code: 982479

USING GIVEN SOLUTIONS TO FIND A QUADRATIC EQUATION

To find a quadratic equation with given numbers as solutions, simply find a quadratic polynomial that has those numbers as zeros and set that polynomial equal to zero. This is easy because a polynomial has the number p as a zero precisely when it has the binomial $x - p$ as a factor. Thus, for instance, to find a quadratic polynomial with zeros at $x = 3$ and $x = -5$, construct the polynomial $P(x) = (x - 3)(x - (-5)) = (x - 3)(x + 5) = x^2 + 2x - 15$. Setting this equal to zero produces an equation, $x^2 + 2x - 15 = 0$, whose solutions are $x = 3$ and $x = -5$.

Of course, any constant multiple $P(x) = a(x - 3)(x + 5)$ will also have the same zeros. For instance, if you choose $a = 4$, then you get the polynomial $P(x) = 4(x - 3)(x + 5) = 4x^2 + 8x - 60$, which also has zeros at $x = 3$ and $x = -5$. From this you can get another equation, $4x^2 + 8x - 60 = 0$, with solutions $x = 3$ and $x = -5$.

Basics of Functions

DEFINITION OF A FUNCTION

A function is a rule that assigns to every number in a given set (called the **domain**) exactly one corresponding value. For example, if our domain is the set $\{-2,1,2,3\}$, we can define a function by assigning to each number its square. This function assigns to -2 the value 4, to 1 the value 1, to 2 the value 4, and to 3 the value 9 (since $(-2)^2 = 4$, $1^2 = 1$, $2^2 = 4$, and $3^2 = 9$). The set of all the values assigned by a function is the **range** of the function. The range of the function in our example is the set $\{1, 4, 9\}$. We may think of a function as a kind of machine: we give it a number as an input, and it uses its rule to produce a number as an output. In the squaring function above, the input 3 produces the output 9.

> **Review Video: What is a Function?**
> Visit mometrix.com/academy and enter code: 784611

FUNCTION NOTATION

We usually name a function by a letter, often the letter f (for *function*—if we need to talk about more than one function, we name the second one g, the third one h, etc.). To specify the value (the output) corresponding to a particular number in the domain (the input), we write the function letter followed by the input number in parentheses. For instance, in the example above the notation $f(3)$ means the value that the function assigns to the number 3, namely 9—that is, $f(3) = 9$. We read the symbols $f(3)$ as, "f of 3," and we call 3 the **argument** of the function and 9 the **value** of the function (so *argument* means *input* and *value* means *output*).

Using function notation we can define the squaring function above by listing the values the function assigns to each argument in the domain: $f(-2) = 4$, $f(1) = 1$, $f(2) = 4$, and $f(3) = 9$. More efficiently, we can define the function by the single equation $f(x) = x^2$, which says that if x is a number from the domain, then we calculate the value assigned to it by substituting the number x in the formula x^2. For instance, we calculate $f(5) = 5^2 = 25$. Similarly, if we define a function g by the equation $g(x) = x^2 - 4x + 7$, then we calculate the value $g(3)$ by substituting 3 for each x in the formula: $g(3) = 3^2 - 4 \cdot 3 + 7 = 9 - 12 + 7 = 4$.

OTHER WAYS TO DEFINE FUNCTIONS

Instead of denoting the value of the function by $f(x)$, sometimes we simply use another letter, usually y. For instance, instead of defining the squaring function by the equation $f(x) = x^2$, we might use the equation $y = x^2$. In this case, we refer to x (the input) as the **independent variable** and y (the output) as the **dependent variable** because the value, y, depends on the number we choose for x.

A formula (with y or $f(x)$) is the most common way to define a function; but sometimes, if the domain is small enough, we prefer to list explicitly the possible inputs and their corresponding outputs. Some ways of doing this appear above, but a more common approach is to put the input-output pairs in a table. For instance, we can define the squaring function above by the table

x	-2	1	2	3
y	4	1	4	9

We see that the domain of this function is the set of all numbers in the x-row and the range is the set of all numbers in the y-row. We note that numbers cannot repeat in the x-row (because a function assigns exactly one value to each argument in the domain) but they can repeat in the y-row (because the function can assign the same value to multiple arguments—for instance, the number 4 appears twice in the y-row).

We can also define a function by writing the inputs and corresponding outputs as ordered pairs of x- and y-values. For instance, we can write the squaring function above as the set of ordered pairs $\{(-2,4),(1,1),(2,4),(3,9)\}$. Further, by treating these ordered pairs as coordinates and plotting the corresponding points on the coordinate plane, we get the **graph** of the function:

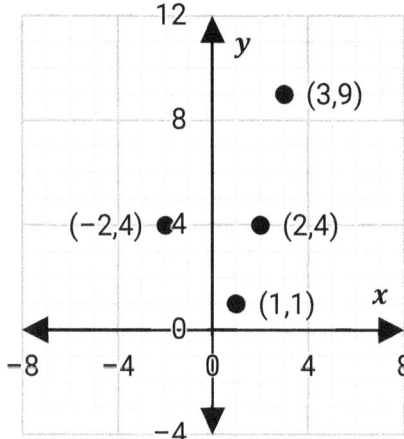

Turning this around, we can potentially use a graph to define a function, namely the function consisting of the coordinate pairs of all the points in the graph. This always works unless the graph has two points with the same x-coordinate (because then the function would assign two different y-values to the same x). It is easy to detect such points: because they have the same x-coordinate, a vertical line passes through both of them. Thus, a graph always defines a function unless it is possible to draw a vertical line that intersects the graph in two or more points. We call this condition the **vertical line test**. For example, if our graph is a circle, then by the Vertical Line Test the graph does not define a function because there are vertical lines that will intersect the circle in two different points.

MORE ON DOMAINS AND RANGES

When we define a function by a formula and do not specify the domain, then by default the domain consists of all real numbers for which the formula produces an answer. For instance, suppose we define a function f by the formula $f(x) = 1/x$. If $x = 0$, then $1/x = 1/0$, which is undefined. But if x is any other real number, then we can calculate the value of $1/x$. So, the default domain of this function is all real numbers except zero. Because of this domain convention, the graph of a function defined by a formula usually consists of infinitely many points that "connect to" each other in a way that produces a line or curve (see examples below) rather than the isolated points we see in the squaring function above.

If we have the graph of a function, its domain consists of all numbers on the x-axis with corresponding points on the graph and its range consists of all numbers on the y-axis with corresponding points on the graph. For example, consider the function $f(x) = x^2 + 3$:

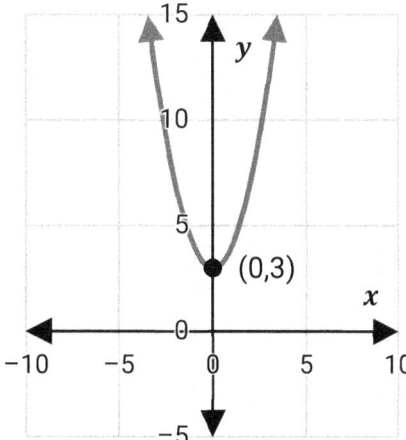

Since the graph continues infinitely to the left and right beyond what we can see, every point on the x-axis has a corresponding point on the graph; so, the domain of this function is all real numbers. On the other hand, the lowest point on this graph has a y-value of 3, and the graph passes through all higher y-values. So, the range of this function is all real numbers greater than or equal to 3, which we can denote algebraically by $y \geq 3$ or, using interval notation, by $[3, \infty)$.

> **Review Video: How to Find Domain and Range**
> Visit mometrix.com/academy and enter code: 778133
>
> **Review Video: Domain and Range of Quadratic Functions**
> Visit mometrix.com/academy and enter code: 331768

MONOTONIC AND EVEN/ODD FUNCTIONS

A function, f, is **increasing** if it always assigns larger values to larger arguments. It is **decreasing** if it always assigns smaller values to larger arguments. That is, f is increasing if $a < b$ always guarantees $f(a) < f(b)$, and it is decreasing if $a < b$ always guarantees $f(a) > f(b)$. The graph of an increasing function consistently rises from left to right, and the graph of a decreasing function consistently falls from left to right. For example, the function $f(x) = 2x$ is an increasing function because doubling a larger number always gives us a larger result than doubling a smaller number.

The graph of $f(x) = 2x$ is a line with slope $m = 2$, which, as we expect, rises from left to right. We call a function **monotonic** if it is either increasing or decreasing.

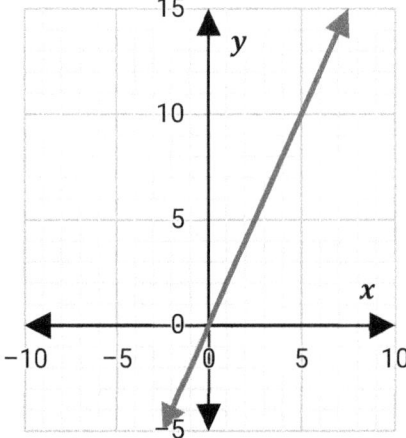

A function, f, is **even** if changing the sign of its argument produces the same value. It is **odd** if changing the sign of its argument produces the same value except with the opposite sign. That is, f is even if $f(-x) = f(x)$ and odd if $f(-x) = -f(x)$ for every argument x. The function $f(x) = x^2 + 3$ is even because substituting opposite arguments always produces the same value. For instance, $f(5) = 28$ and $f(-5) = 28$ because $5^2 + 3 = 25 + 3 = 28$ and $(-5)^2 + 3 = 25 + 3 = 28$. The function $f(x) = 2x$ is odd because substituting opposite arguments always produces opposite values. For instance, $f(10) = 20$ and $f(-10) = -20$ because $2(10) = 20$ and $2(-10) = -20$. The graph of an even function is always symmetric with respect to the y-axis, making the left and right halves of the graph mirror images of each other, as in the graph of the even function $f(x) = x^2 + 3$ above. The graph of an odd function is always symmetric with respect to the origin. This means that if we rotate the graph 180° around the origin (think of sticking a pin through the origin on a sheet of graph paper and rotating the paper halfway around) the graph looks the same, as in the graph of the odd function $f(x) = 2x$ above.

It is worth noting that most functions are neither increasing nor decreasing (that is, they are not monotonic) and most functions are neither even nor odd. For example, the function $f(x) = x^2 -$

x is neither increasing nor decreasing and neither even nor odd: its graph neither rises nor falls consistently, and it is symmetric with respect to neither the y-axis nor the origin.

> **Review Video: Even and Odd Functions**
> Visit mometrix.com/academy and enter code: 278985

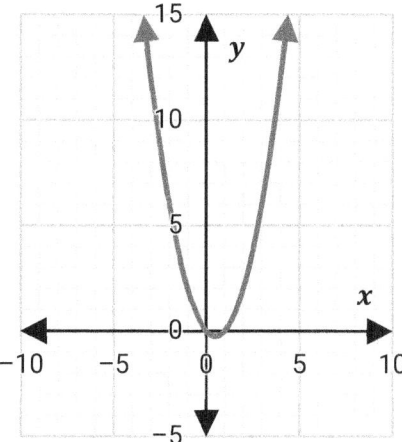

INVERTIBLE (ONE-TO-ONE) FUNCTIONS

A function, f, is one-to-one if it never assigns the same value to different arguments—that is, if $f(a)$ and $f(b)$ are different whenever a and b are different. The graph of a one-to-one function never has two points that lie on the same horizontal line because such points would have different x-values but the same y-value. Thus, a function is one-to-one if it is impossible to draw a horizontal line that intersects its graph in more than one point. We call this condition the **horizonal line test**. For example, the graph of the function $f(x) = 2x$ above is a line that rises from left to right. Every horizontal line intersects this line in exactly one point, so the function $f(x) = 2x$ is one-to-one. This is also clear without the graph because it is impossible to double two different numbers and get the same answer.

When a function, f, is one-to-one, it is possible to define its inverse function, f^{-1}, that "undoes" what f does, assigning to each output from f the input that produced it. That is, for each x in the domain of f, if $y = f(x)$, then $f^{-1}(y) = x$. For example, the inverse of the function $f(x) = 2x$ above is $f^{-1}(y) = y/2$. So, for instance, $f(5) = 2 \cdot 5 = 10$, and $f^{-1}(10) = 10/2 = 5$ (and similarly for every other value of x). Thus, the domain of f^{-1} is the range of f and vice versa. If a function, f, has an inverse, we say that f is **invertible**. Since a function has an inverse precisely when it is one-to-one, the terms *invertible* and *one-to-one* are synonyms.

If f is an invertible function defined by a formula, then to find its inverse we simply write the equation $y = f(x)$ and solve it for x (that is, we isolate the x). The result will be the equation $f^{-1}(y) = x$. For instance, starting with the function $f(x) = 2x$, we write $y = 2x$ and isolate the x by dividing both sides of the equation by 2. This gives us $y/2 = x$, so we know that $f^{-1}(y) = y/2$. Although this procedure is theoretically simple, in practice the algebra can be difficult.

Common Functions

Certain functions and certain kinds of functions are particularly useful, coming up frequently in mathematics and its applications. Once we know some basic function terminology and concepts, it is useful to begin developing a mental library of the most common and useful functions.

> **Review Video: Common Functions**
> Visit mometrix.com/academy and enter code: 629798

CONSTANT FUNCTIONS

A function of the form $f(x) = a$, where a is a real number, is a **constant function**. This function assigns the same value, a, to every real argument x. For instance, given the constant function $f(x) = 5$, we have $f(2) = 5$, $f(100) = 5$, and $f(-7.1) = 5$.

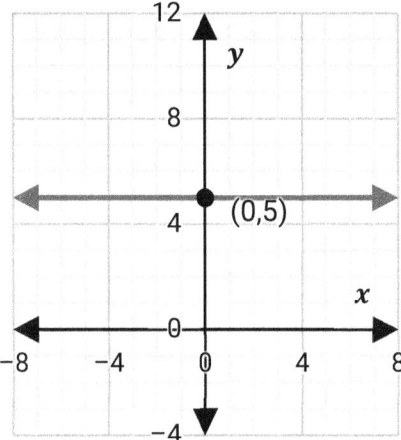

The domain of a constant function is the set of all real numbers, and the range is the set containing the single number a. Its graph is a horizontal line passing through the number $y = a$ on the y-axis (we call the number at which a function's graph intersects the y-axis the **y-intercept** of the function).

THE IDENTITY FUNCTION

The function $f(x) = x$ is the **identity function**. Its value always equals its argument. Thus, for instance, $f(2) = 2$, $f(100) = 100$, and $f(-7.1) = -7.1$.

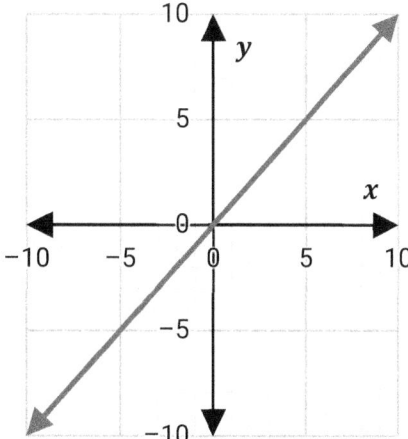

Its domain and range are the set of all real numbers. It is both an increasing function and an odd function. Its graph is a line that passes through the origin and rises from left to right at a 45° angle to the horizontal. Since it passes through the origin, its y intercept is $y = 0$ and it also has an **x-intercept** (a number at which the function's graph intersects the x-axis) of $x = 0$.

LINEAR FUNCTIONS

A function of the form $f(x) = ax + b$, where a and b are real numbers (with $a \neq 0$), is a **linear function** (the identity function is a linear function with $a = 1$ and $b = 0$). Its domain and range are the set of all real numbers. Its graph is a line (the word _linear_ contains the root word _line_) with one x-intercept (at $x = -b/a$), with a y-intercept at $y = b$, and with a direction and steepness that depend on the coefficient a, which we call the **slope**. Specifically, the slope a is the amount the y-value increases for each increase of 1 in the x-value. Thus, for $a > 0$, the line rises from left to right (making f an increasing function), and larger values of a produce steeper ascents. Similarly, for $a < 0$, the line falls from left to right (making f a decreasing function), and smaller (more negative) values of a produce steeper descents. For instance, the graph of the linear function

$f(x) = (1/2)x + 3$ is a line that passes through the point $y = 3$ on the y-axis and that rises by $1/2$ unit for every unit that x increases.

> **Review Video: Graphing Linear Functions**
> Visit mometrix.com/academy and enter code: 699478

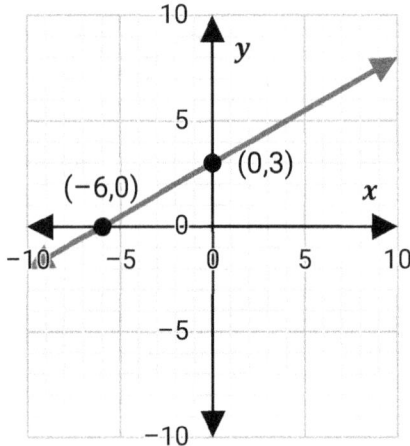

In many contexts it is standard to use the letter m for slope and thus to write the general form of a linear function as $f(x) = mx + b$, known as **slope-intercept form**.

THE SQUARING FUNCTION

The function $f(x) = x^2$ is the **squaring function**.

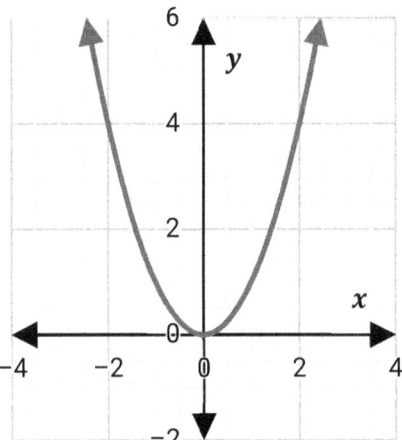

Its graph is U-shaped, opening upward as shown, a shape known as a **parabola**. It has a lowest point, its **vertex**, at the origin, which is also the location of its single x-intercept and single y-intercept. Thus, its **minimum** is $y = 0$, its domain is the set of all real numbers, and its range is the set of nonnegative real numbers (that is, $y \geq 0$). It is an even function and thus symmetric with respect to the y-axis (which we call the **axis of symmetry**), meaning that the left half of the graph is the mirror image of the right half, with the mirror standing on the y-axis.

QUADRATIC FUNCTIONS

A function of the form $f(x) = ax^2 + bx + c$, where a, b, and c are real numbers (with $a \neq 0$), is a **quadratic function** (the squaring function is a quadratic function with $a = 1$, $b = 0$, and $c = 0$). Its domain is the set of all real numbers, and its graph is a parabola. It is symmetric with respect to its axis of symmetry, the vertical line $x = -b/(2a)$. If $a > 0$, the parabola opens upward, so that its vertex is at its lowest point (its minimum) and its range consists of all real numbers greater than or equal to this minimum y-value. If $a < 0$, the parabola opens downward, so that its vertex is at its highest point (its maximum) and its range consists of all real numbers less than or equal to this maximum y-value. Its y-intercept is $y = c$ since $f(0) = c$, and it may have zero, one, or two x-intercepts. For example, the function $f(x) = x^2 - 6x + 5$ has $a = 1$, $b = -6$, and $c = 5$.

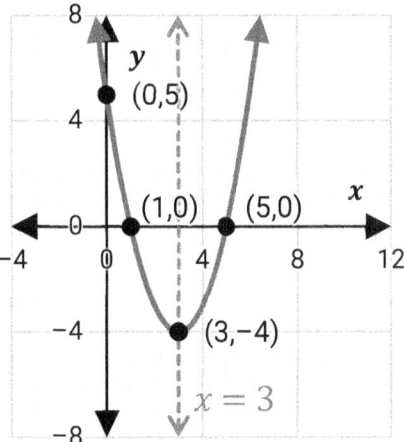

Its graph opens upward (because $a > 0$) and its axis of symmetry is the vertical line $x = 3$ (since $-b/(2a) = -(-6)/(2 \cdot 1) = 3$). Its y-intercept is at $y = 5$. It turns out to have its vertex at the point $(3, -4)$, making its minimum value $y = -4$. So, its domain is the set of all real numbers, and its range is $y \geq -4$. It also turns out to have two x-intercepts, at $x = 1$ and at $x = 5$ (since $f(1) = 0$ and $f(5) = 0$).

POLYNOMIAL FUNCTIONS

A function of the form $f(x) = a^n x^n + a^{n-1} x^{n-1} + \cdots + a_2 x^2 + a_1 x + a_0$, where n is a whole number and $a_0, a_1, a_2, \ldots a_{n-1}, a_n$ are real numbers, is a **polynomial function of degree n**. Its domain is the set of all real numbers (it is complicated to describe its range in general), and its y-intercept is $y = a_0$ (since $f(0) = a_0$). Constant functions, linear functions, and quadratic functions are polynomial functions of degrees 0, 1, and 2, respectively. In general, a polynomial function of degree n has up to n zeros (x-intercepts) and up to $n - 1$ "bends." For example, the fourth degree polynomial function $f(x) = x^4 - 11x^3 + 41x^2 - 61x + 30$, whose graph appears here, has four x-intercepts (at $x = 1$, $x = 2$, $x = 3$, and $x = 5$) and three "bends," and its y-intercept (not visible on the graph) is at $y = 30$.

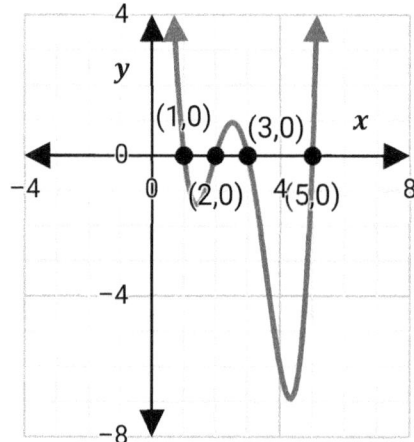

RATIONAL FUNCTIONS

A function of the form $f(x) = P(x)/Q(x)$, where P and Q are polynomials, is a rational function (we note that the word <u>rational</u> includes the root word <i>ratio</i>, indicating that a rational function is a ratio of polynomial functions). The domain of a rational function is all real numbers except the zeros of $Q(x)$ since division by zero is undefined (the range can be difficult to describe in general). Its y-intercept is $f(0)$, if this is defined; and its x-intercepts are the zeros of $P(x)$ that are in the domain of f, if there are any. A rational function may also have vertical asymptotes (vertical lines that the graph approaches without crossing) and a horizontal asymptote (a horizontal line that the curve approaches as x becomes very small or very large (toward the left and right edges of the graph). For example, the rational function $f(x) = (2x^2 + x - 1)/(x^2 + x - 2)$ has as its domain the set of all real numbers except $x = -2$ and $x = 1$ (since those numbers make the denominator zero).

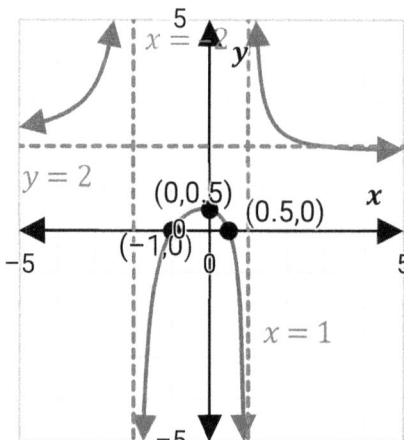

It has a y-intercept of $y = 1/2$ since $f(0) = (-1)/(-2) = 1/2$, and it has x-intercepts at $x = -1$ and at $x = 1/2$ since those numbers make the numerator zero. It has vertical asymptotes at $x = -2$ and $x = 1$ (not coincidentally, these are the numbers omitted from the domain) and a horizontal asymptote at $y = 2$. It is important to note that vertical asymptotes cannot be crossed in rational functions, but horizontal asymptotes can be crossed if the function tends near the asymptote at infinity and does not go past all possible turning points.

THE SQUARE ROOT FUNCTION

The function $f(x) = \sqrt{x}$ is the square root function.

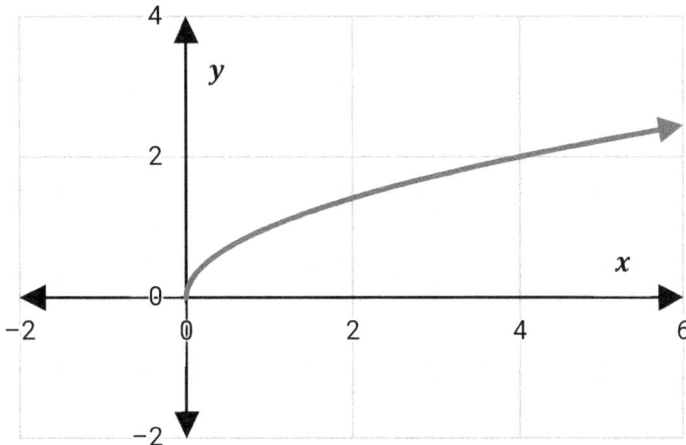

It is an increasing function, and its domain and range are both the set of all nonnegative real numbers. It has one x-intercept and one y-intercept, both appearing at the origin. Its graph is the upper half of a parabola opening to the right. The square root function is the inverse of the squaring function with domain restricted to the nonnegative real numbers (that is, $f(x) = x^2$ for $x \geq 0$).

PIECEWISE-DEFINED FUNCTIONS

As the name suggests, a **piecewise-defined function** (or, simply, a **piecewise function**) is a function defined by different rules on different pieces of the domain. We define such a function using the following form:

Function Name	Rule to Apply	Piece of the Domain on Which the Rule Applies
$f(x) =$	$\begin{cases} \text{Rule 1,} \\ \text{Rule 2,} \\ \text{Rule 3,} \\ \text{etc.,} \end{cases}$	First Piece of the Domain Second Piece of the Domain Third Piece of the Domain etc.

The pieces of the domain should not overlap, and together they should cover the whole domain. For example, we might craft a piecewise-defined function by

$$f(x) = \begin{cases} x^2, & \text{if } x < 2 \\ 3x - 5, & \text{if } x \geq 2 \end{cases}$$

The two pieces of the domain—namely, $x < 2$ and $x \geq 2$—do not overlap, and together they include all real numbers. To evaluate the function for a particular argument x, we determine which piece of the domain includes x and then apply the corresponding rule. For instance, to find $f(4)$, we note that $4 \geq 2$; so, we apply the rule $3x - 5$ to get the value $f(4) = 3 \cdot 4 - 5 = 7$. Similarly, to find $f(-6)$, we note that $-6 < 2$; so, we apply the rule x^2 to get the value $f(-6) = (-6)^2 = 36$.

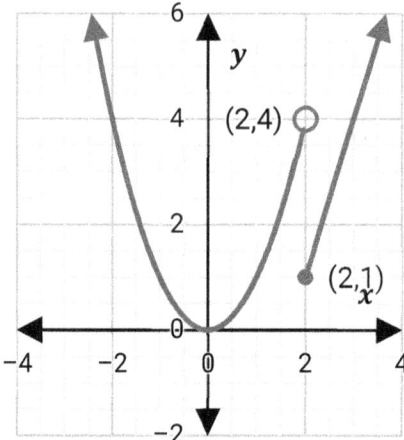

To graph this function, we sketch the graph of the parabola $y = x^2$ on the part of the plane where $x < 2$ and we sketch the line $y = 3x - 5$ on the part of the plane where $x \geq 2$. This produces a graph with a jump at $x = 2$ (a discontinuity—piecewise-defined functions are useful for producing graphs with discontinuities). We plot an open circle at the point $(2,4)$, the end of the left part of the graph, to show that this point is not part of the graph. And we plot a solid dot at the point $(2,1)$, the start of the right part of the graph, to show that this point *is* part of the graph.

THE ABSOLUTE VALUE FUNCTION

A particularly useful piecewise-defined function is the absolute value function. It is so important that instead of naming it $f(x)$ or $g(x)$, we denote it using the special notation $|x|$. Its definition is

$$|x| = \begin{cases} -x, & \text{if } x < 0 \\ x, & \text{if } x \geq 0 \end{cases}$$

For instance, $|8| = 8$ (since $8 \geq 0$) and $|-5| = -(-5) = 5$, since $-5 < 0$. So, the absolute value function acts like the identity function for nonnegative numbers (it leaves them unchanged), and it gives the opposite of negative numbers (it effectively strips off the minus sign). Thus, we can think of the absolute value of a real number as its distance from zero on the number line, without taking into consideration whether the number is larger than or smaller than zero. For instance, $|-3| = 3$ and $|3| = 3$, showing that both -3 and 3 are three units away from zero. The absolute value function is an even function with a V-shaped graph that looks like the line $y = x$ (the identity function) on the right "half" of the plane (for $x \geq 0$) and the line $y = -x$ on the left "half" of the plane (for $x < 0$).

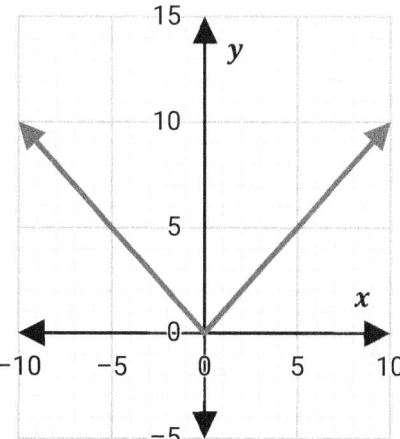

Geometric and Spatial Reasoning

Metric and Customary Measurements

METRIC MEASUREMENT PREFIXES

Giga-	One billion	1 *giga*watt is one billion watts
Mega-	One million	1 *mega*hertz is one million hertz
Kilo-	One thousand	1 *kilo*gram is one thousand grams
Deci-	One-tenth	1 *deci*meter is one-tenth of a meter
Centi-	One-hundredth	1 *centi*meter is one-hundredth of a meter
Milli-	One-thousandth	1 *milli*liter is one-thousandth of a liter
Micro-	One-millionth	1 *micro*gram is one-millionth of a gram

> **Review Video: How the Metric System Works**
> Visit mometrix.com/academy and enter code: 163709

MEASUREMENT CONVERSION

When converting between units, the goal is to maintain the same meaning but change the way it is displayed. In order to go from a larger unit to a smaller unit, multiply the number of the known amount by the equivalent amount. When going from a smaller unit to a larger unit, divide the number of the known amount by the equivalent amount.

For complicated conversions, it may be helpful to set up conversion fractions. In these fractions, one fraction is the **conversion factor**. The other fraction has the unknown amount in the numerator. So, the known value is placed in the denominator. Sometimes, the second fraction has the known value from the problem in the numerator and the unknown in the denominator. Multiply the two fractions to get the converted measurement. Note that since the numerator and the denominator of the factor are equivalent, the value of the fraction is 1. That is why we can say that the result in the new units is equal to the result in the old units even though they have different numbers.

It can often be necessary to chain known conversion factors together. As an example, consider converting 512 square inches to square meters. We know that there are 2.54 centimeters in an inch and 100 centimeters in a meter, and we know we will need to square each of these factors to achieve the conversion we are looking for.

$$\frac{512 \text{ in}^2}{1} \times \left(\frac{2.54 \text{ cm}}{1 \text{ in}}\right)^2 \times \left(\frac{1 \text{ m}}{100 \text{ cm}}\right)^2 = \frac{512 \text{ in}^2}{1} \times \left(\frac{6.4516 \text{ cm}^2}{1 \text{ in}^2}\right) \times \left(\frac{1 \text{ m}^2}{10,000 \text{ cm}^2}\right) = 0.330 \text{ m}^2$$

> **Review Video: Measurement Conversions**
> Visit mometrix.com/academy and enter code: 316703
>
> **Review Video: Converting Kilograms to Pounds**
> Visit mometrix.com/academy and enter code: 241463

COMMON UNITS AND EQUIVALENTS
METRIC EQUIVALENTS

1000 μg (microgram)	1 mg
1000 mg (milligram)	1 g
1000 g (gram)	1 kg
1000 kg (kilogram)	1 metric ton
1000 mL (milliliter)	1 L
1000 μm (micrometer)	1 mm
1000 mm (millimeter)	1 m
100 cm (centimeter)	1 m
1000 m (meter)	1 km

DISTANCE AND AREA MEASUREMENT

Unit	Abbreviation	US equivalent	Metric equivalent
Inch	in	1 inch	2.54 centimeters
Foot	ft	12 inches	0.305 meters
Yard	yd	3 feet	0.914 meters
Mile	mi	5280 feet	1.609 kilometers
Acre	ac	4840 square yards	0.405 hectares
Square Mile	sq. mi. or mi.^{2}	640 acres	2.590 square kilometers

CAPACITY MEASUREMENTS

Unit	Abbreviation	US equivalent	Metric equivalent
Fluid Ounce	fl oz	8 fluid drams	29.573 milliliters
Cup	c	8 fluid ounces	0.237 liter
Pint	pt.	16 fluid ounces	0.473 liter
Quart	qt.	2 pints	0.946 liter
Gallon	gal.	4 quarts	3.785 liters
Teaspoon	t or tsp.	1 fluid dram	5 milliliters
Tablespoon	T or tbsp.	4 fluid drams	15 or 16 milliliters
Cubic Centimeter	cc or cm^3	0.271 drams	1 milliliter

WEIGHT MEASUREMENTS

Unit	Abbreviation	US equivalent	Metric equivalent
Ounce	oz	16 drams	28.35 grams
Pound	lb	16 ounces	453.6 grams
Ton	tn.	2,000 pounds	907.2 kilograms

VOLUME AND WEIGHT MEASUREMENT CLARIFICATIONS

Always be careful when using ounces and fluid ounces. They are not equivalent.

1 pint = 16 fluid ounces	1 fluid ounce ≠ 1 ounce
1 pound = 16 ounces	1 pint ≠ 1 pound

Having one pint of something does not mean you have one pound of it. In the same way, just because something weighs one pound does not mean that its volume is one pint.

In the United States, the word "ton" by itself refers to a short ton or a net ton. Do not confuse this with a long ton (also called a gross ton) or a metric ton (also spelled *tonne*), which have different measurement equivalents.

$$1 \text{ US ton} = 2000 \text{ pounds} \quad \neq \quad 1 \text{ metric ton} = 1000 \text{ kilograms}$$

Polygons

A **polygon** is a closed, two-dimensional figure with three or more straight line segments called **sides**. The point at which two sides of a polygon intersect is called the **vertex**. In a polygon, the number of sides is always equal to the number of vertices. A polygon with all sides congruent and all angles equal is called a **regular polygon**. Common polygons are:

$$\text{Triangle} = 3 \text{ sides}$$
$$\text{Quadrilateral} = 4 \text{ sides}$$
$$\text{Pentagon} = 5 \text{ sides}$$
$$\text{Hexagon} = 6 \text{ sides}$$
$$\text{Heptagon} = 7 \text{ sides}$$
$$\text{Octagon} = 8 \text{ sides}$$
$$\text{Nonagon} = 9 \text{ sides}$$
$$\text{Decagon} = 10 \text{ sides}$$
$$\text{Dodecagon} = 12 \text{ sides}$$

More generally, an n-gon is a polygon that has n angles and n sides.

> **Review Video: Intro to Polygons**
> Visit mometrix.com/academy and enter code: 271869

The sum of the interior angles of an n-sided polygon is $(n - 2) \times 180°$. For example, in a triangle $n = 3$. So the sum of the interior angles is $(3 - 2) \times 180° = 180°$. In a quadrilateral, $n = 4$, and the sum of the angles is $(4 - 2) \times 180° = 360°$.

> **Review Video: Sum of Interior Angles**
> Visit mometrix.com/academy and enter code: 984991

CONVEX AND CONCAVE POLYGONS

A **convex polygon** is a polygon whose diagonals all lie within the interior of the polygon. A **concave polygon** is a polygon with at least one diagonal that is outside the polygon. In the diagram below, quadrilateral $ABCD$ is concave because diagonal $\overline{AC}$ lies outside the polygon and quadrilateral $EFGH$ is convex because both diagonals lie inside the polygon.

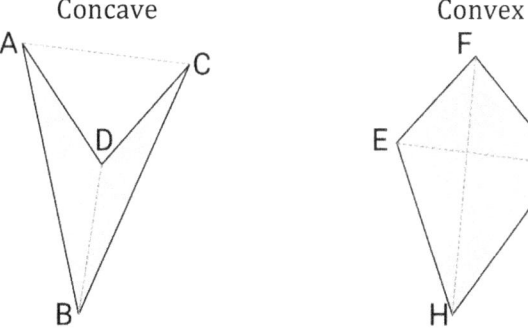

Apothem and Radius

A line segment from the center of a regular polygon that is perpendicular to a side of the polygon is called the **apothem**. A line segment from the center of a regular polygon to a vertex of the polygon is called a **radius**. In a regular polygon, the apothem can be used to find the area of the polygon using the formula $A = \frac{1}{2}ap$, where a is the apothem, and p is the perimeter.

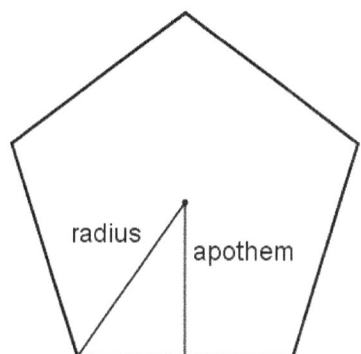

A **diagonal** is a line segment that joins two non-adjacent vertices of a polygon. The number of diagonals a polygon has can be found by using the formula:

$$\text{number of diagonals} = \frac{n(n-3)}{2}$$

Note that n is the number of sides in the polygon. This formula works for all polygons, not just regular polygons.

Congruence and Similarity

Congruent figures are geometric figures that have the same size and shape. For congruent polygons all corresponding angle measures are equal, and all corresponding side lengths are equal. Congruence is indicated by the symbol $\cong$. For instance, the expression $ABC \cong DEF$ indicates that the triangles below are congruent. The order of the letters is important, indicating which parts of the polygons correspond to each other. For example, since the letters A and D both come first, ∠A and ∠D have the same measure.

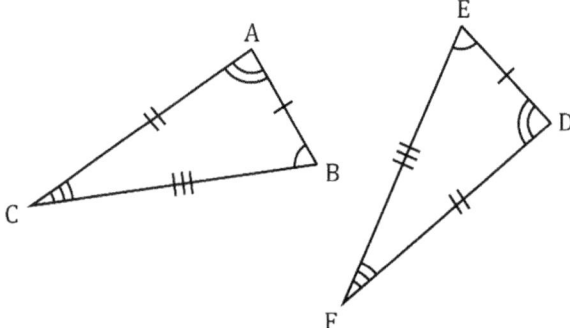

Similar figures are geometric figures that have the same shape, but do not necessarily have the same size. For similar polygons all corresponding angle measures are equal, and all corresponding side lengths are proportional, but they do not have to be equal. It is indicated by the symbol ~. For instance, the expression $ABC \sim DEF$ indicates that the triangles below are similar. Again, the order of the letters indicates which parts of the polygons correspond to each other.

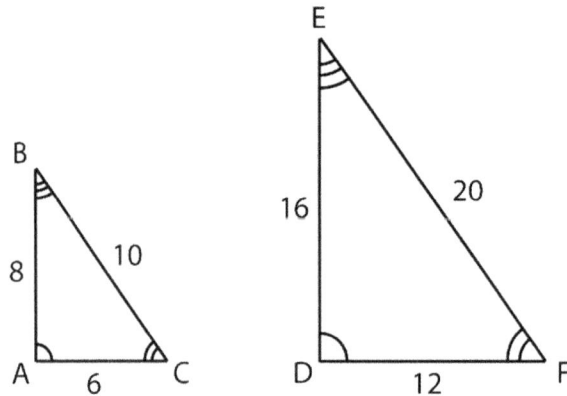

Note that all congruent figures are also similar, but not all similar figures are congruent.

> **Review Video: Congruent Shapes**
> Visit mometrix.com/academy and enter code: 492281

Line of Symmetry

A line that divides a figure or object into congruent parts that are mirror images of each other across the line is called a **line of symmetry**. An object may have no lines of symmetry, one line of symmetry, or multiple (i.e., more than one) lines of symmetry.

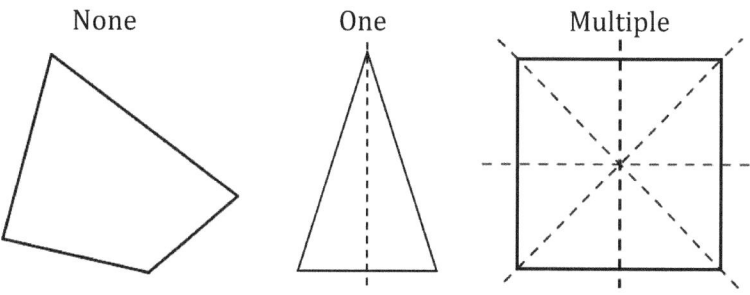

Review Video: Symmetry
Visit mometrix.com/academy and enter code: 528106

Triangles

A triangle is a three-sided figure with the sum of its interior angles being 180°. The **perimeter of any triangle** is found by summing the three side lengths; $P = a + b + c$. For an equilateral triangle, this is the same as $P = 3a$, where a is any side length, since all three sides are the same length.

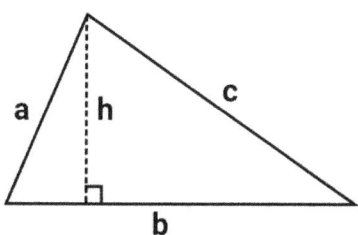

Review Video: Proof that a Triangle is 180 Degrees
Visit mometrix.com/academy and enter code: 687591

Review Video: Area and Perimeter of a Triangle
Visit mometrix.com/academy and enter code: 853779

The **area of any triangle** can be found by taking half the product of one side length referred to as the base, often given the variable b and the perpendicular distance from that side to the opposite vertex called the altitude or height and given the variable h. In equation form that is $A = \frac{1}{2}bh$. Another formula that works for any triangle is $A = \sqrt{s(s-a)(s-b)(s-c)}$, where s is the semiperimeter: $\frac{a+b+c}{2}$, and a, b, and c are the lengths of the three sides. Special cases include isosceles triangles, $A = \frac{1}{2}b\sqrt{a^2 - \frac{b^2}{4}}$, where b is the unique side and a is the length of one of the two congruent sides, and equilateral triangles, $A = \frac{\sqrt{3}}{4}a^2$, where a is the length of a side.

Review Video: Area of Any Triangle
Visit mometrix.com/academy and enter code: 138510

PARTS OF A TRIANGLE

An **altitude** of a triangle is a line segment drawn from one vertex perpendicular to the opposite side. In the diagram that follows, $\overline{BE}$, $\overline{AD}$, and $\overline{CF}$ are altitudes. The length of an altitude is also called the height of the triangle. The three altitudes in a triangle are always concurrent. The point of concurrency of the altitudes of a triangle, O, is called the **orthocenter**. Note that in an obtuse triangle, the orthocenter will be outside the triangle, and in a right triangle, the orthocenter is the vertex of the right angle.

A **median** of a triangle is a line segment drawn from one vertex to the midpoint of the opposite side. In the diagram that follows, $\overline{BH}$, $\overline{AG}$, and $\overline{CI}$ are medians. This is not the same as the altitude, except the altitude to the base of an isosceles triangle and all three altitudes of an equilateral triangle. The point of concurrency of the medians of a triangle, T, is called the **centroid**. This is the same point as the orthocenter only in an equilateral triangle. Unlike the orthocenter, the centroid is always inside the triangle. The centroid can also be considered the exact center of the triangle. Any shape triangle can be perfectly balanced on a tip placed at the centroid. The centroid is also the point that is two-thirds the distance from the vertex to the opposite side.

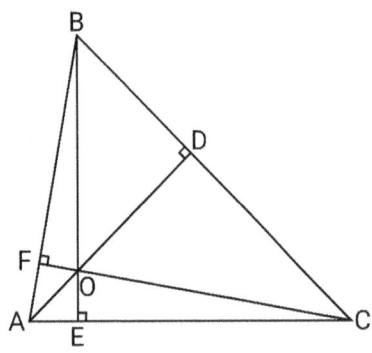 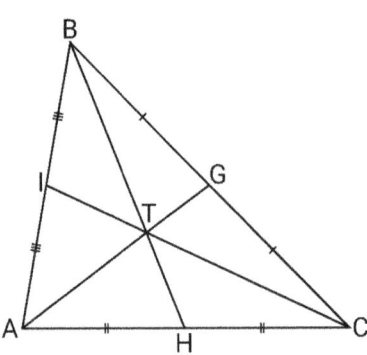

Review Video: Centroid, Incenter, Circumcenter, and Orthocenter
Visit mometrix.com/academy and enter code: 598260

Triangle Properties

CLASSIFICATIONS OF TRIANGLES

A **scalene triangle** is a triangle with no congruent sides. A scalene triangle will also have three angles of different measures. The angle with the largest measure is opposite the longest side, and the angle with the smallest measure is opposite the shortest side. An **acute triangle** is a triangle whose three angles are all less than 90°. If two of the angles are equal, the acute triangle is also an **isosceles triangle**. An isosceles triangle will also have two congruent angles opposite the two congruent sides. If the three angles are all equal, the acute triangle is also an **equilateral triangle**. An equilateral triangle will also have three congruent angles, each 60°. All equilateral triangles are also acute triangles. An **obtuse triangle** is a triangle with exactly one angle greater than 90°. The other two angles may or may not be equal. If the two remaining angles are equal, the obtuse triangle is also an isosceles triangle. A **right triangle** is a triangle with exactly one angle equal to 90°. All right triangles follow the Pythagorean theorem. A right triangle can never be acute or obtuse.

The table below illustrates how each descriptor places a different restriction on the triangle:

Sides \ Angles	Acute: All angles < 90°	Obtuse: One angle > 90°	Right: One angle = 90°
Scalene: No equal side lengths	$90° > \angle a > \angle b > \angle c$ $x > y > z$	$\angle a > 90° > \angle b > \angle c$ $x > y > z$	$90° = \angle a > \angle b > \angle c$ $x > y > z$
Isosceles: Two equal side lengths	$90° > \angle a, \angle b, \text{ or } \angle c$ $\angle b = \angle c, \quad y = z$	$\angle a > 90° > \angle b = \angle c$ $x > y = z$	$\angle a = 90°$ $\angle b = \angle c = 45°$ $x > y = z$
Equilateral: Three equal side lengths	$60° = \angle a = \angle b = \angle c$ $x = y = z$		

> **Review Video: Introduction to Types of Triangles**
> Visit mometrix.com/academy and enter code: 511711

GENERAL RULES FOR TRIANGLES

The **triangle inequality theorem** states that the sum of the measures of any two sides of a triangle is always greater than the measure of the third side. If the sum of the measures of two sides were equal to the third side, a triangle would be impossible because the two sides would lie flat across the third side and there would be no vertex. If the sum of the measures of two of the sides was less than the third side, a closed figure would be impossible because the two shortest sides would never meet. In other words, for a triangle with sides lengths A, B, and C: $A + B > C$, $B + C > A$, and $A + C > B$.

The sum of the measures of the interior angles of a triangle is always 180°. Therefore, a triangle can never have more than one angle greater than or equal to 90°.

In any triangle, the angles opposite congruent sides are congruent, and the sides opposite congruent angles are congruent. The largest angle is always opposite the longest side, and the smallest angle is always opposite the shortest side.

The line segment that joins the midpoints of any two sides of a triangle is always parallel to the third side and exactly half the length of the third side.

> **Review Video: General Rules (Triangle Inequality Theorem)**
> Visit mometrix.com/academy and enter code: 166488

SIMILARITY AND CONGRUENCE RULES

Similar triangles are triangles whose corresponding angles are equal and whose corresponding sides are proportional. Represented by AAA. Similar triangles whose corresponding sides are congruent are also congruent triangles.

Triangles can be shown to be **congruent** in 5 ways:

- **SSS**: Three sides of one triangle are congruent to the three corresponding sides of the second triangle.
- **SAS**: Two sides and the included angle (the angle formed by those two sides) of one triangle are congruent to the corresponding two sides and included angle of the second triangle.
- **ASA**: Two angles and the included side (the side that joins the two angles) of one triangle are congruent to the corresponding two angles and included side of the second triangle.
- **AAS**: Two angles and a non-included side of one triangle are congruent to the corresponding two angles and non-included side of the second triangle.
- **HL**: The hypotenuse and leg of one right triangle are congruent to the corresponding hypotenuse and leg of the second right triangle.

> **Review Video: Similar Triangles**
> Visit mometrix.com/academy and enter code: 398538

Quadrilaterals

A **quadrilateral** is a closed two-dimensional geometric figure that has four straight sides. The sum of the interior angles of any quadrilateral is 360°.

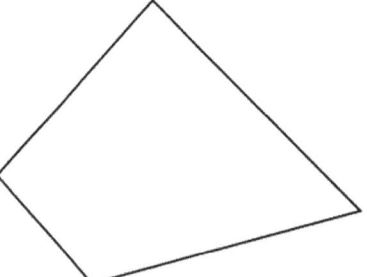

> **Review Video: Diagonals of Parallelograms, Rectangles, and Rhombi**
> Visit mometrix.com/academy and enter code: 320040

KITE

A **kite** is a quadrilateral with two pairs of adjacent sides that are congruent. A result of this is perpendicular diagonals. A kite can be concave or convex and has one line of symmetry.

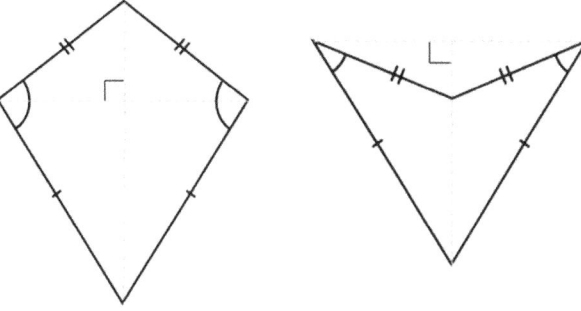

TRAPEZOID

Trapezoid: A trapezoid is defined as a quadrilateral that has at least one pair of parallel sides. There are no rules for the second pair of sides. So, there are no rules for the diagonals and no lines of symmetry for a trapezoid.

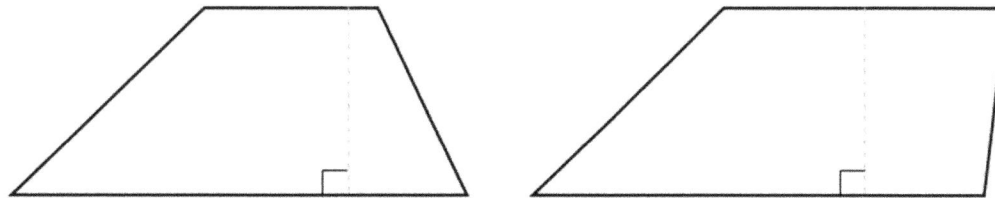

The **area of a trapezoid** is found by the formula $A = \frac{1}{2}h(b_1 + b_2)$, where h is the height (segment joining and perpendicular to the parallel bases), and b_1 and b_2 are the two parallel sides (bases). Do not use one of the other two sides as the height unless that side is also perpendicular to the parallel bases.

The **perimeter of a trapezoid** is found by the formula $P = a + b_1 + c + b_2$, where a, b_1, c, and b_2 are the four sides of the trapezoid.

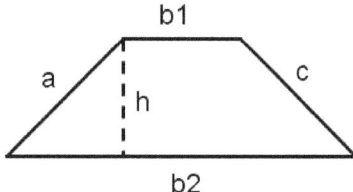

Review Video: Area and Perimeter of a Trapezoid
Visit mometrix.com/academy and enter code: 587523

Isosceles trapezoid: A trapezoid with equal base angles. This gives rise to other properties including: the two nonparallel sides have the same length, the two non-base angles are also equal, and there is one line of symmetry through the midpoints of the parallel sides.

PARALLELOGRAM

A **parallelogram** is a quadrilateral that has two pairs of opposite parallel sides. As such it is a special type of trapezoid. The sides that are parallel are also congruent. The opposite interior angles are always congruent, and the consecutive interior angles are supplementary. The diagonals of a parallelogram divide each other. Each diagonal divides the parallelogram into two congruent triangles. A parallelogram has no line of symmetry, but does have 180-degree rotational symmetry about the midpoint.

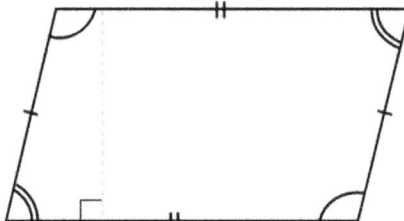

The **area of a parallelogram** is found by the formula $A = bh$, where b is the length of the base, and h is the height. Note that the base and height correspond to the length and width in a rectangle, so this formula would apply to rectangles as well. Do not confuse the height of a parallelogram with the length of the second side. The two are only the same measure in the case of a rectangle.

The **perimeter of a parallelogram** is found by the formula $P = 2a + 2b$ or $P = 2(a + b)$, where a and b are the lengths of the two sides.

> **Review Video: Area and Perimeter of a Parallelogram**
> Visit mometrix.com/academy and enter code: 718313

RECTANGLE

A **rectangle** is a quadrilateral with four right angles. All rectangles are parallelograms and trapezoids, but not all parallelograms or trapezoids are rectangles. The diagonals of a rectangle are congruent. Rectangles have two lines of symmetry (through each pair of opposing midpoints) and 180-degree rotational symmetry about the midpoint.

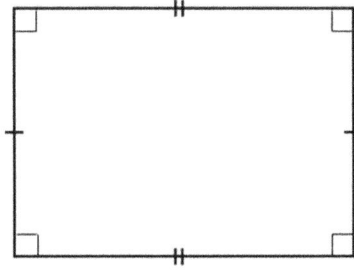

The **area of a rectangle** is found by the formula $A = lw$, where A is the area of the rectangle, l is the length (usually considered to be the longer side) and w is the width (usually considered to be the shorter side). The numbers for l and w are interchangeable.

The **perimeter of a rectangle** is found by the formula $P = 2l + 2w$ or $P = 2(l + w)$, where l is the length, and w is the width. It may be easier to add the length and width first and then double the result, as in the second formula.

Rhombus

A **rhombus** is a quadrilateral with four congruent sides. All rhombuses are parallelograms and kites; thus, they inherit all the properties of both types of quadrilaterals. The diagonals of a rhombus are perpendicular to each other. Rhombi have two lines of symmetry (along each of the diagonals) and 180° rotational symmetry. The **area of a rhombus** is half the product of the diagonals: $A = \frac{d_1 d_2}{2}$ and the perimeter of a rhombus is: $P = 2\sqrt{(d_1)^2 + (d_2)^2}$.

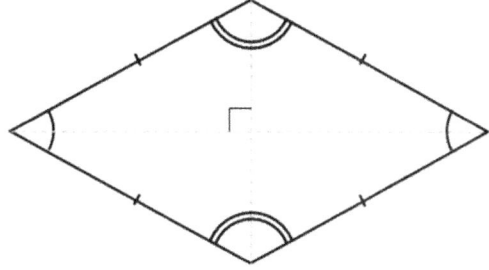

Square

A **square** is a quadrilateral with four right angles and four congruent sides. Squares satisfy the criteria of all other types of quadrilaterals. The diagonals of a square are congruent and perpendicular to each other. Squares have four lines of symmetry (through each pair of opposing midpoints and along each of the diagonals) as well as 90° rotational symmetry about the midpoint.

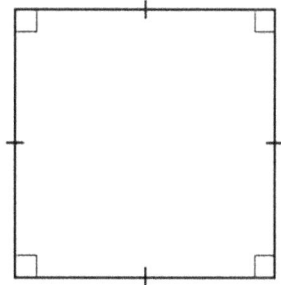

The **area of a square** is found by using the formula $A = s^2$, where s is the length of one side. The **perimeter of a square** is found by using the formula $P = 4s$, where s is the length of one side. Because all four sides are equal in a square, it is faster to multiply the length of one side by 4 than to add the same number four times. You could use the formulas for rectangles and get the same answer.

> **Review Video: Area and Perimeter of Rectangles and Squares**
> Visit mometrix.com/academy and enter code: 428109

HIERARCHY OF QUADRILATERALS

The hierarchy of quadrilaterals is as follows:

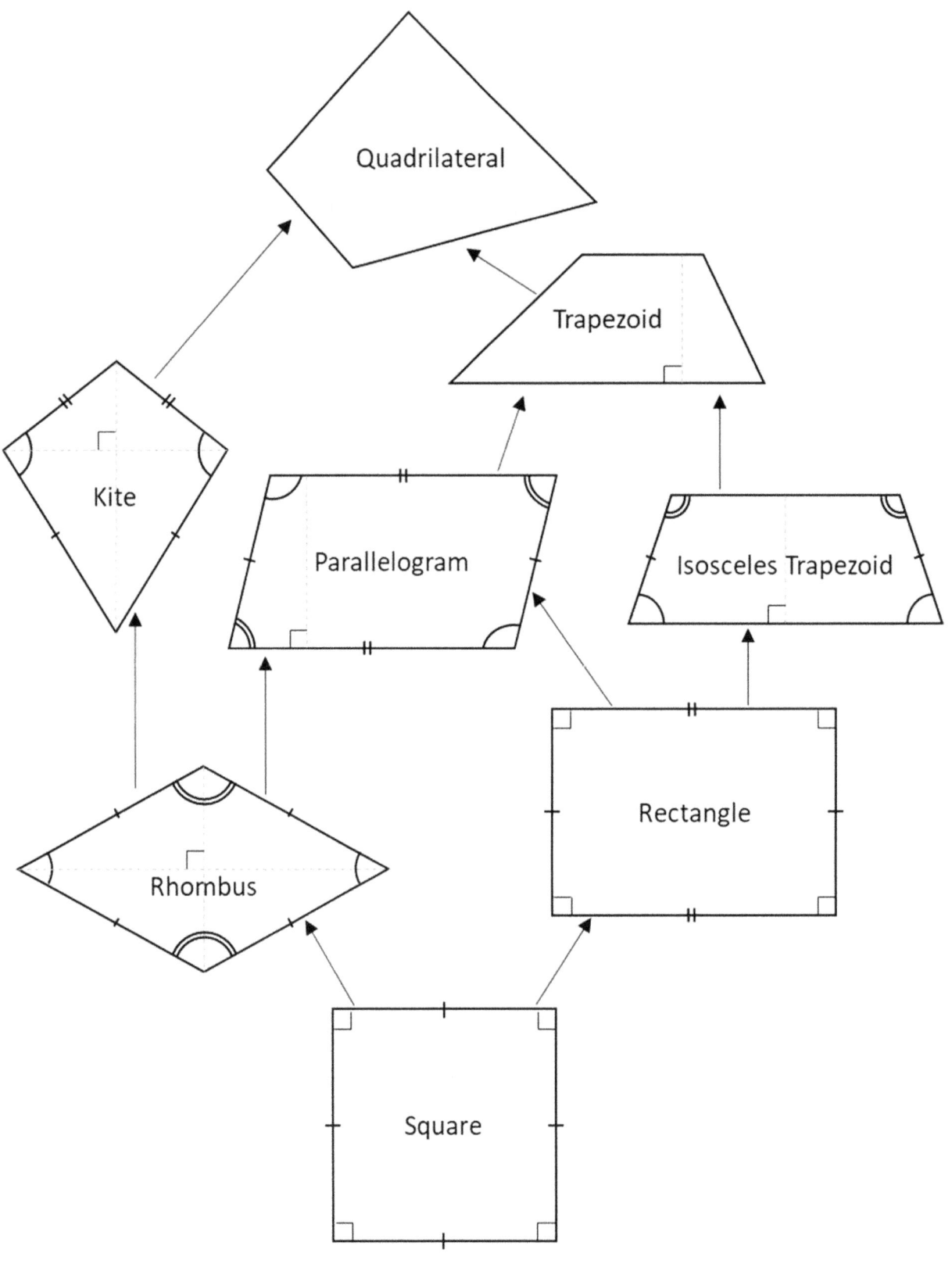

Circles

The **center** of a circle is the single point from which every point on the circle is **equidistant**. The **radius** is a line segment that joins the center of the circle and any one point on the circle. All radii of a circle are equal. Circles that have the same center but not the same length of radii are **concentric**. The **diameter** is a line segment that passes through the center of the circle and has both endpoints on the circle. The length of the diameter is exactly twice the length of the radius. Point O in the diagram below is the center of the circle, segments $\overline{OX}$, $\overline{OY}$, and $\overline{OZ}$ are radii; and segment $\overline{XZ}$ is a diameter.

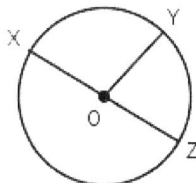

> **Review Video: Points of a Circle**
> Visit mometrix.com/academy and enter code: 420746
>
> **Review Video: Diameter, Radius, and Circumference**
> Visit mometrix.com/academy and enter code: 448988

The **area of a circle** is found by the formula $A = \pi r^2$, where r is the length of the radius. If the diameter of the circle is given, remember to divide it in half to get the length of the radius before proceeding.

The **circumference** of a circle is found by the formula $C = 2\pi r$, where r is the radius. Again, remember to convert the diameter if you are given that measure rather than the radius.

> **Review Video: Area and Circumference of a Circle**
> Visit mometrix.com/academy and enter code: 243015

INSCRIBED AND CIRCUMSCRIBED FIGURES

These terms can both be used to describe a given arrangement of figures, depending on perspective. If each of the vertices of figure A lie on figure B, then it can be said that figure A is **inscribed** in figure B, but it can also be said that figure B is **circumscribed** about figure A. The following table and examples help to illustrate the concept. Note that the figures cannot both be circles, as they would be completely overlapping and neither would be inscribed or circumscribed.

Given	Description	Equivalent Description	Figures
Each of the sides of a pentagon is tangent to a circle	The circle is inscribed in the pentagon	The pentagon is circumscribed about the circle	
Each of the vertices of a pentagon lie on a circle	The pentagon is inscribed in the circle	The circle is circumscribed about the pentagon	

3D Shapes

SOLIDS

The **surface area of a solid object** is the area of all sides or exterior surfaces. For objects such as prisms and pyramids, a further distinction is made between base surface area (B) and lateral surface area (LA). For a prism, the total surface area (SA) is $SA = LA + 2B$. For a pyramid or cone, the total surface area is $SA = LA + B$.

The **surface area of a sphere** can be found by the formula $A = 4\pi r^2$, where r is the radius. The volume is given by the formula $V = \frac{4}{3}\pi r^3$, where r is the radius. Both quantities are generally given in terms of π.

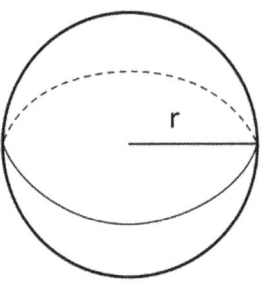

Review Video: Volume and Surface Area of a Sphere
Visit mometrix.com/academy and enter code: 786928

Review Video: How to Calculate the Volume of 3D Objects
Visit mometrix.com/academy and enter code: 163343

The **volume of any prism** is found by the formula $V = Bh$, where B is the area of the base, and h is the height (perpendicular distance between the bases). The surface area of any prism is the sum of the areas of both bases and all sides. It can be calculated as $SA = 2B + Ph$, where P is the perimeter of the base.

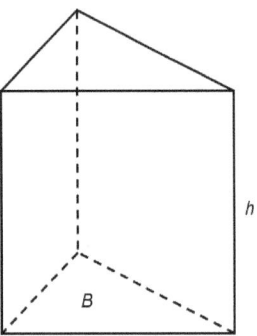

Review Video: Volume and Surface Area of a Prism
Visit mometrix.com/academy and enter code: 420158

For a **rectangular prism**, the volume can be found by the formula $V = lwh$, where V is the volume, l is the length, w is the width, and h is the height. The surface area can be calculated as $SA = 2lw + 2hl + 2wh$ or $SA = 2(lw + hl + wh)$.

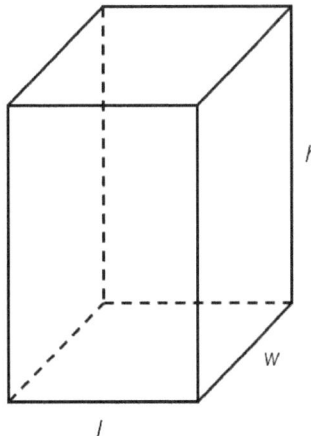

Review Video: Volume and Surface Area of a Rectangular Prism
Visit mometrix.com/academy and enter code: 282814

The **volume of a cube** can be found by the formula $V = s^3$, where s is the length of a side. The surface area of a cube is calculated as $SA = 6s^2$, where SA is the total surface area and s is the length of a side. These formulas are the same as the ones used for the volume and surface area of a rectangular prism, but simplified since all three quantities (length, width, and height) are the same.

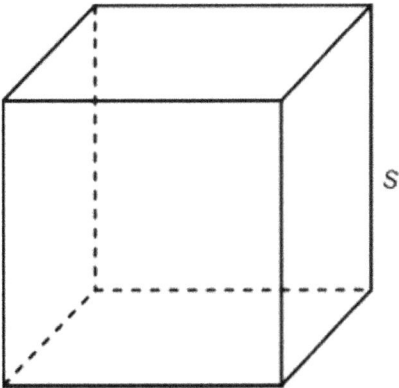

Review Video: Volume and Surface Area of a Cube
Visit mometrix.com/academy and enter code: 664455

The **volume of a cylinder** can be calculated by the formula $V = \pi r^2 h$, where r is the radius, and h is the height. The surface area of a cylinder can be found by the formula $SA = 2\pi r^2 + 2\pi r h$. The first term is the base area multiplied by two, and the second term is the perimeter of the base multiplied by the height.

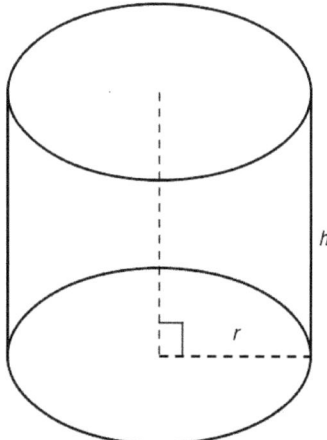

Review Video: Volume and Surface Area of a Right Circular Cylinder
Visit mometrix.com/academy and enter code: 226463

The **volume of a pyramid** is found by the formula $V = \frac{1}{3}Bh$, where B is the area of the base, and h is the height (perpendicular distance from the vertex to the base). Notice this formula is the same as $\frac{1}{3}$ times the volume of a prism. Like a prism, the base of a pyramid can be any shape.

Finding the **surface area of a pyramid** is not as simple as the other shapes we've looked at thus far. If the pyramid is a right pyramid, meaning the base is a regular polygon and the vertex is directly over the center of that polygon, the surface area can be calculated as $SA = B + \frac{1}{2}Ph_s$, where P is the perimeter of the base, and h_s is the slant height (distance from the vertex to the midpoint of one side of the base). If the pyramid is irregular, the area of each triangle side must be calculated individually and then summed, along with the base.

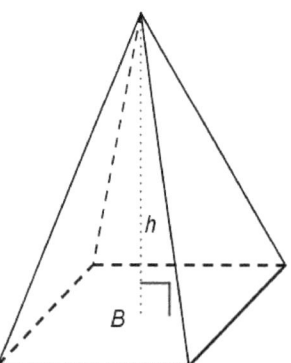

Review Video: Volume and Surface Area of a Pyramid
Visit mometrix.com/academy and enter code: 621932

The **volume of a cone** is found by the formula $V = \frac{1}{3}\pi r^2 h$, where r is the radius, and h is the height. Notice this is the same as $\frac{1}{3}$ times the volume of a cylinder. The surface area can be calculated as

$SA = \pi r^2 + \pi rs$, where s is the slant height. The slant height can be calculated using the Pythagorean theorem to be $\sqrt{r^2 + h^2}$, so the surface area formula can also be written as $SA = \pi r^2 + \pi r\sqrt{r^2 + h^2}$.

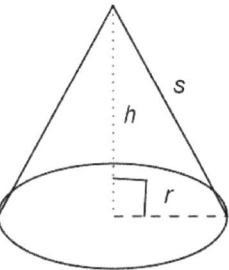

Review Video: <u>Volume and Surface Area of a Right Circular Cone</u>
Visit mometrix.com/academy and enter code: 573574

Pythagorean Theorem

The side of a triangle opposite the right angle is called the **hypotenuse**. The other two sides are called the legs. The Pythagorean theorem states a relationship among the legs and hypotenuse of a right triangle: $(a^2 + b^2 = c^2)$, where a and b are the lengths of the legs of a right triangle, and c is the length of the hypotenuse. Note that this formula will only work with right triangles.

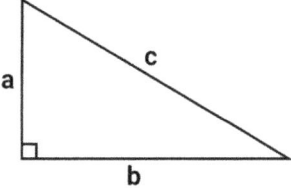

Review Video: <u>Pythagorean Theorem</u>
Visit mometrix.com/academy and enter code: 906576

Trigonometric Formulas

In the diagram below, angle C is the right angle, and side c is the hypotenuse. Side a is the side opposite to angle A and side b is the side opposite to angle B. Using ratios of side lengths as a means to calculate the sine, cosine, and tangent of an acute angle only works for right triangles.

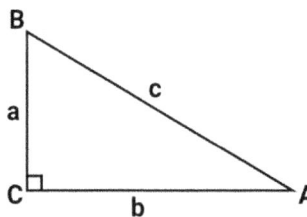

$\sin A = \dfrac{\text{opposite side}}{\text{hypotenuse}} = \dfrac{a}{c}$ $\csc A = \dfrac{1}{\sin A} = \dfrac{\text{hypotenuse}}{\text{opposite side}} = \dfrac{c}{a}$

$\cos A = \dfrac{\text{adjacent side}}{\text{hypotenuse}} = \dfrac{b}{c}$ $\sec A = \dfrac{1}{\cos A} = \dfrac{\text{hypotenuse}}{\text{adjacent side}} = \dfrac{c}{b}$

$\tan A = \dfrac{\text{opposite side}}{\text{adjacent side}} = \dfrac{a}{b}$ $\cot A = \dfrac{1}{\tan A} = \dfrac{\text{adjacent side}}{\text{opposite side}} = \dfrac{b}{a}$

LAWS OF SINES AND COSINES

The **law of sines** states that $\frac{\sin A}{a} = \frac{\sin B}{b} = \frac{\sin C}{c}$, where A, B, and C are the angles of a triangle, and a, b, and c are the sides opposite their respective angles. This formula will work with all triangles, not just right triangles.

The **law of cosines** is given by the formula $c^2 = a^2 + b^2 - 2ab(\cos C)$, where a, b, and c are the sides of a triangle, and C is the angle opposite side c. This is a generalized form of the Pythagorean theorem that can be used on any triangle.

> **Review Video: Law of Sines**
> Visit mometrix.com/academy and enter code: 206844
>
> **Review Video: Law of Cosines**
> Visit mometrix.com/academy and enter code: 158911

Probabilistic and Statistical Reasoning

Probability

Probability is the likelihood of a certain outcome occurring for a given event. An **event** is any situation that produces a result. It could be something as simple as flipping a coin or as complex as launching a rocket. Determining the probability of an outcome for an event can be equally simple or complex. As such, there are specific terms used in the study of probability that need to be understood:

- **Compound event**—an event that involves two or more independent events (rolling a pair of dice and taking the sum)
- **Desired outcome** (or success)—an outcome that meets a particular set of criteria (a roll of 1 or 2 if we are looking for numbers less than 3)
- **Independent events**—two or more events whose outcomes do not affect one another (two coins tossed at the same time)
- **Dependent events**—two or more events whose outcomes affect one another (two cards drawn consecutively from the same deck)
- **Certain outcome**—probability of outcome is 100% or 1
- **Impossible outcome**—probability of outcome is 0% or 0
- **Mutually exclusive outcomes**—two or more outcomes whose criteria cannot all be satisfied in a single event (a coin coming up heads and tails on the same toss)
- **Random variable**—refers to all possible outcomes of a single event which may be discrete or continuous.

> **Review Video: Intro to Probability**
> Visit mometrix.com/academy and enter code: 212374

SAMPLE SPACE

The total set of all possible results of a test or experiment is called a **sample space**, or sometimes a universal sample space. The sample space, represented by one of the variables S, Ω, or U (for universal sample space) has individual elements called outcomes. Other terms for outcome that may be used interchangeably include elementary outcome, simple event, or sample point. The number of outcomes in a given sample space could be infinite or finite, and some tests may yield multiple unique sample sets. For example, tests conducted by drawing playing cards from a standard deck would have one sample space of the card values, another sample space of the card suits, and a third sample space of suit-denomination combinations. For most tests, the sample spaces considered will be finite.

An **event**, represented by the variable E, is a portion of a sample space. It may be one outcome or a group of outcomes from the same sample space. If an event occurs, then the test or experiment will generate an outcome that satisfies the requirement of that event. For example, given a standard deck of 52 playing cards as the sample space, and defining the event as the collection of face cards, then the event will occur if the card drawn is a J, Q, or K. If any other card is drawn, the event is said to have not occurred.

For every sample space, each possible outcome has a specific likelihood, or probability, that it will occur. The probability measure, also called the **distribution**, is a function that assigns a real number probability, from zero to one, to each outcome. For a probability measure to be accurate, every outcome must have a real number probability measure that is greater than or equal to zero and less than or equal to one. Also, the probability measure of the sample space must equal one, and the probability measure of the union of multiple outcomes must equal the sum of the individual probability measures.

Probabilities of events are expressed as real numbers from zero to one. They give a numerical value to the chance that a particular event will occur. The probability of an event occurring is the sum of the probabilities of the individual elements of that event. For example, in a standard deck of 52 playing cards as the sample space and the collection of face cards as the event, the probability of drawing a specific face card is $\frac{1}{52} = 0.019$, but the probability of drawing any one of the twelve face cards is $12(0.019) = 0.228$. Note that rounding of numbers can generate different results. If you multiplied 12 by the fraction $\frac{1}{52}$ before converting to a decimal, you would get the answer $\frac{12}{52} = 0.231$.

THEORETICAL AND EXPERIMENTAL PROBABILITY

Theoretical probability can usually be determined without actually performing the event. The likelihood of an outcome occurring, or the probability of an outcome occurring, is given by the formula:

$$P(A) = \frac{\text{Number of acceptable outcomes}}{\text{Number of possible outcomes}}$$

Note that $P(A)$ is the probability of an outcome A occurring, and each outcome is just as likely to occur as any other outcome. If each outcome has the same probability of occurring as every other possible outcome, the outcomes are said to be equally likely to occur. The total number of acceptable outcomes must be less than or equal to the total number of possible outcomes. If the two are equal, then the outcome is certain to occur and the probability is 1. If the number of acceptable outcomes is zero, then the outcome is impossible and the probability is 0. For example, if there are 20 marbles in a bag and 5 are red, then the theoretical probability of randomly selecting a red marble is 5 out of 20, $\left(\frac{5}{20} = \frac{1}{4}, 0.25, \text{ or } 25\%\right)$.

If the theoretical probability is unknown or too complicated to calculate, it can be estimated by an experimental probability. **Experimental probability**, also called empirical probability, is an estimate of the likelihood of a certain outcome based on repeated experiments or collected data. In other words, while theoretical probability is based on what *should* happen, experimental probability is based on what *has* happened. Experimental probability is calculated in the same way as theoretical probability, except that actual outcomes are used instead of possible outcomes. The more experiments performed or datapoints gathered, the better the estimate should be.

Theoretical and experimental probability do not always line up with one another. Theoretical probability says that out of 20 coin-tosses, 10 should be heads. However, if we were actually to toss 20 coins, we might record just 5 heads. This doesn't mean that our theoretical probability is incorrect; it just means that this particular experiment had results that were different from what was predicted. A practical application of empirical probability is the insurance industry. There are no set functions that define lifespan, health, or safety. Insurance companies look at factors from hundreds of thousands of individuals to find patterns that they then use to set the formulas for insurance premiums.

> **Review Video: Empirical Probability**
> Visit mometrix.com/academy and enter code: 513468

OBJECTIVE AND SUBJECTIVE PROBABILITY

Objective probability is based on mathematical formulas and documented evidence. Examples of objective probability include raffles or lottery drawings where there is a pre-determined number of possible outcomes and a predetermined number of outcomes that correspond to an event. Other cases of objective probability include probabilities of rolling dice, flipping coins, or drawing cards. Most gambling games are based on objective probability.

In contrast, **subjective probability** is based on personal or professional feelings and judgments. Often, there is a lot of guesswork following extensive research. Areas where subjective probability is applicable include sales trends and business expenses. Attractions set admission prices based on subjective probabilities of attendance based on varying admission rates in an effort to maximize their profit.

COMPLEMENT OF AN EVENT

Sometimes it may be easier to calculate the possibility of something not happening, or the **complement of an event**. Represented by the symbol $\bar{A}$, the complement of A is the probability that event A does not happen. When you know the probability of event A occurring, you can use the formula $P(\bar{A}) = 1 - P(A)$, where $P(\bar{A})$ is the probability of event A not occurring, and $P(A)$ is the probability of event A occurring.

ADDITION RULE

The **addition rule** for probability is used for finding the probability of a compound event. Use the formula $P(A \cup B) = P(A) + P(B) - P(A \cap B)$, where $P(A \cap B)$ is the probability of both events occurring to find the probability of a compound event. The probability of both events occurring at the same time must be subtracted to eliminate any overlap in the first two probabilities.

CONDITIONAL PROBABILITY

Given two events A and B, the **conditional probability** $P(A|B)$ is the probability that event A will occur, given that event B has occurred. The conditional probability cannot be calculated simply from $P(A)$ and $P(B)$; these probabilities alone do not give sufficient information to determine the conditional probability. It can, however, be determined if you are also given the probability of the intersection of events A and B, $P(A \cap B)$, the probability that events A and B both occur. Specifically, $P(A|B) = \frac{P(A \cap B)}{P(B)}$. For instance, suppose you have a jar containing two red marbles and two blue marbles, and you draw two marbles at random. Consider event A being the event that the first marble drawn is red, and event B being the event that the second marble drawn is blue. If we want to find the probability that B occurs given that A occurred, $P(B|A)$, then we can compute it using the fact that $P(A)$ is $\frac{1}{2}$, and $P(A \cap B)$ is $\frac{1}{3}$. (The latter may not be obvious, but may be determined by finding the product of $\frac{1}{2}$ and $\frac{2}{3}$). Therefore $P(B|A) = \frac{P(A \cap B)}{P(A)} = \frac{1/3}{1/2} = \frac{2}{3}$.

CONDITIONAL PROBABILITY IN EVERYDAY SITUATIONS

Conditional probability often arises in everyday situations in, for example, estimating the risk or benefit of certain activities. The conditional probability of having a heart attack given that you exercise daily may be smaller than the overall probability of having a heart attack. The conditional probability of having lung cancer given that you are a smoker is larger than the overall probability of having lung cancer. Note that changing the order of the conditional probability changes the meaning: the conditional probability of having lung cancer given that you are a smoker is a very different thing from the probability of being a smoker given that you have lung cancer. In an extreme case, suppose that a certain rare disease is caused only by eating a certain food, but even then, it is unlikely. Then the conditional probability of having that disease given that you eat the dangerous food is nonzero but low, but the conditional probability of having eaten that food given that you have the disease is 100%!

> **Review Video: Conditional Probability**
> Visit mometrix.com/academy and enter code: 397924

INDEPENDENCE

The conditional probability $P(A|B)$ is the probability that event A will occur given that event B occurs. If the two events are independent, we do not expect that whether or not event B occurs should have any effect on whether or not event A occurs. In other words, we expect $P(A|B) = P(A)$.

This can be proven using the usual equations for conditional probability and the joint probability of independent events. The conditional probability $P(A|B) = \frac{P(A \cap B)}{P(B)}$. If A and B are independent, then $P(A \cap B) = P(A)P(B)$. So $P(A|B) = \frac{P(A)P(B)}{P(B)} = P(A)$. By similar reasoning, if A and B are independent then $P(B|A) = P(B)$.

MULTIPLICATION RULE

The **multiplication rule** can be used to find the probability of two independent events occurring using the formula $P(A \cap B) = P(A) \times P(B)$, where $P(A \cap B)$ is the probability of two independent events occurring, $P(A)$ is the probability of the first event occurring, and $P(B)$ is the probability of the second event occurring.

The multiplication rule can also be used to find the probability of two dependent events occurring using the formula $P(A \cap B) = P(A) \times P(B|A)$, where $P(A \cap B)$ is the probability of two dependent events occurring and $P(B|A)$ is the probability of the second event occurring after the first event has already occurred.

Use a **combination of the multiplication** rule and the rule of complements to find the probability that at least one outcome of the element will occur. This is given by the general formula $P(\text{at least one event occurring}) = 1 - P(\text{no outcomes occurring})$. For example, to find the probability that at least one even number will show when a pair of dice is rolled, find the probability that two odd numbers will be rolled (no even numbers) and subtract from one. You can always use a tree diagram or make a chart to list the possible outcomes when the sample space is small, such as in the dice-rolling example, but in most cases it will be much faster to use the multiplication and complement formulas.

> **Review Video: Multiplication Rule**
> Visit mometrix.com/academy and enter code: 782598

UNION AND INTERSECTION OF TWO SETS OF OUTCOMES

If A and B are each a set of elements or outcomes from an experiment, then the **union** (symbol ∪) of the two sets is the set of elements found in set A or set B. For example, if $A = \{2, 3, 4\}$ and $B = \{3, 4, 5\}$, $A \cup B = \{2, 3, 4, 5\}$. Note that the outcomes 3 and 4 appear only once in the union. For statistical events, the union is equivalent to "or"; $P(A \cup B)$ is the same thing as $P(A \text{ or } B)$. The **intersection** (symbol ∩) of two sets is the set of outcomes common to both sets. For the above sets A and B, $A \cap B = \{3, 4\}$. For statistical events, the intersection is equivalent to "and"; $P(A \cap B)$ is the same thing as $P(A \text{ and } B)$. It is important to note that union and intersection operations commute. That is:

$$A \cup B = B \cup A \text{ and } A \cap B = B \cap A$$

Two-Way Frequency Tables

If we have a two-way frequency table, it is generally a straightforward matter to read off the probabilities of any two events A and B, as well as the joint probability of both events occurring, $P(A \cap B)$. We can then find the conditional probability $P(A|B)$ by calculating $P(A|B) = \frac{P(A \cap B)}{P(B)}$. We could also check whether or not events are independent by verifying whether $P(A)P(B) = P(A \cap B)$.

For example, a certain store's recent T-shirt sales:

	Small	Medium	Large	Total
Blue	25	40	35	100
White	27	25	22	74
Black	8	23	15	46
Total	60	88	72	220

Suppose we want to find the conditional probability that a customer buys a black shirt (event A), given that the shirt he buys is size small (event B). From the table, the probability $P(B)$ that a customer buys a small shirt is $\frac{60}{220} = \frac{3}{11}$. The probability $P(A \cap B)$ that he buys a small, black shirt is $\frac{8}{220} = \frac{2}{55}$. The conditional probability $P(A|B)$ that he buys a black shirt, given that he buys a small shirt, is therefore $P(A|B) = \frac{2/55}{3/11} = \frac{2}{15}$.

Similarly, if we want to check whether the event a customer buys a blue shirt, A, is independent of the event that a customer buys a medium shirt, B. From the table, $P(A) = \frac{100}{220} = \frac{5}{11}$ and $P(B) = \frac{88}{220} = \frac{4}{10}$. Also, $P(A \cap B) = \frac{40}{220} = \frac{2}{11}$. Since $\left(\frac{5}{11}\right)\left(\frac{4}{10}\right) = \frac{20}{110} = \frac{2}{11}$, $P(A)P(B) = P(A \cap B)$ and these two events are indeed independent.

Data Analysis

DISPERSION

A **measure of dispersion** is a single value that helps to "interpret" the measure of central tendency by providing more information about how the data values in the set are distributed about the measure of central tendency. The measure of dispersion helps to eliminate or reduce the disadvantages of using the mean, median, or mode as a single measure of central tendency, and give a more accurate picture of the dataset as a whole. To have a measure of dispersion, you must know or calculate the range, standard deviation, or variance of the data set.

RANGE

The **range** of a set of data is the difference between the greatest and lowest values of the data in the set. To calculate the range, you must first make sure the units for all data values are the same, and then identify the greatest and lowest values. If there are multiple data values that are equal for the highest or lowest, just use one of the values in the formula. Write the answer with the same units as the data values you used to do the calculations.

> **Review Video: Statistical Range**
> Visit mometrix.com/academy and enter code: 778541

SAMPLE STANDARD DEVIATION

Standard deviation is a measure of dispersion that compares all the data values in the set to the mean of the set to give a more accurate picture. To find the **standard deviation of a sample**, use the formula

$$s = \sqrt{\frac{\sum_{i=1}^{n}(x_i - \bar{x})^2}{n-1}}$$

Note that s is the standard deviation of a sample, x_i represents the individual values in the data set, $\bar{x}$ is the mean of the data values in the set, and n is the number of data values in the set. The higher the value of the standard deviation is, the greater the variance of the data values from the mean. The units associated with the standard deviation are the same as the units of the data values.

> **Review Video: Standard Deviation**
> Visit mometrix.com/academy and enter code: 419469

SAMPLE VARIANCE

The **variance of a sample** is the square of the sample standard deviation (denoted s^2). While the mean of a set of data gives the average of the set and gives information about where a specific data value lies in relation to the average, the variance of the sample gives information about the degree to which the data values are spread out and tells you how close an individual value is to the average compared to the other values. The units associated with variance are the same as the units of the data values squared.

PERCENTILE

Percentiles and quartiles are other methods of describing data within a set. **Percentiles** tell what percentage of the data in the set fall below a specific point. For example, achievement test scores are often given in percentiles. A score at the 80th percentile is one which is equal to or higher than 80 percent of the scores in the set. In other words, 80 percent of the scores were lower than that score.

Quartiles are percentile groups that make up quarter sections of the data set. The first quartile is the 25th percentile. The second quartile is the 50th percentile; this is also the median of the dataset. The third quartile is the 75th percentile.

SKEWNESS

Skewness is a way to describe the symmetry or asymmetry of the distribution of values in a dataset. If the distribution of values is symmetrical, there is no skew. In general the closer the mean of a data set is to the median of the data set, the less skew there is. Generally, if the mean is to the right of the median, the data set is *positively skewed*, or right-skewed, and if the mean is to the left of the median, the data set is *negatively skewed*, or left-skewed. However, this rule of thumb is not infallible. When the data values are graphed on a curve, a set with no skew will be a perfect bell curve.

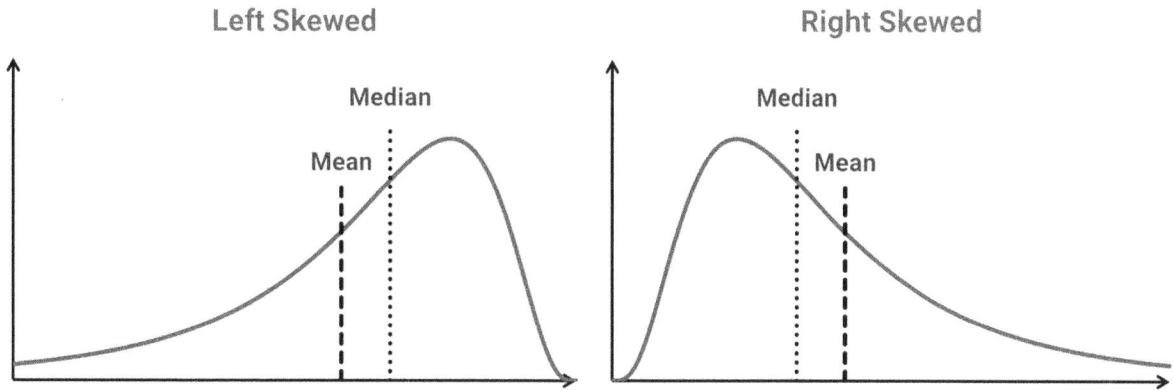

To estimate skew, use the formula:

$$\text{skew} = \frac{\sqrt{n(n-1)}}{n-2} \left(\frac{\frac{1}{n}\sum_{i=1}^{n}(x_i - \bar{x})^3}{\left(\frac{1}{n}\sum_{i=1}^{n}(x_i - \bar{x})^2\right)^{\frac{3}{2}}} \right)$$

Note that n is the datapoints in the set, x_i is the ith value in the set, and $\bar{x}$ is the mean of the set.

> **Review Video: Skew**
> Visit mometrix.com/academy and enter code: 661486

UNIMODAL VS. BIMODAL

If a distribution has a single peak, it would be considered **unimodal**. If it has two discernible peaks it would be considered **bimodal**. Bimodal distributions may be an indication that the set of data being considered is actually the combination of two sets of data with significant differences. A **uniform distribution** is a distribution in which there is *no distinct peak or variation* in the data. No values or ranges are particularly more common than any other values or ranges.

OUTLIER

An outlier is an extremely high or extremely low value in the data set. It may be the result of measurement error, in which case, the outlier is not a valid member of the data set. However, it may also be a valid member of the distribution. Unless a measurement error is identified, the experimenter cannot know for certain if an outlier is or is not a member of the distribution. There are arbitrary methods that can be employed to designate an extreme value as an outlier. One method designates an outlier (or possible outlier) to be any value less than $Q_1 - 1.5(IQR)$ or any value greater than $Q_3 + 1.5(IQR)$.

DATA ANALYSIS
SIMPLE REGRESSION

In statistics, **simple regression** is using an equation to represent a relation between independent and dependent variables. The independent variable is also referred to as the explanatory variable or the predictor and is generally represented by the variable x in the equation. The dependent variable, usually represented by the variable y, is also referred to as the response variable. The equation may be any type of function – linear, quadratic, exponential, etc. The best way to handle this task is to use the regression feature of your graphing calculator. This will easily give you the curve of best fit and provide you with the coefficients and other information you need to derive an equation.

LINE OF BEST FIT

In a scatter plot, the **line of best fit** is the line that best shows the trends of the data. The line of best fit is given by the equation $\hat{y} = ax + b$, where a and b are the regression coefficients. The regression coefficient a is also the slope of the line of best fit, and b is also the y-coordinate of the point at which the line of best fit crosses the y-axis. Not every point on the scatter plot will be on the line of best fit. The differences between the y-values of the points in the scatter plot and the corresponding y-values according to the equation of the line of best fit are the residuals. The line of best fit is also called the least-squares regression line because it is also the line that has the lowest sum of the squares of the residuals.

CORRELATION COEFFICIENT

The **correlation coefficient** is the numerical value that indicates how strong the relationship is between the two variables of a linear regression equation. A correlation coefficient of –1 is a perfect negative correlation. A correlation coefficient of +1 is a perfect positive correlation. Correlation coefficients close to –1 or +1 are very strong correlations. A correlation coefficient equal to zero indicates there is no correlation between the two variables. This test is a good indicator of whether or not the equation for the line of best fit is accurate. The formula for the correlation coefficient is

$$r = \frac{\sum_{i=1}^{n}(x_i - \bar{x})(y_i - \bar{y})}{\sqrt{\sum_{i=1}^{n}(x_i - \bar{x})^2}\sqrt{\sum_{i=1}^{n}(y_i - \bar{y})^2}}$$

where r is the correlation coefficient, n is the number of data values in the set, (x_i, y_i) is a point in the set, and $\bar{x}$ and $\bar{y}$ are the means.

Z-SCORE

A **z-score** is an indication of how many standard deviations a given value falls from the sample mean. To calculate a z-score, use the formula:

$$\frac{x - \bar{x}}{\sigma}$$

In this formula x is the data value, $\bar{x}$ is the mean of the sample data, and σ is the standard deviation of the population. If the z-score is positive, the data value lies above the mean. If the z-score is negative, the data value falls below the mean. These scores are useful in interpreting data such as standardized test scores, where every piece of data in the set has been counted, rather than just a small random sample. In cases where standard deviations are calculated from a random sample of the set, the z-scores will not be as accurate.

CENTRAL LIMIT THEOREM

According to the **central limit theorem**, regardless of what the original distribution of a sample is, the distribution of the means tends to get closer and closer to a normal distribution as the sample size gets larger and larger (this is necessary because the sample is becoming more all-encompassing of the elements of the population). As the sample size gets larger, the distribution of the sample mean will approach a normal distribution with a mean of the population mean and a variance of the population variance divided by the sample size.

Measures of Central Tendency

A **measure of central tendency** is a statistical value that gives a reasonable estimate for the center of a group of data. There are several different ways of describing the measure of central tendency. Each one has a unique way it is calculated, and each one gives a slightly different perspective on the data set. Whenever you give a measure of central tendency, always make sure the units are the same. If the data has different units, such as hours, minutes, and seconds, convert all the data to the same unit, and use the same unit in the measure of central tendency. If no units are given in the data, do not give units for the measure of central tendency.

MEAN

The **statistical mean** of a group of data is the same as the arithmetic average of that group. To find the mean of a set of data, first convert each value to the same units, if necessary. Then find the sum of all the values, and count the total number of data values, making sure you take into consideration each individual value. If a value appears more than once, count it more than once. Divide the sum of the values by the total number of values and apply the units, if any. Note that the mean does not have to be one of the data values in the set, and may not divide evenly.

$$\text{mean} = \frac{\text{sum of the data values}}{\text{quantity of data values}}$$

For instance, the mean of the data set {88, 72, 61, 90, 97, 68, 88, 79, 86, 93, 97, 71, 80, 84, 89} would be the sum of the fifteen numbers divided by 15:

$$\frac{88 + 72 + 61 + 90 + 97 + 68 + 88 + 79 + 86 + 93 + 97 + 71 + 80 + 84 + 89}{15} = \frac{1242}{15} = 82.8$$

While the mean is relatively easy to calculate and averages are understood by most people, the mean can be very misleading if it is used as the sole measure of central tendency. If the data set has outliers (data values that are unusually high or unusually low compared to the rest of the data values), the mean can be very distorted, especially if the data set has a small number of values. If unusually high values are countered with unusually low values, the mean is not affected as much. For example, if five of twenty students in a class get a 100 on a test, but the other 15 students have an average of 60 on the same test, the class average would appear as 70. Whenever the mean is skewed by outliers, it is always a good idea to include the median as an alternate measure of central tendency.

A **weighted mean**, or weighted average, is a mean that uses "weighted" values. The formula is weighted mean $= \frac{w_1 x_1 + w_2 x_2 + w_3 x_3 \ldots + w_n x_n}{w_1 + w_2 + w_3 + \cdots + w_n}$. Weighted values, such as $w_1, w_2, w_3, \ldots w_n$ are assigned to

each member of the set $x_1, x_2, x_3, \ldots x_n$. When calculating the weighted mean, make sure a weight value for each member of the set is used.

> **Review Video: All About Averages**
> Visit mometrix.com/academy and enter code: 176521

MEDIAN

The **statistical median** is the value in the middle of the set of data. To find the median, list all data values in order from smallest to largest or from largest to smallest. Any value that is repeated in the set must be listed the number of times it appears. If there are an odd number of data values, the median is the value in the middle of the list. If there is an even number of data values, the median is the arithmetic mean of the two middle values.

For example, the median of the data set {88, 72, 61, 90, 97, 68, 88, 79, 86, 93, 97, 71, 80, 84, 88} is 86 since the ordered set is {61, 68, 71, 72, 79, 80, 84, **86**, 88, 88, 88, 90, 93, 97, 97}.

The big disadvantage of using the median as a measure of central tendency is that is relies solely on a value's relative size as compared to the other values in the set. When the individual values in a set of data are evenly dispersed, the median can be an accurate tool. However, if there is a group of rather large values or a group of rather small values that are not offset by a different group of values, the information that can be inferred from the median may not be accurate because the distribution of values is skewed.

MODE

The **statistical mode** is the data value that occurs the greatest number of times in the data set. It is possible to have exactly one mode, more than one mode, or no mode. To find the mode of a set of data, arrange the data like you do to find the median (all values in order, listing all multiples of data values). Count the number of times each value appears in the data set. If all values appear an equal number of times, there is no mode. If one value appears more than any other value, that value is the mode. If two or more values appear the same number of times, but there are other values that appear fewer times and no values that appear more times, all of those values are the modes.

For example, the mode of the data set {**88**, 72, 61, 90, 97, 68, **88**, 79, 86, 93, 97, 71, 80, 84, **88**} is 88.

The main disadvantage of the mode is that the values of the other data in the set have no bearing on the mode. The mode may be the largest value, the smallest value, or a value anywhere in between in the set. The mode only tells which value or values, if any, occurred the greatest number of times. It does not give any suggestions about the remaining values in the set.

> **Review Video: Mean, Median, and Mode**
> Visit mometrix.com/academy and enter code: 286207

Displaying Information

Frequency Tables

Frequency tables show how frequently each unique value appears in a set. A **relative frequency table** is one that shows the proportions of each unique value compared to the entire set. Relative frequencies are given as percentages; however, the total percent for a relative frequency table will not necessarily equal 100 percent due to rounding. An example of a frequency table with relative frequencies is below.

Favorite Color	Frequency	Relative Frequency
Blue	4	13%
Red	7	22%
Green	3	9%
Purple	6	19%
Cyan	12	38%

> Review Video: **Data Interpretation of Graphs**
> Visit mometrix.com/academy and enter code: 200439

Circle Graphs

Circle graphs, also known as *pie charts*, provide a visual depiction of the relationship of each type of data compared to the whole set of data. The circle graph is divided into sections by drawing radii to create central angles whose percentage of the circle is equal to the individual data's percentage of the whole set. Each 1% of data is equal to 3.6° in the circle graph. Therefore, data represented by a 90° section of the circle graph makes up 25% of the whole. When complete, a circle graph often looks like a pie cut into uneven wedges. The pie chart below shows the data from the frequency table referenced earlier where people were asked their favorite color.

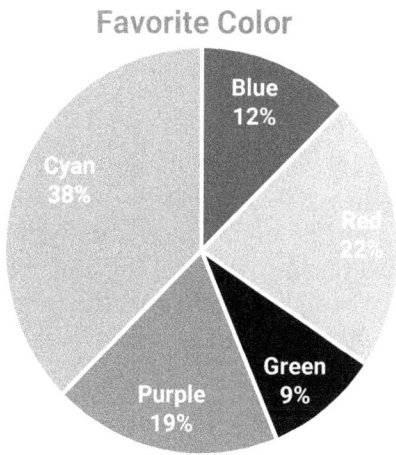

PICTOGRAPHS

A **pictograph** is a graph, generally in the horizontal orientation, that uses pictures or symbols to represent the data. Each pictograph must have a key that defines the picture or symbol and gives the quantity each picture or symbol represents. Pictures or symbols on a pictograph are not always shown as whole elements. In this case, the fraction of the picture or symbol shown represents the same fraction of the quantity a whole picture or symbol stands for. For example, a row with $3\frac{1}{2}$ ears of corn, where each ear of corn represents 100 stalks of corn in a field, would equal $3\frac{1}{2} \times 100 = 350$ stalks of corn in the field.

Name	Number of ears of corn eaten	Field	Number of stalks of corn
Michael	🌽🌽🌽🌽	Field 1	🌽🌽🌽🌽🌽
Tara	🌽🌽	Field 2	🌽🌽🌽(½)
John	🌽🌽🌽	Field 3	🌽🌽🌽🌽
Sara	🌽	Field 4	🌽
Jacob	🌽🌽🌽	Field 5	🌽🌽🌽(½)

Each 🌽 represents 1 ear of corn eaten.   Each 🌽 represents 100 stalks of corn.

> **Review Video: Pictographs**
> Visit mometrix.com/academy and enter code: 147860

LINE GRAPHS

Line graphs have one or more lines of varying styles (solid or broken) to show the different values for a set of data. The individual data are represented as ordered pairs, much like on a Cartesian plane. In this case, the x- and y-axes are defined in terms of their units, such as dollars or time. The individual plotted points are joined by line segments to show whether the value of the data is increasing (line sloping upward), decreasing (line sloping downward), or staying the same (horizontal line). Multiple sets of data can be graphed on the same line graph to give an easy visual comparison. An example of this would be graphing achievement test scores for different groups of students over the same time period to see which group had the greatest increase or decrease in performance from year to year (as shown below).

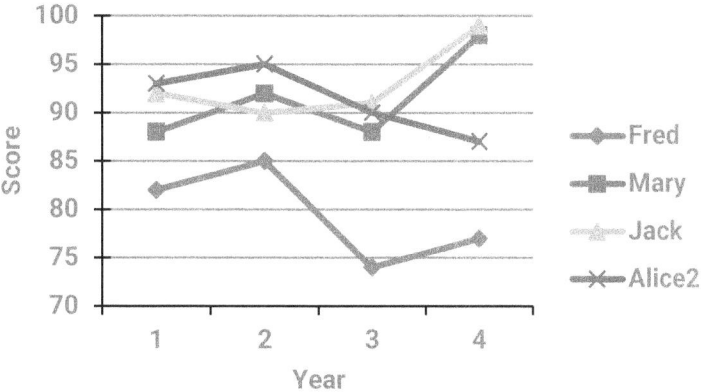

Review Video: **How to Create a Line Graph**
Visit mometrix.com/academy and enter code: 480147

LINE PLOTS

A **line plot**, also known as a *dot plot*, has plotted points that are not connected by line segments. In this graph, the horizontal axis lists the different possible values for the data, and the vertical axis lists the number of times the individual value occurs. A single dot is graphed for each value to show the number of times it occurs. This graph is more closely related to a bar graph than a line graph. Do not connect the dots in a line plot or it will misrepresent the data.

Review Video: **Line Plot**
Visit mometrix.com/academy and enter code: 754610

STEM AND LEAF PLOTS

A **stem and leaf plot** is useful for depicting groups of data that fall into a range of values. Each piece of data is separated into two parts: the first, or left, part is called the stem; the second, or right, part is called the leaf. Each stem is listed in a column from smallest to largest. Each leaf that has the common stem is listed in that stem's row from smallest to largest. For example, in a set of two-digit numbers, the digit in the tens place is the stem, and the digit in the ones place is the leaf. With a stem and leaf plot, you can easily see which subset of numbers (10s, 20s, 30s, etc.) is the largest. This information is also readily available by looking at a histogram, but a stem and leaf plot also allows you to look closer and see exactly which values fall in that range. Using a sample set of test scores (82, 88, 92, 93, 85, 90, 92, 95, 74, 88, 90, 91, 78, 87, 98, 99), we can assemble a stem and leaf plot like the one below.

Test Scores

7	4	8						
8	2	5	7	8	8			
9	0	0	1	2	2	3	5	8	9

Review Video: **Stem and Leaf Plots**
Visit mometrix.com/academy and enter code: 302339

BAR GRAPHS

A **bar graph** is one of the few graphs that can be drawn correctly in two different configurations – both horizontally and vertically. A bar graph is similar to a line plot in the way the data is organized on the graph. Both axes must have their categories defined for the graph to be useful. Rather than placing a single dot to mark the point of the data's value, a bar, or thick line, is drawn from zero to the exact value of the data, whether it is a number, percentage, or other numerical value. Longer bar lengths correspond to greater data values. To read a bar graph, read the labels for the axes to find the units being reported. Then, look where the bars end in relation to the scale given on the corresponding axis and determine the associated value.

The bar chart below represents the responses from our favorite-color survey.

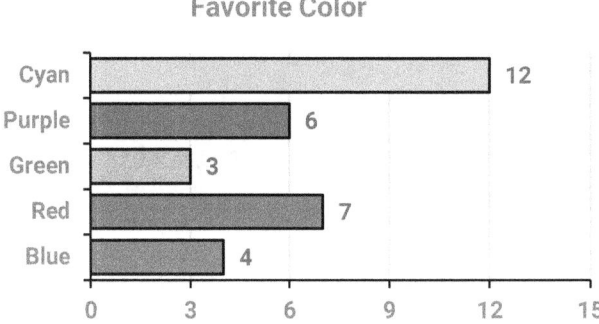

HISTOGRAMS

At first glance, a **histogram** looks like a vertical bar graph. The difference is that a bar graph has a separate bar for each piece of data and a histogram has one continuous bar for each *range* of data. For example, a histogram may have one bar for the range 0–9, one bar for 10–19, etc. While a bar graph has numerical values on one axis, a histogram has numerical values on both axes. Each range is of equal size, and they are ordered left to right from lowest to highest. The height of each column on a histogram represents the number of data values within that range. Like a stem and leaf plot, a histogram makes it easy to glance at the graph and quickly determine which range has the greatest quantity of values. A simple example of a histogram is below.

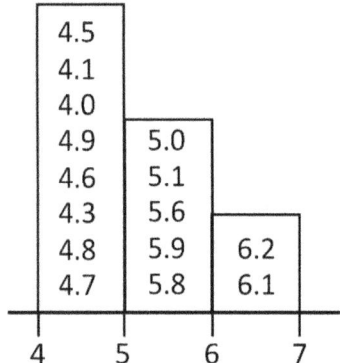

5-NUMBER SUMMARY

The **5-number summary** of a set of data gives a very informative picture of the set. The five numbers in the summary include the minimum value, maximum value, and the three quartiles. This information gives the reader the range and median of the set, as well as an indication of how the data is spread about the median.

BOX AND WHISKER PLOTS

A **box-and-whiskers plot** is a graphical representation of the 5-number summary. To draw a box-and-whiskers plot, plot the points of the 5-number summary on a number line. Draw a box whose ends are through the points for the first and third quartiles. Draw a vertical line in the box through the median to divide the box in half. Draw a line segment from the first quartile point to the minimum value, and from the third quartile point to the maximum value.

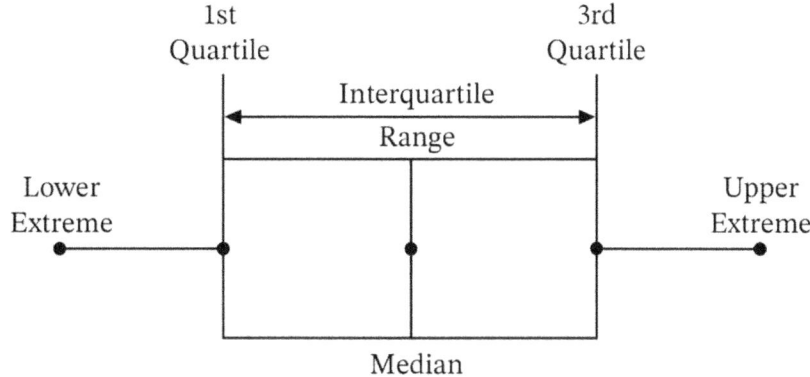

Review Video: Box and Whisker Plots
Visit mometrix.com/academy and enter code: 810817

EXAMPLE

Given the following data (32, 28, 29, 26, 35, 27, 30, 31, 27, 32), we first sort it into numerical order: 26, 27, 27, 28, 29, 30, 31, 32, 32, 35. We can then find the median. Since there are ten values, we take the average of the 5th and 6th values to get 29.5. We find the lower quartile by taking the median of the data smaller than the median. Since there are five values, we take the 3rd value, which is 27. We find the upper quartile by taking the median of the data larger than the overall median, which is 32. Finally, we note our minimum and maximum, which are simply the smallest and largest values in the set: 26 and 35, respectively. Now we can create our box plot:

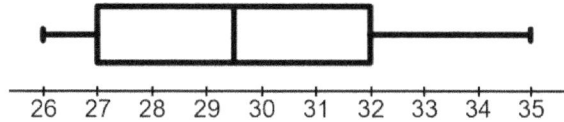

This plot is fairly "long" on the right whisker, showing one or more unusually high values (but not quite outliers). The other quartiles are similar in length, showing a fairly even distribution of data.

INTERQUARTILE RANGE

The **interquartile range, or IQR**, is the difference between the upper and lower quartiles. It measures how the data is dispersed: a high IQR means that the data is more spread out, while a low IQR means that the data is clustered more tightly around the median. To find the IQR, subtract the lower quartile value (Q_1) from the upper quartile value (Q_3).

EXAMPLE

To find the upper and lower quartiles, we first find the median and then take the median of all values above it and all values below it. In the following data set (16, 18, 13, 24, 16, 51, 32, 21, 27, 39), we first rearrange the values in numerical order: 13, 16, 16, 18, 21, 24, 27, 32, 39, 51. There are 10 values, so the median is the average of the 5th and 6th: $\frac{21+24}{2} = \frac{45}{2} = 22.5$. We do not actually need this value to find the upper and lower quartiles. We look at the set of numbers below the median: 13, 16, 16, 18, 21. There are five values, so the 3rd is the median (16), or the value of the lower quartile (Q_1). Then we look at the numbers above the median: 24, 27, 32, 39, 51. Again there are five values, so the 3rd is the median (32), or the value of the upper quartile (Q_3). We find the IQR by subtracting Q_1 from Q_3: $32 - 16 = 16$.

68-95-99.7 RULE

The **68–95–99.7 rule** describes how a normal distribution of data should appear when compared to the mean. This is also a description of a normal bell curve. According to this rule, 68 percent of the data values in a normally distributed set should fall within one standard deviation of the mean (34 percent above and 34 percent below the mean), 95 percent of the data values should fall within two standard deviations of the mean (47.5 percent above and 47.5 percent below the mean), and 99.7 percent of the data values should fall within three standard deviations of the mean, again, equally distributed on either side of the mean. This means that only 0.3 percent of all data values should fall more than three standard deviations from the mean. On the graph below, the normal curve is centered on the y-axis. The x-axis labels are how many standard deviations away from the center you are. Therefore, it is easy to see how the 68-95-99.7 rule can apply.

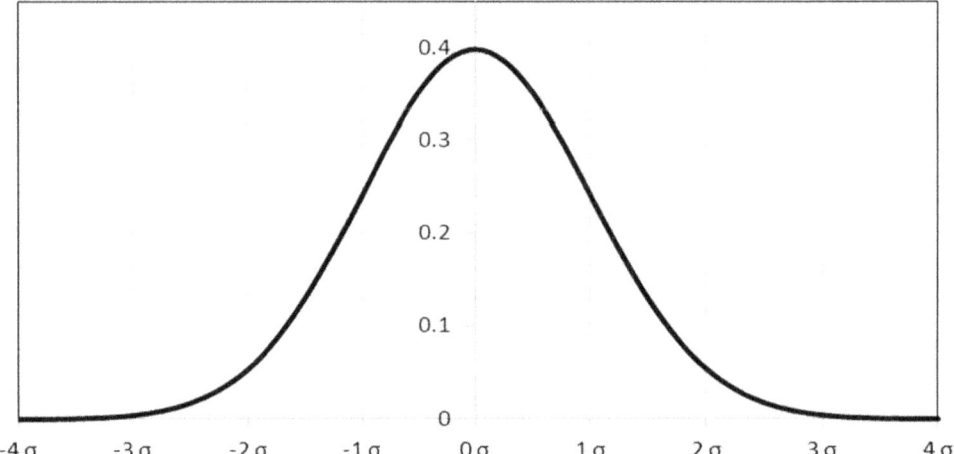

Scatter Plots

BIVARIATE DATA

Bivariate data is simply data from two different variables. (The prefix *bi-* means *two*.) In a *scatter plot*, each value in the set of data is plotted on a grid similar to a Cartesian plane, where each axis represents one of the two variables. By looking at the pattern formed by the points on the grid, you can often determine whether or not there is a relationship between the two variables, and what that relationship is, if it exists. The variables may be directly proportionate, inversely proportionate, or show no proportion at all. It may also be possible to determine if the data is linear, and if so, to find an equation to relate the two variables. The following scatter plot shows the relationship between preference for brand "A" and the age of the consumers surveyed.

SCATTER PLOTS

Scatter plots are also useful in determining the type of function represented by the data and finding the simple regression. Linear scatter plots may be positive or negative. Nonlinear scatter plots are generally exponential or quadratic. Below are some common types of scatter plots:

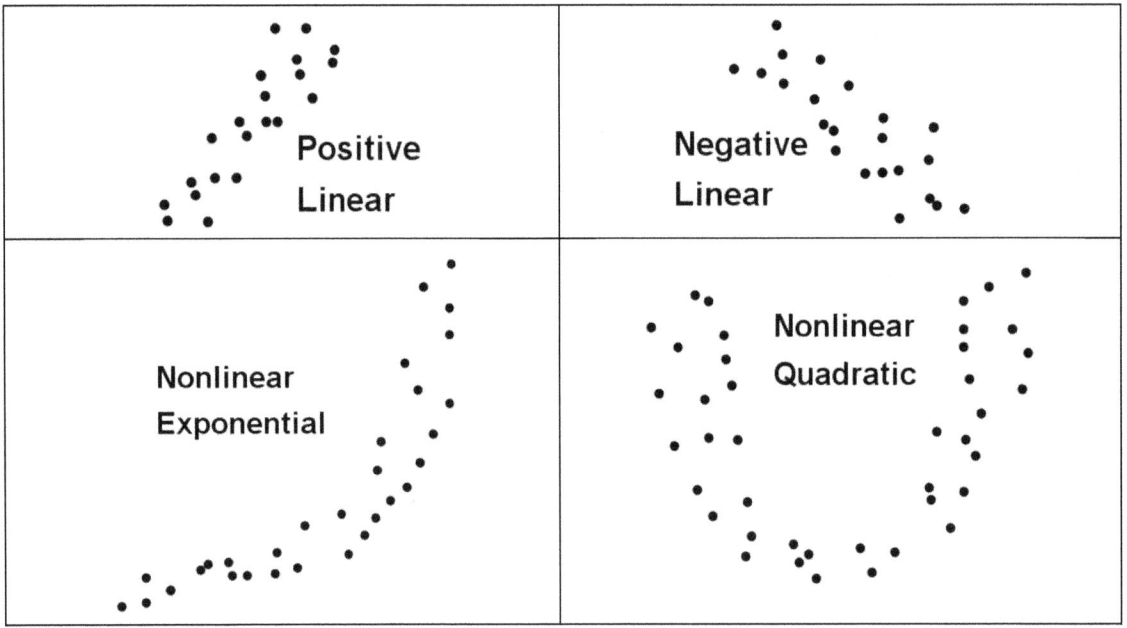

Review Video: Scatter Plot
Visit mometrix.com/academy and enter code: 596526

TSI Math Practice Test #1

Want to take this practice test in an online interactive format? Check out the online resources page, which includes interactive practice questions and much more: **mometrix.com/resources719/tsimath-27346**

1. Elizabeth has a standard die that is labeled 1 to 6, and she rolls it 100 times. Which of the following experimental outcomes is NOT likely?
   A. 67 rolls will show a number greater than 2.
   B. 50 rolls will show an even number.
   C. 75 rolls will show a number less than 4.
   D. 33 rolls will show a number less than 3.

2. Janelle bought 3 movie tickets and an order of popcorn for her family for $32.50. Jon bought 4 movie tickets and 2 orders of popcorn for his family for $46. How much does a movie ticket cost?
   A. $4.00
   B. $6.50
   C. $7.75
   D. $9.50

3. If $2^4 = 4^x$, what is the value of x?
   A. 2
   B. 4
   C. 6
   D. 8

4. Rafael has a business selling computers. He buys computers from the manufacturer for $450 each and sells them for $800. Each month, he must also pay fixed costs of $3,000 for rent and utilities for his store. If he sells n computers in a month, which of the following equations can be used to find his profit?
   A. $P = n(\$800 - \$450)$
   B. $P = n(\$800 - \$450 - \$3{,}000)$
   C. $P = \$3{,}000 \times n(\$800 - \$450)$
   D. $P = n(\$800 - \$450) - \$3{,}000$

5. Given the double bar graph shown below, which of the following statements is true?

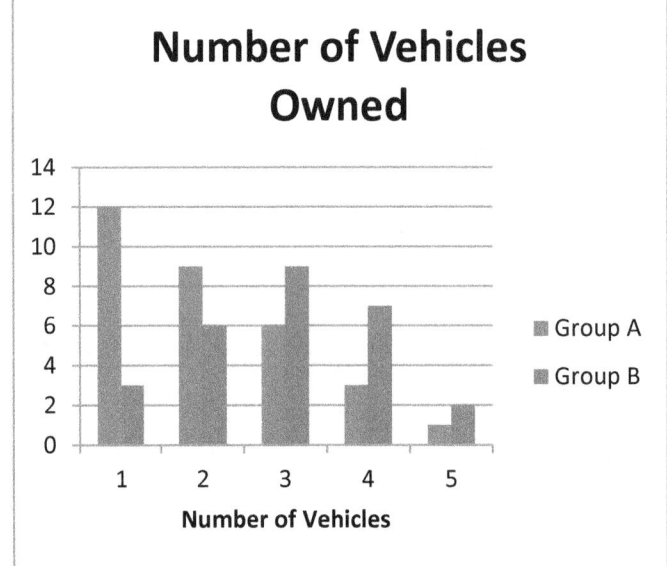

A. Group A is negatively skewed, while Group B is approximately normal.
B. Group A is positively skewed, while Group B is approximately normal.
C. Group A is approximately normal, while Group B is negatively skewed.
D. Group A is approximately normal, while Group B is positively skewed.

6. For what real number x is it true that $3(2x - 10) = x$?

A. –6
B. –5
C. 5
D. 6

Refer to the following for question 7:

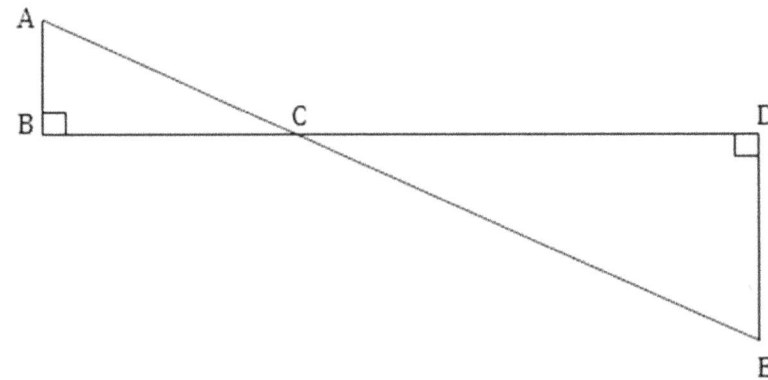

7. In the figure above, $\overline{BC}$ is 4 units long. Segment $\overline{CD}$ is 8 units long. Segment $\overline{DE}$ is 6 units long. What is the length of segment $\overline{AC}$?

A. 7 units
B. 5 units
C. 3 units
D. 2.5 units

8. Under the condition that $x > y$, which of the following CANNOT be true following the inequality $x + y > 0$?

   A. $x = 3$ and $y = 0$
   B. $x = 6$ and $y = -1$
   C. $x = -3$ and $y = 0$
   D. $x = 3$ and $y = -3$

9. Given the histograms shown below, which of the following statements is true?

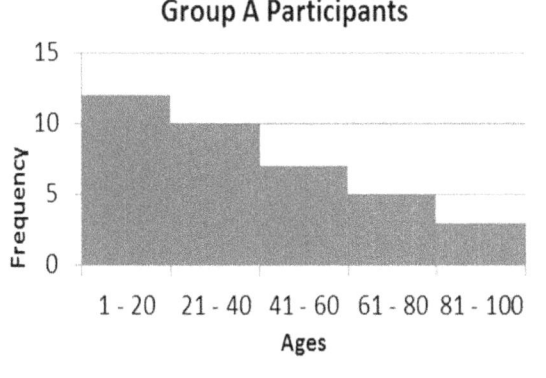
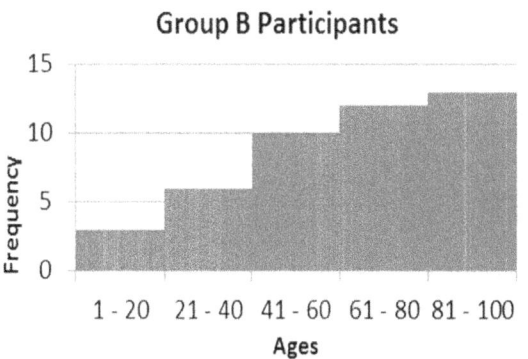

   A. Group A is negatively skewed and has a mean that is less than the mean of Group B.
   B. Group A is positively skewed and has a mean that is more than the mean of Group B.
   C. Group B is negatively skewed and has a mean that is more than the mean of Group A.
   D. Group B is positively skewed and has a mean that is less than the mean of Group A.

10. Janice weighs x pounds. Elaina weighs 23 pounds more than Janice. June weighs 14 pounds more than Janice. In terms of x, what is the sum of their weights minus 25 pounds?

    A. $3x + 37$ pounds
    B. $3x + 12$ pounds
    C. $x + 12$ pounds
    D. $3x - 25$ pounds

11. A bag contains 8 red marbles, 3 blue marbles, and 4 green marbles. What is the probability Carlos draws a red marble, does not replace it, and then draws another red marble?

    A. $\frac{2}{15}$
    B. $\frac{4}{15}$
    C. $\frac{32}{105}$
    D. $\frac{64}{225}$

12. Given the equation $2^x = 64$, what is the value of x?

    A. 4
    B. 5
    C. 6
    D. 7

13. How many integers are solutions of the inequality $|x| < 4$?
    A. 0
    B. 3
    C. 7
    D. ∞

14. Expand the following expression: $(x + 2)(x - 3)$
    A. $x^2 - 1$
    B. $x^2 - 6$
    C. $x^2 - x - 6$
    D. $x^2 - 5x - 1$

15. If $520 \div x = 40n$, then which of the following is equal to nx?
    A. 13
    B. 26
    C. 40
    D. $40nx$

16. How many 3-inch segments can a 4.5-yard line be divided into?
    A. 15
    B. 45
    C. 54
    D. 64

17. A building has a number of floors of equal height, as well as a thirty-foot spire on top. If the height of each floor in feet is h, and there are n floors in the building, which of the following represents the building's total height in feet?
    A. $n + h + 30$
    B. $nh + 30$
    C. $30n + h$
    D. $30h + n$

18. If the area of a rectangular game board is 336 square inches and its perimeter is 76 inches, what is the length of the shorter side?
    A. 10 inches
    B. 14 inches
    C. 19 inches
    D. 24 inches

19. A regular toilet uses 3.2 gallons of water per flush. A low-flow toilet uses 1.6 gallons of water per flush. What is the difference between the number of gallons used by the regular toilet and the low-flow toilet after 375 flushes?
    A. 100 gallons
    B. 525 gallons
    C. 600 gallons
    D. 1,200 gallons

20. If $-\frac{1}{3}x + 7 = 4$, what is the value for $\frac{1}{3}x + 3$?
    A. 3
    B. 6
    C. 9
    D. 12

Answer Key and Explanations for Test #1

1. C: The theoretical probability of rolling a number less than 4 is the same as the theoretical probability of rolling an even number; the probability is $\frac{1}{2}$. The expected number of rolls showing a number less than 4 is equal to the product of the total number of rolls (100) and the probability $\frac{1}{2}$: $100 \times \frac{1}{2} = 50$. Thus, it is likely that 50 of the rolls will show a number less than 4, not 75 of the rolls.

2. D: We can create a system of equations to solve for the cost of tickets and popcorn. If Janelle purchased 3 tickets and 1 order of popcorn for $32.50, we can write the equation $3t + p = 32.5$, where t is the price of a ticket and p is the price of popcorn. If Jon purchased 4 tickets and 2 orders of popcorn for $46, this can be written as $4t + 2p = 46$. We can multiply the first equation by 2 and the second equation by −1 to eliminate a variable.

$$6t + 2p = 65$$
$$-4t - 2p = -46$$

We add these two equations together.

$$2t = 19$$

From here, divide both sides by 2.

$$t = 9.5$$

So, each ticket costs $9.50.

3. A: Start by solving 2^4: $2^4 = 2 \times 2 \times 2 \times 2 = 16$. Therefore, $4^x = 16$. $4^2 = 16$, so $x = 2$.

4. D: Rafael's profit on each computer is given by the difference between the price he pays and the price he charges his customer, or $800 − $450. If he sells n computers in a month, his total profit will be n times this difference, or $n(\$800 − \$450)$. However, it is necessary to subtract his fixed costs of $3,000 from this to compute his final profit per month. This gives the complete equation:

$$P = n(\$800 - \$450) - \$3,000$$

5. B: Data is said to be positively skewed when there are a higher number of lower values, indicating data that is skewed right. Data is said to be negatively skewed when there are a higher number of higher values, indicating that the data is skewed left. An approximately normal distribution shows an increase in frequency, followed by a decrease in frequency, of approximately the same rate, following a general bell curve. Therefore, Group A is positively skewed, and Group B is approximately normal.

6. D: To solve $3(2x − 10) = x$, first expand the left side by distributing the 3 into the parentheses.

$$6x - 30 = x$$

Next, subtract $6x$ from both sides.

$$-30 = -5x$$

Finally, divide both sides by –5.

$$6 = x$$

7. B: The two right triangles are similar because they share a pair of vertical angles. Vertical angles are always congruent (e.g., ∠ACB and ∠DCE). Both right angles (e.g., ∠B and ∠D) are also congruent. So, ∠A and ∠E are congruent because of the triangular sum theorem.

With similar triangles, corresponding sides will be proportional. $\overline{BC}$ is $\frac{1}{2}$ the length of $\overline{CD}$. So, $\overline{AC}$ will be $\frac{1}{2}$ the length of $\overline{CE}$. The length of $\overline{CE}$ can be computed from the Pythagorean theorem because it is the hypotenuse of a right triangle where the lengths of the other two sides are known.

$$\overline{CE} = \sqrt{6^2 + 8^2} = \sqrt{36 + 64} = \sqrt{100} = 10$$

The length of $\overline{AC}$ will be $\frac{1}{2}$ of this value, or 5 units.

8. D: First, test each expression to see which satisfies the condition $x > y$. This condition is met for all the answer choices except for the third choice, so this doesn't need to be considered further. Next, test the remaining choices to see which satisfy the inequality $x + y > 0$. It can be seen that this inequality holds for the first two choices, but it does not for the last choice, since $x + y = 3 + (-3) = 3 - 3 = 0$. In this case, the sum $x + y$ is not greater than 0.

9. C: Skew in histograms refers to asymmetry in a histogram. Data is said to be positively skewed when there is a higher frequency of lower values, skewing the data to the right. Another way of determining skew is to compare the median and the mean. When the mean is greater than the median, the data is considered to be skewed right.

Conversely, data is skewed left (or negatively) when there is a higher frequency of larger values or when the mean is less than the median.

Group A is positively skewed because there is a higher number of low frequencies. Group B is negatively skewed because there is a higher value of high frequencies. Since Group B generally has higher frequencies than Group A, Group B has a mean that is more than Group A.

10. B: Translate this word problem into a mathematical equation. Janice's weight is x. Let Elaina's weight be $x + 23$, since she weighs 23 pounds more than Janice. Let June's weight be $x + 14$, since she weighs 14 pounds more than Janice. Add their weights together and subtract 25 pounds.

$$x + (x + 23) + (x + 14) - 25$$
$$3x + 37 - 25$$
$$3x + 12$$

Therefore, the sum of their weights minus 25 pounds is $3x + 12$ pounds.

11. B: The events are dependent since the first marble was not replaced. The sample space of the second draw will decrease by 1 because there will be one fewer marble to choose from. The number of possible red marbles for the second draw will also decrease by 1. Thus, the probability may be written as $P(A \text{ and } B) = \frac{8}{15} \times \frac{7}{14} = \frac{8}{15} \times \frac{1}{2} = \frac{8}{30} = \frac{4}{15}$. The probability he draws a red marble, does not replace it, and draws another red marble is $\frac{4}{15}$.

12. C: The power to which 2 is raised to give 64 is 6: $2^6 = 64$. Thus, $x = 6$.

13. C: Absolute value represents a number's distance from 0 on a number line. There are seven integers whose absolute value (or distance from 0) is less than 4: –3, –2, –1, 0, 1, 2, 3.

14. C: A method commonly taught to multiply binomials is the FOIL method, an acronym for *first, outer, inner, last*: multiply the first terms of each factor, then the outer terms, then the inner terms, and finally, the last terms.

$$(x+2)(x-3)$$
$$(x)(x) + (x)(-3) + (2)(x) + (2)(-3)$$

From here, simplify and combine like terms.

$$x^2 - 3x + 2x - 6$$
$$x^2 - x - 6$$

15. A: To solve for nx, rearrange the equation so nx is by itself on one side.

$$520 \div x = 40n$$

Start by multiplying by x on both sides.

$$520 = 40nx$$

Then, divide by 40 on both sides.

$$13 = nx$$

16. C: For this problem there are 3 inches in each segment, 12 inches in a foot, and 3 feet in a yard. Set up a conversion problem and simplify.

$$4.5 \text{ yd} \times \frac{3 \text{ ft}}{1 \text{ yd}} \times \frac{12 \text{ in}}{1 \text{ ft}} \times \frac{1 \text{ segment}}{3 \text{ in}} = 4.5 \times 12 \text{ segments} = 54 \text{ segments}$$

Therefore, a 4.5-yard line can be divided into 54 3-inch segments.

17. B: If there are n floors and each floor has a height of h feet, then to find the total height of the floors, we just multiply the number of floors by the height of each floor: nh. To find the total height of the building, we must also add the height of the spire, 30 feet. The building's total height in feet is $nh + 30$.

18. B: Using the formula for the perimeter of a rectangle, we know that $P = 2l + 2w$. Substituting the value given, we get $76 = 2l + 2w$. Solve this for l.

$$76 - 2w = 2l$$
$$38 - w = l$$

Using the formula for the area of a rectangle, we know that $A = l \times w$. Substituting the value given, we get $336 = l \times w$.

If we substitute the $38 - w$ for l, we get $(38 - w)w = 336$. Solve this for w.

$$38w - w^2 = 336$$
$$0 = w^2 - 38w + 336$$
$$0 = (w - 14)(w - 24)$$
$$w = 14 \text{ or } w = 24$$

The shorter of these two possibilities is 14, so the length of the shorter side is 14 inches.

19. C: To solve this problem, first calculate how many gallons each toilet uses in 375 flushes.

$$3.2 \times 375 = 1{,}200 \text{ gallons}$$
$$1.6 \times 375 = 600 \text{ gallons}$$

The problem is asking for the difference, so find the difference between the regular toilet and the low-flow toilet: $1{,}200 - 600 = 600$ gallons. Note that you could also find the difference in water use for one flush, and then multiply that amount by 375.

$$3.2 - 1.6 = 1.6$$
$$1.6 \times 375 = 600$$

With both methods of solving, the regular toilet uses 600 gallons more than the low-flow toilet after 375 flushes.

20. B: Subtract 7 from both sides of the equation.

$$-\frac{1}{3}x + 7 = 4$$
$$-\frac{1}{3}x = -3$$

In order to get the term x by itself, multiply both sides by -3.

$$x = 9$$

Now we substitute this value into the given equation $\frac{1}{3}x + 3$.

$$\frac{1}{3}(9) + 3 = 3 + 3 = 6$$

TSI Math Practice Test #2

1. Michaela can finish 3 problems in 10 minutes. How many problems can she complete in 3 hours?

    A. 90
    B. 54
    C. 18
    D. 9

2. If 120 customers purchased coffee today, and this is $\frac{1}{4}$ less than yesterday, how many people purchased coffee yesterday?

    A. 90
    B. 150
    C. 160
    D. 240

3. If $\frac{3}{s} = 7$ and $\frac{4}{t} = 12$, then what is the value of $s - t$?

    A. $-\frac{1}{7}$
    B. $\frac{2}{7}$
    C. $\frac{2}{12}$
    D. $\frac{2}{21}$

4. If the average of 7 and x is equal to the average of 9, 4, and x, what is the value of x?

    A. $x = 4$
    B. $x = 5$
    C. $x = 6$
    D. $x = 7$

5. If a number is increased by 30% and then decreased by 25%, how does the final number differ from the original?

    A. It is 5% greater than the original.
    B. It is 7.5% greater than the original.
    C. It is the same as the original.
    D. It is 2.5% less than the original.

6. Abram rolls a 6-sided die with each side labeled 1-6. What is the probability he rolls an even number or a number greater than 4?

    A. $\frac{1}{6}$
    B. $\frac{2}{3}$
    C. $\frac{3}{4}$
    D. $\frac{5}{6}$

7. In the following figure, if $\frac{b}{a+b+c} = \frac{3}{5}$, then what is the value of b?

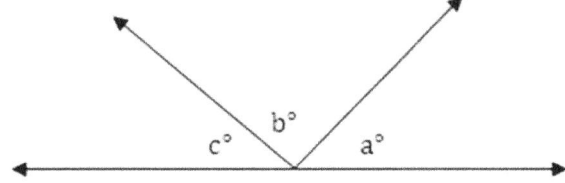

- A. 60
- B. 72
- C. 108
- D. 120

8. A communications company charges $5.00 for the first 10 minutes of a call and $1.20 for each minute thereafter. Which of the following equations correctly relates the price in dollars, d, to the number of minutes, m (when $m \geq 10$)?
   - A. $d = 5 + 1.2m$
   - B. $d = 5 + 1.2(m - 10)$
   - C. $d = 5m + 1.2(m + 10)$
   - D. $d = (m + 10)(5 + 1.2)$

9. If an item with an original price of $25.98 is marked down by 25%, and a coupon for 20% off is additionally applied, what is the final price?
   - A. $19.49
   - B. $17.77
   - C. $15.59
   - D. $13.28

10. If the ratio of the measures of the three angles in a triangle are 2 : 6 : 10, what is the actual measure of the smallest angle?
    - A. 20 degrees
    - B. 40 degrees
    - C. 60 degrees
    - D. 80 degrees

11. If $2x + 3y = 13$ and $4x - y = 5$, then what is the value of $3x + 2y$?
    - A. 3
    - B. 6
    - C. 12
    - D. 24

12. What is the expanded form of $(x + 6)(x - 6)$?
    - A. $x^2 - 12x - 36$
    - B. $x^2 + 12x - 36$
    - C. $x^2 + 12x + 36$
    - D. $x^2 - 36$

13. Andi wants to put tile on her shower floor, which is 3 ft by 5.5 ft. If the tile costs $5.75 per square foot, how much will it cost her to buy the tile, rounded to the nearest dollar?

    A. $17
    B. $72
    C. $95
    D. $131

14. If $a - 16 = 8b + 6$, what does $a + 3$ equal?

    A. $b + 3$
    B. $8b + 19$
    C. $8b + 22$
    D. $8b + 25$

15. Drawing cards from a regular deck, what is the probability that Ana draws a jack, replaces the card, and then draws an ace?

    A. $\frac{1}{52}$
    B. $\frac{17}{52}$
    C. $\frac{1}{169}$
    D. $\frac{3}{208}$

16. If $x + 2y = 3$ and $-x - 3y = 4$, then what is the value of x?

    A. 1
    B. 5
    C. 7
    D. 17

17. Expand the following expression: $(y + 1)(y + 2)(y + 3)$

    A. $y^3 + 3y + 2$
    B. $3y^2 + 6y + 3$
    C. $y^3 + 6y^2 + 11y + 6$
    D. $8y^3 + 6y + 8$

18. If $x > 2$, then what is the value of $\left(\frac{x^2 - 5x + 6}{x+1}\right) \times \left(\frac{x+1}{x-2}\right)$?

    A. $x + 1$
    B. $x - 3$
    C. $\frac{x^2 + 2x + 1}{x - 2}$
    D. $\frac{x^2 - 2x - 3}{x + 1}$

19. Max reads three books averaging 360 pages. Lucy reads five books averaging 200 pages. What is the average length of all the books that Max and Lucy read?

    A. 212 pages
    B. 232 pages
    C. 260 pages
    D. 295 pages

20. If $x - 2$ is the least of three consecutive even integers, what is the sum of the three integers?

   A. $3x - 3$
   B. x
   C. $3x$
   D. $x - 3$

Answer Key and Explanations for Test #2

1. B: We need to find how many problems Michaela can finish in 3 hours, so we start with converting the 3 hours to minutes. Because 1 hour is 60 minutes, 3 hours is $3 \times 60 = 180$ minutes. We can set up a ratio: $\frac{3 \text{ problems}}{10 \text{ minutes}} = \frac{x \text{ problems}}{180 \text{ minutes}}$. To solve for x, we cross-multiply and divide: $10x = 3(180)$, so $x = \frac{3(180)}{10} = 54$. Therefore, Michaela can complete 54 problems in 3 hours.

2. C: If 120 is $\frac{1}{4}$ less than yesterday's number, we can write this as: $120 = y - \frac{1}{4}y$, where y is yesterday's number. We combine terms on the right to solve: $120 = \frac{3}{4}y$, so $y = 120\left(\frac{4}{3}\right) = 160$. Therefore, 160 people purchased coffee yesterday.

3. D: Multiply both sides of the first equation by s to get $3 = 7s$. Then divide both sides by 7 to find that $s = \frac{3}{7}$. Multiply both sides of the second equation by t to get $4 = 12t$. Then divide both sides by 12 to find that $t = \frac{4}{12}$, which reduces to $\frac{1}{3}$. To find the difference, we must convert to a common denominator. In this case, the common denominator is 21. Multiplying by appropriate fractional equivalents of 1, we find that $\frac{3}{7}\left(\frac{3}{3}\right) = \frac{9}{21}$ and $\frac{1}{3}\left(\frac{7}{7}\right) = \frac{7}{21}$. Therefore, $s - t = \frac{9}{21} - \frac{7}{21} = \frac{2}{21}$.

4. B: The average of 7 and x is $\frac{7+x}{2}$. The average of 9, 4, and x is $\frac{9+4+x}{3}$.

$$\frac{7+x}{2} = \frac{13+x}{3}$$

To solve, start by cross-multiplying.

$$3(7+x) = 2(13+x)$$

Then, distribute and solve for x.

$$21 + 3x = 26 + 2x$$
$$3x = 5 + 2x$$
$$x = 5$$

5. D: We can choose a value for the original number and calculate the increase and decrease. For example, we can let the original value equal 100. We increase this by 30% by multiplying by 1.3: $100(1.3) = 130$. Then we decrease it by 25% by multiplying by 0.75: $130(0.75) = 97.5$. This is 2.5 less than 100, and 2.5 out of 100 is 2.5%, so the final value is 2.5% less than the original.

6. B: The probability of non-mutually exclusive events A and B occurring may be written as $P(A \text{ or } B) = P(A) + P(B) - P(A \text{ and } B)$. There are 3 even numbers on the die, so the probability of rolling an even number is $\frac{3}{6}$. There are 2 numbers greater than 4, so this probability is $\frac{2}{6}$. There is 1 number, 6, that is both even and greater than 4, so this probability is $\frac{1}{6}$. Thus, $P(A \text{ or } B) = \frac{3}{6} + \frac{2}{6} - \frac{1}{6} = \frac{4}{6} = \frac{2}{3}$.

7. C: The angles a, b, and c form a straight line, so $a + b + c = 180$. Substituting 180 for $a + b + c$ in the proportion, we have $\frac{b}{180} = \frac{3}{5}$. By cross-multiplying, we can solve for b.

$$5b = 3(180)$$
$$b = 108$$

8. B: The charge is $1.20 for each minute after the first ten minutes. The number of minutes after the first ten minutes is $m - 10$, so $1.20 per minute charged for the part of the phone call exceeding 10 minutes is $1.2(m - 10)$. Adding this to the $5.00 charge for the first ten minutes gives $d = 5 + 1.2(m - 10)$.

9. C: An item is first marked down by 25% and then by an additional 20%. If 25% is taken off the price, the remaining cost is 75% of the original price, so we can calculate the first markdown: $25.98(0.75) = 19.485$. If 20% is taken off this price, the remaining cost is 80% of this price, so we can calculate the second and final markdown: $19.485(0.8) = 15.588$. We round to the hundredths place to find the final cost: $15.59.

10. A: The sum of the measures of the three angles of any triangle is 180 degrees. The equation for the sum of the angles of this triangle can be written as $2x + 6x + 10x = 180$, or $18x = 180$. Therefore, $x = 10$. We multiply 2 by 10 to find that the measure of the smallest angle is 20 degrees.

11. C: This system of equations can be solved using the substitution method. Solve for y in the second equation.

$$y = 4x - 5$$

Plug this into the first equation and simplify.

$$2x + 3(4x - 5) = 13$$
$$2x + 12x - 15 = 13$$

From here, solve for x.

$$14x - 15 = 13$$
$$14x = 28$$
$$x = 2$$

Then we plug the value of x into either equation and solve for y.

$$4(2) - y = 5$$
$$8 - y = 5$$
$$-y = -3$$
$$y = 3$$

Finally, substitute these values into the expression $3x + 2y$.

$$3x + 2y = 3(2) + 2(3) = 12$$

12. D: Use the difference of squares rule that states that $(a + b)(a - b) = a^2 - b^2$, or multiply the binomials using the FOIL method: multiply together the *first* term of each factor, then the *outer* terms, then the *inner* terms, and finally the *last* terms. Then add the products together.

$$(x + 6)(x - 6) = x \times x + x \times (-6) + 6 \times x + 6 \times (-6)$$
$$= x^2 - 6x + 6x - 36$$
$$= x^2 - 36$$

13. C: First, calculate the square footage (or area) of the shower floor by multiplying the length by the width.

$$A = 3 \times 5.5 = 16.5 \text{ ft}^2$$

Then, multiply the number of square feet by the cost per square foot to find the total cost of tiling the floor.

$$16.5 \times 5.75 = 94.875$$

We round this to the nearest dollar to find that Andi's total cost is $95.

14. D: Start by isolating a on one side of the equation.

$$a - 16 = 8b + 6$$
$$a = 8b + 6 + 16$$
$$a = 8b + 22$$

Next, add 3 to both side of the equation.

$$a + 3 = 8b + 22 + 3$$
$$a + 3 = 8b + 25$$

15. C: The probability of drawing a jack is $\frac{4}{52} = \frac{1}{13}$ because there are 4 jacks and a total of 52 cards. Likewise, the probability of drawing an ace is $\frac{4}{52} = \frac{1}{13}$. We can find the probability of independent events A and B using the formula $P(A \text{ and } B) = P(A) \times P(B)$. Thus, the probability she draws a jack, replaces it, and then draws an ace may be represented as $P(A \text{ and } B) = \frac{1}{13} \times \frac{1}{13}$, which simplifies to $P(A \text{ and } B) = \frac{1}{169}$.

16. D: There are several ways to solve a system of equations like this. In this case, the simplest way to solve is by elimination. Add the two equations together to cancel out the x-values.

$$(x + 2y = 3) + (-x - 3y = 4)$$
$$x + 2y - x - 3y = 3 + 4$$
$$-y = 7$$
$$y = -7$$

Now, put that value for y back into one of the original equations.

$$x + 2(-7) = 3$$
$$x - 14 = 3$$
$$x = 17$$

Therefore, the value of x is 17.

17. C: This question requires us to multiply three algebraic expressions. When multiplying more than two binomials, multiply any two binomials using the FOIL method, and then multiply the result by the remaining binomial. Start by multiplying the first two binomials.

$$(y + 1)(y + 2) = (y \times y) + (y \times 2) + (1 \times y) + (1 \times 2)$$
$$= y^2 + 2y + y + 2$$
$$= y^2 + 3y + 2$$

Then multiply the result by the third expression.

$$(y^2 + 3y + 2)(y + 3) = (y^2 + 3y + 2)(y) + (y^2 + 3y + 2)(3)$$
$$= (y^3 + 3y^2 + 2y) + (3y^2 + 9y + 6)$$
$$= y^3 + 3y^2 + 3y^2 + 2y + 9y + 6$$
$$= y^3 + 6y^2 + 11y + 6$$

18. B: Before carrying out the multiplication of the polynomials, notice that there is a factor of $x + 1$ in both the right numerator and left denominator, so this term can be canceled out. The expression then multiplies to $\frac{x^2-5x+6}{x-2}$. We can simplify further by factoring the numerator.

One way to factor a quadratic expression with a leading coefficient of 1 is to look for two numbers that add up to the coefficient of x (in this case –5) and multiply to the constant term (in this case 6). Two such numbers are –2 and –3: $(-2) + (-3) = -5$ and $(-2) \times (-3) = 6$. So $x^2 - 5x + 6 = (x - 2)(x - 3)$. That means $\frac{x^2-5x+6}{x-2} = \frac{(x-2)(x-3)}{x-2}$. The $x - 2$ in the numerator and denominator can cancel, so we are left with just $x - 3$. (Note that if $x = -1$ or $x = 2$, the obtained simplified expression would not be true: either value of x would result in a denominator of zero in the original expression, so the whole expression would be undefined. Therefore, it is necessary to state that these values of x are excluded from the domain. For a domain of $x > 2$, both $x = -1$ and $x = 2$ would be excluded.)

19. C: To find the average, we need to add up each part and divide by the number of parts. If Max reads 3 books and Lucy reads 5 books, there are 8 books in total. We can find the total number of pages by multiplying 360 by 3 and 200 by 5, and then dividing the sum by 8.

$$\frac{360 \times 3 + 200 \times 5}{8} = \frac{1{,}080 + 1{,}000}{8} = \frac{2{,}080}{8} = 260$$

Therefore, the average length of all the books that Max and Lucy read is 260 pages.

20. C: Consecutive even integers increase by 2. So if the first integer is $x - 2$, the second is $x - 2 + 2 = x$, and the third is $x + 2$. Adding the three integers together yields: $x - 2 + x + x + 2 = 3x$.

TSI Math Practice Test #3

1. What is the solution to the equation: $4\sqrt{x} + 8 = 24$?
   A. $x = 2$
   B. $x = 4$
   C. $x = 12$
   D. $x = 16$

2. Every person attending a meeting hands out a business card to every other person at the meeting. If a total of 30 cards are handed out, how many people are at the meeting?
   A. 5 people
   B. 6 people
   C. 10 people
   D. 15 people

3. Which of the following could be a graph of the function $y = \frac{1}{x}$?

A.

B.

C.

D.

4. The table below shows the cost of renting a bicycle for 1, 2, or 3 hours. Which answer choice shows the equation that best represents the data? Let C represent the cost of the rental and h stand for the number of hours of rental time.

Hours	1	2	3
Cost	$3.60	$7.20	$10.80

A. $C = 3.60h$
B. $C = h + 3.60$
C. $C = 3.60h + 10.80$
D. $C = \frac{10.80}{h}$

5. Which of the following inequalities is correct?
   A. $\frac{1}{3} < \frac{2}{7} < \frac{5}{12}$
   B. $\frac{2}{7} < \frac{1}{3} < \frac{5}{12}$
   C. $\frac{5}{12} < \frac{2}{7} < \frac{1}{3}$
   D. $\frac{5}{12} < \frac{1}{3} < \frac{2}{7}$

6. Simplify $\frac{x^6}{y^4} \cdot x^2 y^3$.
   A. $x^4 y$
   B. $\frac{x^4}{y}$
   C. $x^8 y$
   D. $\frac{x^8}{y}$

7. Given the equation: $\frac{2}{x+4} = \frac{3}{x}$, what is the value of x?
   A. -14
   B. -12
   C. 10
   D. 12

8. An exam has 30 questions. A student gets 1 point for each correctly answered question and loses $\frac{1}{2}$ point for each incorrectly answered question. The student neither gains nor loses any points for a question left blank. If C is the number of questions a student gets right and B is the number of questions the student leaves blank, which of the following represents the student's score on the exam?
   A. $C - \frac{1}{2} B$
   B. $C - \frac{1}{2}(30 - B)$
   C. $C - \frac{1}{2}(30 - B - C)$
   D. $(30 - C) - \frac{1}{2}(30 - B)$

9. Examine the triangles below:

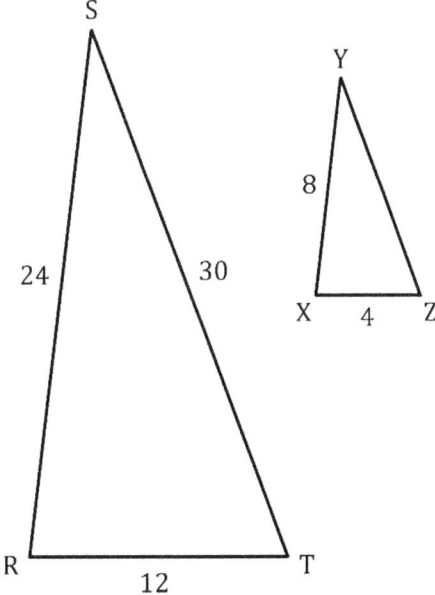

In order for $\triangle RST$ to be similar to $\triangle XYZ$, what must the length of $\overline{YZ}$ be?

A. 10
B. 14
C. 15
D. 22

10. Elisha spins a spinner with 8 equally spaced sections labeled 1–8. What is the probability that the spinner lands either on a number greater than 5 or on 2?

A. $\frac{1}{2}$
B. $\frac{1}{8}$
C. $\frac{3}{8}$
D. $\frac{3}{64}$

11. In the figure pictured below, find the value of x.

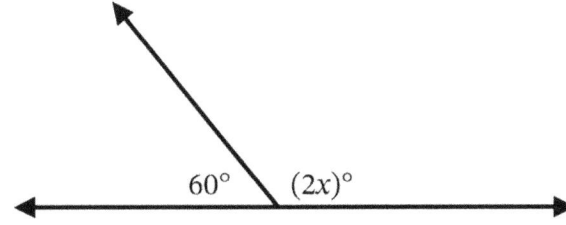

A. $x = 30$
B. $x = 60$
C. $x = 100$
D. $x = 120$

12. If $6q + 3 = 8q - 7$, what is q?
    A. -7
    B. $-\frac{5}{7}$
    C. $\frac{5}{7}$
    D. 5

13. The formula for finding the volume of a cone is $V = \frac{1}{3}\pi r^2 h$. Which of the following equations is correctly solved for r?
    A. $r = \frac{1}{3}\pi h$
    B. $r = \sqrt{\frac{3V}{\pi h}}$
    C. $r = \frac{3V}{\pi h}$
    D. $r = V - \frac{1}{3}\pi h$

14. If the radius of circle O is one-quarter the diameter of circle P, what is the ratio of the circumference of circle O to the circumference of circle P?
    A. $\frac{1}{4}$
    B. $\frac{1}{2}$
    C. 2
    D. 4

15. A bag contains 2 red marbles, 3 blue marbles, and 5 green marbles. What is the probability Gitta draws a red marble, does not replace it, and then draws another red marble?
    A. $\frac{1}{25}$
    B. $\frac{1}{45}$
    C. $\frac{2}{45}$
    D. $\frac{14}{45}$

16. Solve for n in the equation: $4n - p = 3r$
    A. $\frac{3r}{4} - p$
    B. $p + 3r$
    C. $p - 3r$
    D. $\frac{3r}{4} + \frac{p}{4}$

17. Which of the following is equivalent to this expression: $x(y - 2) + y(3 - x)$?
    A. $xy + y$
    B. $-2x + 3y$
    C. $2xy - 2x + 3y$
    D. $xy + 3y - x - 2$

18. Which of the following expressions is equivalent to $(a+b)(a-b)$?
    A. $a^2 - b^2$
    B. $(a+b)^2$
    C. $(a-b)^2$
    D. $ab(a-b)$

19. At a school carnival, three students spend an average of $10. Six other students spend an average of $4. What is the average amount of money spent by all nine students?
    A. $5
    B. $6
    C. $7
    D. $8

20. Edward draws a card from a standard deck of cards, does not replace it, and then draws another card. What is the probability that he draws a heart and then a spade?
    A. $\frac{1}{16}$
    B. $\frac{1}{2}$
    C. $\frac{1}{17}$
    D. $\frac{13}{204}$

Answer Key and Explanations for Test #3

1. D: The radical equation may be solved by first subtracting 8 from both sides of the equation.

$$4\sqrt{x} + 8 = 24$$
$$4\sqrt{x} = 16$$

Then, divide both sides of the equation by 4.

$$\sqrt{x} = 4$$

Finally, square both sides.

$$x = 16$$

2. B: Call the number of people present at the meeting x. If each person hands out a card to every other person (that is, every person besides himself), then each person hands out $x - 1$ cards. The total number of cards handed out is therefore $x(x - 1)$. Since we are told there are a total of 30 cards handed out, we have the equation $x(x - 1) = 30$, which we can rewrite as the quadratic equation $x^2 - x - 30 = 0$. We can solve this equation by factoring the quadratic expression. One way to do this is to find two numbers that add up to the coefficient of x (in this case, –1) and that multiply to the constant term (in this case, –30). Those two numbers are 5 and –6. Our factored equation is therefore $(x + 5)(x - 6) = 0$. To make the equation true, one or both of the factors must be zero: either $x + 5 = 0$, in which case $x = -5$, or $x - 6 = 0$, in which case $x = 6$. Obviously, the number of people at the meeting cannot be negative, so the second solution, $x = 6$, must be correct. There are 6 people at the meeting.

3. A: This is a typical plot of an inverse variation where the product of the dependent and independent variables, x and y, is always equal to the same value. In this case, the product is always equal to 1. So, the plot is in the first and third quadrants of the coordinate plane. As x increases and goes to infinity, y decreases and goes to zero while keeping the constant product. In contrast, choice B is a linear plot for an equation of the form $y = x$. Choice C is a quadratic plot for the equation $y = x^2$. Choice D is an exponential plot for the equation $y = 2^x$.

4. A: This equation is a linear relationship that has a slope of 3.60 and passes through the origin. The table shows that for each hour of rental, the cost increases by $3.60. This matches with the slope of the equation. Of course, if the bicycle is not rented at all (0 hours), there will be no charge ($0). If plotted on the Cartesian plane, the line would have a y-intercept of 0. The first choice is the only one that meets these requirements.

5. B: One way to compare fractions is to convert them to equivalent fractions with common denominators. In this case, the lowest common denominator of the three fractions is $7 \times 12 = 84$. Convert each of the fractions to this denominator: $\frac{1}{3} = \frac{1 \times 28}{3 \times 28} = \frac{28}{84}, \frac{2}{7} = \frac{2 \times 12}{7 \times 12} = \frac{24}{84}$, and $\frac{5}{12} = \frac{5 \times 7}{12 \times 7} = \frac{35}{84}$. Since $24 < 28 < 35$, it must be the case that $\frac{2}{7} < \frac{1}{3} < \frac{5}{12}$.

6. D: When variables are multiplied, their exponents are added together. First, move any variables out of the denominator by reversing the sign on their exponents.

$$\frac{x^6}{y^4} \cdot x^2 y^3 = x^6 y^{-4} \cdot x^2 y^3$$

Next, group sets of like variables to make it easier to combine them accurately.

$$= (x^6 x^2)(y^{-4} y^3)$$

Finally, add the exponents and simplify.

$$= x^{6+2} y^{-4+3}$$
$$= x^8 y^{-1}$$
$$= \frac{x^8}{y}$$

7. B: To solve this equation, start by cross multiplying.

$$\frac{2}{x+4} = \frac{3}{x}$$
$$2x = 3(x+4)$$

Next, distribute 3 into the parentheses on the right side of the equation.

$$2x = 3x + 12$$

Then, subtract $3x$ from both sides.

$$-x = 12$$

Finally, divide both sides by –1.

$$x = -12$$

8. C: If the exam has 30 questions, and the student answered C questions correctly and left B questions blank, then the number of questions the student answered incorrectly must be $30 - B - C$. The student gets 1 point for each correct question, or $1 \times C = C$ points, and loses $\frac{1}{2}$ point for each incorrect question, or $\frac{1}{2}(30 - B - C)$ points. Since the blank questions do not affect the student's score, one way to express his total score is $C - \frac{1}{2}(30 - B - C)$.

9. A: If two triangles are similar, then all pairs of corresponding sides are proportional. For $\triangle RST$ to be similar to $\triangle XYZ$, we need $\frac{RS}{XY} = \frac{RT}{XZ} = \frac{ST}{YZ}$. Substituting the numbers from the figure in for those values gives $\frac{24}{8} = \frac{12}{4} = \frac{30}{YZ}$. Simplifying the fractions results in $\frac{3}{1} = \frac{3}{1} = \frac{30}{YZ}$. Therefore, in order for the triangles to be similar, we need $\frac{3}{1} = \frac{30}{YZ}$. After cross-multiplying the terms, it becomes $3(YZ) = 30(1)$, so $3(YZ) = 30$. Divide both sides by 3 to get $YZ = 10$.

10. A: The probability of the mutually exclusive events A or B occurring may be written as $P(A \text{ or } B) = P(A) + P(B)$. The probability of obtaining a number greater than 5 is $\frac{3}{8}$ because 3 of the 8 sections are greater than 5: 6, 7, and 8. The probability of obtaining a 2 is $\frac{1}{8}$ because this refers to 1 of the 8 sections. Thus, $P(A \text{ or } B) = \frac{3}{8} + \frac{1}{8} = \frac{4}{8} = \frac{1}{2}$.

11. B: Angles that form a straight line add up to 180 degrees. Such angles are sometimes referred to as being supplementary.

$$60 + 2x = 180$$
$$2x = 120$$
$$x = 60$$

12. D: Rearrange the equation to isolate q. First, subtract $6q$ from both sides.

$$6q + 3 = 8q - 7$$
$$3 = 2q - 7$$

Then, add 7 to both sides.

$$10 = 2q$$

Finally, divide both sides by 2.

$$5 = q$$

13. B: Dividing both sides of the equation by $\frac{1}{3}\pi h$ gives $r^2 = \frac{V}{\frac{1}{3}\pi h} = \frac{3V}{\pi h}$. We can then solve for r by taking the square root of both sides, which gives us $r = \sqrt{\frac{3V}{\pi h}}$.

14. B: The radius of circle O is one-fourth the diameter of circle P. The diameter is twice the radius, or $d = 2r$. This means that the radius of circle O is half of the radius of circle P, or $r_O = \frac{1}{4}(2r_P) = \frac{1}{2}r_P$. The circumference of circle P is $2\pi r_P$. The circumference of circle O is $2\pi r_O = 2\pi\left(\frac{1}{2}r_P\right) = \pi r_P$. Since circle P's circumference is twice that of circle O, the ratio of circle O's circumference to circle P's is $\frac{\pi r_P}{2\pi r_P} = \frac{1}{2}$.

15. B: The events are dependent since the first marble was not replaced. The sample space of the second draw will decrease by 1 because there will be one fewer marble to choose from. The number of possible red marbles for the second draw will also decrease by 1. Thus, the probability may be written as $P(A \text{ and } B) = \frac{2}{10} \times \frac{1}{9}$. Thus, the probability Gitta draws a red marble, does not replace it, and draws another red marble is $\frac{2}{90}$, or $\frac{1}{45}$.

16. D: To solve, isolate n by putting all the other terms on the other side of the equal sign.

$$4n - p = 3r$$
$$4n = 3r + p$$
$$n = \frac{3r}{4} + \frac{p}{4}$$

17. B: First, let's distribute the x and y that are outside the parentheses and then combine like terms.

$$\begin{aligned} x(y-2) + y(3-x) &= (xy - 2x) + (3y - xy) \\ &= -2x + 3y + xy - xy \\ &= -2x + 3y \end{aligned}$$

18. A: Compute the product using the FOIL method, in which the first terms, the outer terms, the inner terms, and finally the last terms are figured in sequence of multiplication. As a result, $(a+b)(a-b) = a^2 + ba - ab - b^2$. The middle terms, ba and $-ab$, cancel each other out, which leaves $a^2 - b^2$.

19. B: The average is the total amount spent divided by the number of students. The first three students spend an average of $10, so the total amount they spend is $3 \times \$10 = \$30$. The other six students spend an average of $4, so the total amount they spend is $6 \times \$4 = \$24$. The total amount spent by all nine students is $\$30 + \$24 = \$54$, and the average amount they spend is $\$54 \div 9 = \$6$.

20. D: Since he does not replace the first card, the events are dependent. The sample space will decrease by 1 for the second draw because there will be one fewer card to choose from. Thus, the probability may be written as $P(A \text{ and } B) = \frac{13}{52} \times \frac{13}{51}$, or $P(A \text{ and } B) = \frac{169}{2,652} = \frac{13}{204}$.

TSI Math Practice Test #4

1. Which of the following is the solution to $3 - 2x < 5$?
   A. $x < 1$
   B. $x > 1$
   C. $x < -1$
   D. $x > -1$

2. The graph below shows the number of miles Jen runs each day, Monday through Friday. What fraction of the time does she run at least four miles?

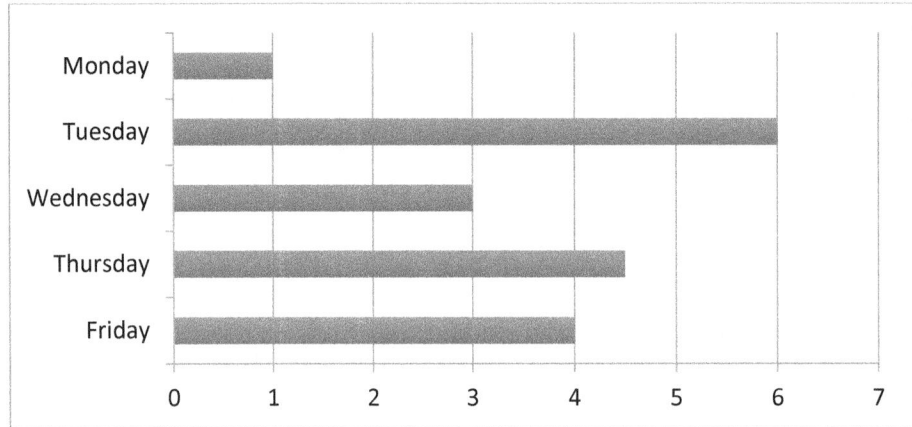

   A. $\frac{3}{7}$
   B. $\frac{3}{2}$
   C. $\frac{2}{5}$
   D. $\frac{3}{5}$

3. Bob decides to go into business selling lemonade. He buys a wooden stand for $45 and sets it up outside his house. He figures that the cost of lemons, sugar, and paper cups for each glass of lemonade sold will be 10¢. Which of these expressions describes his cost for making g glasses of lemonade?
   A. $\$45 + \$0.10g$
   B. $\$44.90g$
   C. $\$44.90g + 10¢$
   D. $\$90$

4. If 1 inch on a map represents 60 feet, how many yards apart are two points if the distance between the points on the map is 10 inches?
   A. 1,800
   B. 600
   C. 200
   D. 2

5. The cost, in dollars, of shipping x computers to California for sale is $3,000 + 100x$. The amount received when selling these computers is $400x$ dollars. What is the least number of computers that must be shipped and sold so that the amount received is at least equal to the shipping cost?
   A. 10 computers
   B. 15 computers
   C. 20 computers
   D. 25 computers

6. Which of the following figures shows parallelogram $WXYZ$ being carried onto its image $W'X'Y'Z'$ by a reflection across the x-axis?

A.

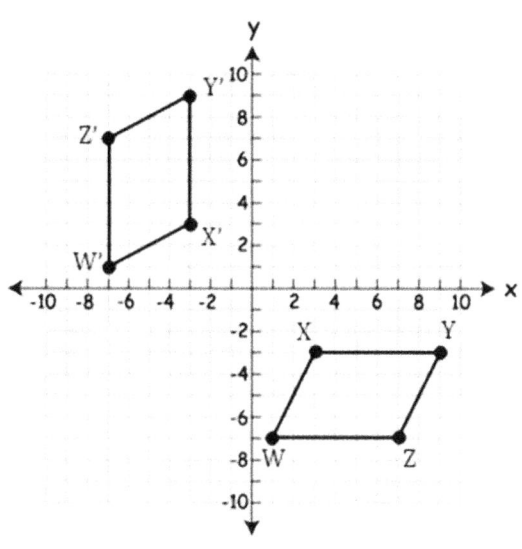

C.

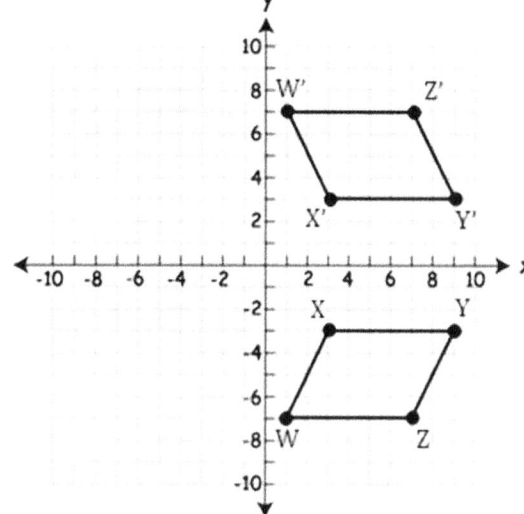

B.

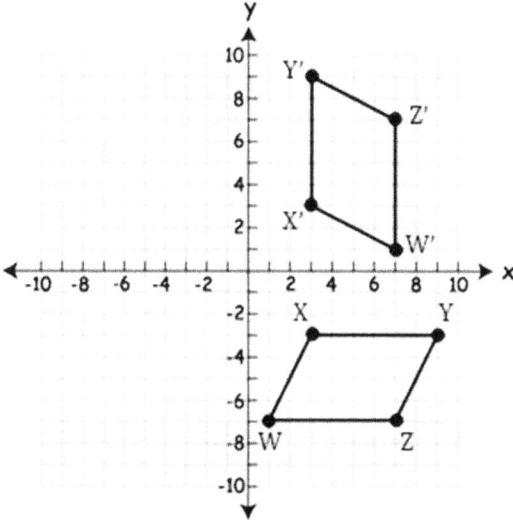

D.

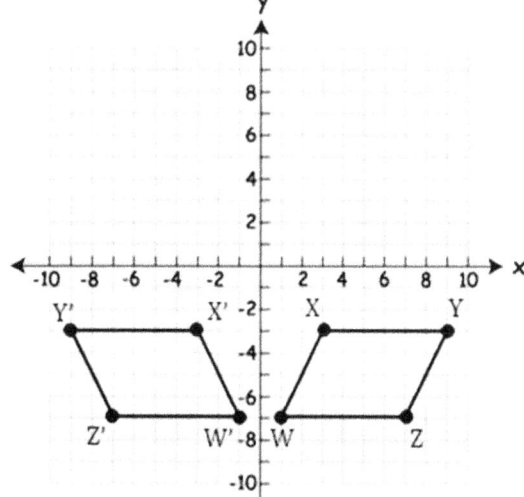

7. If $a = -6$ and $b = 7$, then what is $4a(3b + 5) + 2b$ equal to?
   A. -610
   B. -485
   C. 638
   D. 850

8. Which of the following graphs represents the inequality $-2 < x \leq 4$?

A.
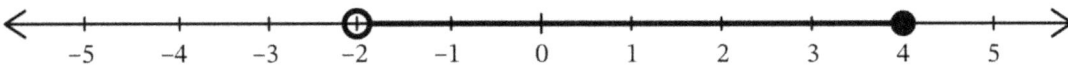

B.
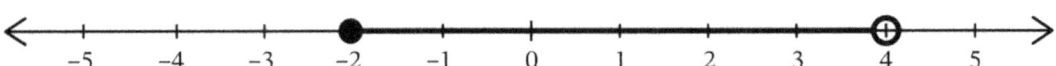

C.
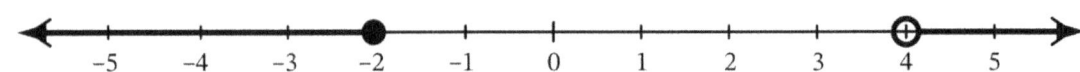

D.
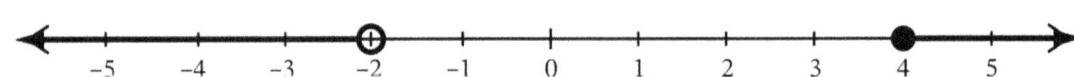

9. Simplify the following: $\frac{x^2}{y^2} + \frac{x}{y^3}$

   A. $\frac{x^3+x}{y^3}$

   B. $\frac{x^2+xy}{y^3}$

   C. $\frac{x^2y+xy}{y^3}$

   D. $\frac{x^2y+x}{y^3}$

10. Which of the following represents the factored form of the expression $x^2 - 3x - 40$?
    A. $(x - 8)(x + 5)$
    B. $(x - 7)(x + 4)$
    C. $(x + 10)(x - 4)$
    D. $(x + 6)(x - 9)$

Refer to the following for question 11:

An MP3 player is set to play songs at random from the 15 songs it contains in memory. Any song can be played at any time, even if it is repeated. There are 5 songs by Band A, 3 songs by Band B, 2 by Band C, and 5 by Band D.

11. If the player has just played two songs in a row by Band D, what is the probability that the next song will also be by Band D?

A. $\frac{1}{3}$
B. $\frac{1}{5}$
C. $\frac{1}{9}$
D. $\frac{1}{27}$

12. What is $|x| + |x - 2|$ when $x = 1$?

A. 0
B. 1
C. 2
D. 3

13. Simplify the following expression: $(2x^2 + 3x + 2) - (x^2 + 2x - 3)$

A. $x^2 + x + 5$
B. $x^2 + x - 1$
C. $x^2 + 5x + 5$
D. $x^2 + 5x - 1$

14. Which frequency table is represented by the histogram shown below?

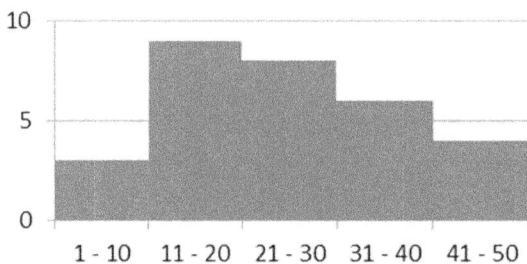

A.

Interval	Frequency
1 – 10	3
11 – 20	9
21 – 30	8
31 – 40	6
41 – 50	4

B.

Interval	Frequency
1 – 10	3
11 – 20	8
21 – 30	8
31 – 40	6
41 – 50	3

C.

Interval	Frequency
1 – 10	3
11 – 20	9
21 – 30	8
31 – 40	5
41 – 50	4

D.

Interval	Frequency
1 – 10	2
11 – 20	9
21 – 30	8
31 – 40	6
41 – 50	5

15. The ratio of Jon's monthly expenses to his savings is 7:1. If he is able to save $725 per month, what are his monthly expenses?

    A. $5,075
    B. $5,800
    C. $6,125
    D. $6,350

16. Two hikers start at a ranger station and leave at the same time. One hiker heads due west at 3 mph. The other hiker heads due north at 4 mph. How far apart are the hikers after 2 hours of hiking?

   A. 5 miles
   B. 7 miles
   C. 10 miles
   D. 14 miles

17. What is the area of the parallelogram in the figure below?

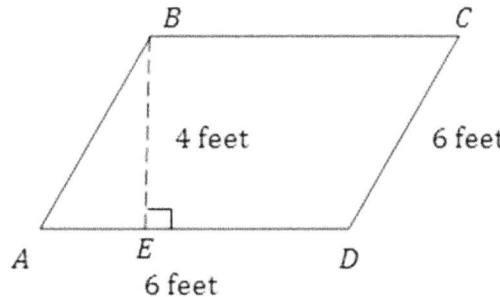

   A. 12 square feet
   B. 24 square feet
   C. 36 square feet
   D. 144 square feet

Refer to the following for question 18:

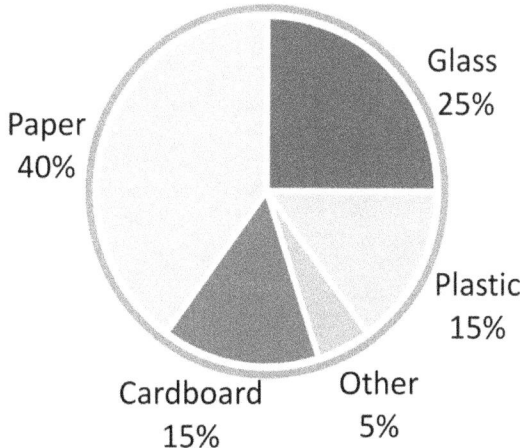

18. The Charleston Recycling Company collects 50,000 tons of recyclable material every month. The chart shows the kinds of materials that are collected by the company's five trucks. What is the second most common material that is recycled?

   A. Cardboard
   B. Glass
   C. Paper
   D. Plastic

19. A metal rod used in manufacturing must be as close as possible to 15 inches in length. The tolerance of the length, L, in inches, is specified by the inequality $|L - 15| \leq 0.01$. What is the minimum length permissible for the rod?
- A. 14.9 inches
- B. 14.99 inches
- C. 15.01 inches
- D. 15.1 inches

20. A recipe calls for 2 cups of water for every 6 cups of flour. Josie wants to make a smaller batch using only 2 cups of flour. How much water should she use?
- A. $\frac{1}{2}$ cup
- B. 2 cups
- C. $\frac{2}{3}$ cup
- D. 12 cups

Answer Key and Explanations for Test #4

1. D: To solve the inequality $3 - 2x < 5$, we can first subtract 3 from both sides to get $-2x < 2$. Now we can divide both sides of the inequality by -2. When an inequality is multiplied or divided by a negative number, its direction changes ($<$ becomes $>$, $\leq$ becomes $\geq$, and vice versa). So $-2x < 2$ becomes $\frac{-2x}{-2} > \frac{2}{-2}$, or $x > -1$.

2. D: The graph shows five days that Jen runs. On three of the days (Tuesday, Thursday, and Friday), she runs four or more miles. So three out of five days, or $\frac{3}{5}$ of the time, she runs at least four miles.

3. A: Each glass of lemonade costs 10¢, or $0.10. So, g glasses will cost $g \times \$0.10$. To this, add the amount Bob initially spent on the wooden stand, $45. This gives the expression in the first choice.

$$\$45 + \$0.10 \times g$$

4. C: Start by setting up a proportion to solve: $\frac{1 \text{ inch}}{60 \text{ feet}} = \frac{10 \text{ inches}}{x \text{ feet}}$. When the numbers are cross-multiplied, you get $x = 600$. Now we need to convert 600 feet to yards. There are 3 feet in 1 yard, so divide 600 by 3 to find the number of yards between the two points: $600 \div 3 = 200$. Therefore, the two points are 200 yards apart.

5. A: Setting the cost of shipping equal to the amount received gives us the equation $3{,}000 + 100x = 400x$. Subtract $100x$ from both sides to get $3{,}000 = 300x$, then divide both sides by 300 to see that $x = 10$. Therefore, the least number of computers that must be shipped and sold is 10.

6. C: A reflection is a transformation producing a mirror image. A figure reflected over the x-axis will have its vertices in the form (x, y) transformed to $(x, -y)$. The point W at $(1, -7)$ reflects to W' at $(1, 7)$. Only choice C shows $WXYZ$ being carried onto its image $W'X'Y'Z'$ by a reflection across the x-axis. Choice A shows a reflection across the line $y = x$. Choice B shows a 90° counterclockwise rotation about the origin. Choice D shows a reflection across the y-axis.

7. A: Start by substituting the given values into the expression.

$$4(-6)(3(7) + 5) + 2(7)$$

From here, simplify the expression using the order of operations. Start by simplifying the expression inside the parentheses.

$$4(-6)(21 + 5) + 2(7)$$
$$4(-6)(26) + 2(7)$$

From here, simplify the multiplication in order from left to right.

$$-24(26) + 2(7)$$
$$-624 + 14$$

Finally, add.

$$-624 + 14 = -610$$

8. A: When graphing an inequality, a solid circle at an endpoint means that the number at that endpoint is included in the range, while a hollow circle means it is not. Since the inequality says that x is strictly greater than –2, the circle at –2 should be hollow. Since the inequality says that x is less than or equal to 4, the circle at 4 should be solid. $-2 < x \leq 4$ indicates that x is between –2 and 4, so the area between the circles should be shaded.

9. D: To add the two fractions, first rewrite them with the least common denominator, which is in this case y^3. This is already the denominator in $\frac{x}{y^3}$, and we can rewrite $\frac{x^2}{y^2}$ as $\frac{x^2 \times y}{y^2 \times y} = \frac{x^2 y}{y^3}$. Thus, $\frac{x^2}{y^2} + \frac{x}{y^3} = \frac{x^2 y}{y^3} + \frac{x}{y^3} = \frac{x^2 y + x}{y^3}$.

10. A: The expression may be factored as $(x - 8)(x + 5)$. The factorization may be checked by distributing each term in the first factor to each term in the second factor by using the FOIL method. Doing so gives $x^2 + 5x - 8x - 40$, which can be rewritten as $x^2 - 3x - 40$.

11. A: The probability of playing a song by any band is proportional to the number of songs by that band over the total number of songs, or $\frac{5}{15} = \frac{1}{3}$ for Band D. The probability of playing any particular song is not affected by what has been played previously, so all 15 songs have an equal probability to be played.

12. C: Substitute and simplify as follows:

$$|x| + |x - 2| = |1| + |1 - 2|$$
$$= |1| + |-1|$$
$$= 1 + 1$$
$$= 2$$

13. A: $(2x^2 + 3x + 2) - (x^2 + 2x - 3) = (2x^2 + 3x + 2) + (-1)(x^2 + 2x - 3)$. First, distribute the –1 to remove the parentheses: $2x^2 + 3x + 2 - x^2 - 2x + 3$. Next, combine like terms: $(2x^2 - x^2) + (3x - 2x) + (2 + 3) = x^2 + x + 5$.

14. A: The frequency table in choice A correctly shows the frequencies represented by the histogram. The frequencies of values falling between 1 and 10 is 3, between 11 and 20 is 9, between 21 and 30 is 8, between 31 and 40 is 6, and between 41 and 50 is 4.

15. A: The ratio of expenses to income is 7: 1. Since we know he saves $725 per month, we need to multiply this value by 7 to find out how much he spends on expenses each month. $725 × 7 = $5,075. So, Jon spends $5,075 on expenses each month.

16. C: Hiking due west at 3 mph, the first hiker will have gone 6 miles after 2 hours. Hiking due north at 4 mph, the second hiker will have gone 8 miles after 2 hours. Since one hiker headed west and the other headed north, their distance from each other can be drawn as:

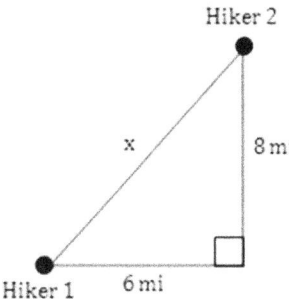

Since the distance between the two hikers is the hypotenuse of a right triangle, and since we know the lengths of the two legs of the right triangle, we can use the Pythagorean theorem ($a^2 + b^2 = c^2$) to find the value of x.

$$6^2 + 8^2 = x^2$$
$$36 + 64 = x^2$$
$$100 = x^2$$
$$10 = x$$

Therefore, the hikers are 10 miles apart after 2 hours of hiking.

17. B: The area of a parallelogram is base × height, or $A = bh$, where b is the length of the base of the parallelogram and h is the length of an altitude to that side. In this problem, $A = 6 \text{ ft} \times 4 \text{ ft} = 24 \text{ ft}^2$. Remember, use the length of BE, not the length of CD for the height.

18. B: This pie chart shows the percentage of the total recyclable material that each material represents. The larger percentages have larger slices of the circle. Also, the percentage for each material is shown next to each slice. In this chart, paper is the most recycled material because it has the largest slice. This is 40% of the total. The next most common is glass at 25% of the total. All of the other materials stand for smaller portions of the total.

19. B: The inequality specifies that the difference between L and 15 inches must be less or equal to 0.01. Note that $|14.99 − 15| = |−0.01| = 0.01$, which is equal to the specified tolerance and therefore meets the condition.

20. C: To start, we can write our ratio in fractional form as $\frac{2 \text{ cups of water}}{6 \text{ cups of flour}}$. We know Josie wants to lessen the flour to only 2 cups, making our proportion $\frac{2 \text{ cups of water}}{6 \text{ cups of flour}} = \frac{x \text{ cups of water}}{2 \text{ cups of flour}}$. To find the value of x, we can cross multiply the two diagonal values we know, 2 and 2, and divide their product by the remaining value, 6. $2 \times 2 = 4$, and $4 \div 6 = \frac{4}{6}$, which simplifies to $\frac{2}{3}$. This means Josie should use $\frac{2}{3}$ of a cup of water for every 2 cups of flour.

TSI Math Practice Test #5

Mathematics

1. Marlon pays $45 for a jacket that has been marked down 25%. What was the original cost of the jacket?

   A. $80
   B. $75
   C. $65
   D. $60

2. Which of the following equations demonstrates the associative property of multiplication?

   A. $2(3 + 4) = 2(3) + 2(4)$
   B. $(3 \times 6) \times 2 = (4 \times 3) \times 3$
   C. $(2 \times 3) \times 4 = 2 \times (3 \times 4)$
   D. $6 \times 4 = 4 \times 6$

3. Which of the following statements is NOT true?

   A. In most cases of a skewed distribution, the mean is pulled towards the longer tail.
   B. In most cases of a skewed distribution, the mean is pulled towards the area with a higher frequency of scores.
   C. In a normal distribution, the mean, median, and mode are the same value.
   D. The area under a normal curve is 1.

4. In a pack of 20 jelly beans, there are two licorice- and four cinnamon-flavored jelly beans. What is the probability of choosing a licorice jelly bean followed by a cinnamon jelly bean?

   A. $\frac{2}{5}$
   B. $\frac{8}{20}$
   C. $\frac{2}{95}$
   D. $\frac{1}{50}$

5. A teacher asks her students to find the error in this algebra problem. What is the error?

$$3x + 4x = (2^2 + 1) + 2(2)$$
$$7x = 5 + 2(2)$$
$$7x = 7(2)$$
$$7x = 14$$
$$x = 2$$

   A. The student incorrectly added before multiplying.
   B. The student incorrectly multiplied before adding.
   C. The student incorrectly applied the exponent.
   D. The student incorrectly combined like terms.

6. Aidan has a plastic container in the shape of a square pyramid. He wants to fill the container with chocolate candies. If the base has a side length of 6 inches and the height of the container is 9 inches, how many cubic inches of space may be filled with candies?

   A. 98
   B. 102
   C. 108
   D. 112

7. Natasha designs a square pyramidal tent for her children. Each of the sides of the square base measures x ft, and the tent's height is h feet. If Natasha were to increase by 1 ft the length of each side of the base, how much more interior space would the tent have?

   A. $\frac{x^2h+2xh+h}{3}$ ft^3
   B. $\frac{2xh+h}{3}$ ft^3
   C. $\frac{x^2h+3}{3}$ ft^3
   D. 1 ft^3

8. Which of the following steps were applied to $\triangle ABC$?

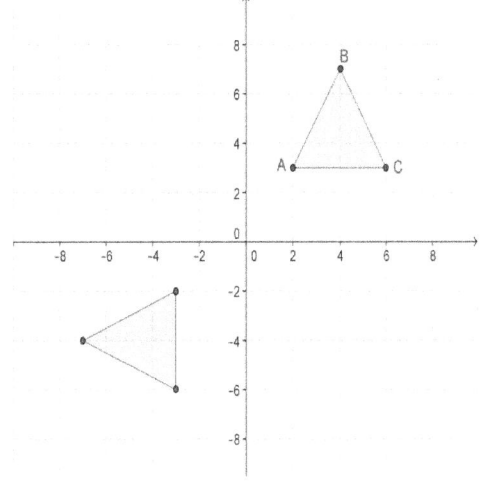

   A. Reflection across the x-axis and counterclockwise rotation of 90 degrees about the origin
   B. Reflection across the x-axis and counterclockwise rotation of 180 degrees about the origin
   C. Reflection across the x-axis and counterclockwise rotation of 270 degrees about the origin
   D. Reflection across the y-axis and counterclockwise rotation of 180 degrees about the origin

9. What is the length of the hypotenuse in the triangle shown below?

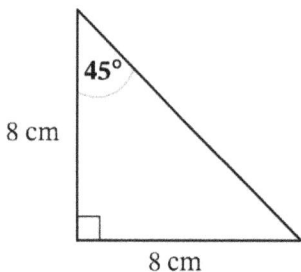

A. 4 cm
B. $8\sqrt{3}$ cm
C. 16 cm
D. $8\sqrt{2}$ cm

10. The 6th grade teachers at Washington Elementary School are doing a collaborative unit on cherry trees. Miss Wilson's math classes are making histograms summarizing the heights of black cherry trees located at a local fruit orchard. How many of the trees at this local orchard are 73 feet tall?

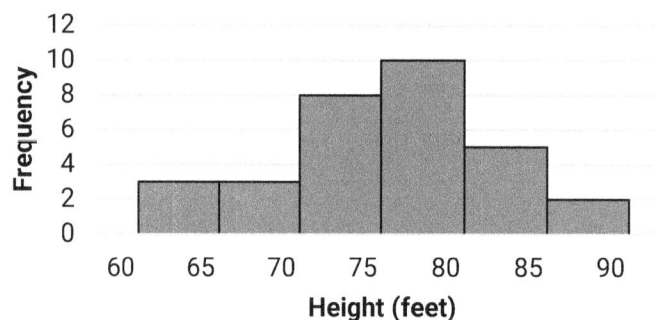

A. 8
B. 9
C. 17
D. That information cannot be obtained from this graph

11. Given that x is a prime number and the greatest common factor of x and y is greater than 1, compare the two quantities.

Quantity A	Quantity B
y	the least common multiple of x and y

A. Quantity A is greater.
B. Quantity B is greater.
C. The two quantities are the same.
D. The relationship cannot be determined from the given information.

12. On his morning run, a jogger records his distance from his front door in meters as a function of time in seconds. If x represents time in seconds, which of the following equations represents the jogger's distance from his front door as a function of time?

Time	0	3	4	6	7
Distance	5.2	25.0	31.6	44.8	51.4

A. $y = 3x + 25$
B. $y = 25.0x + 5.2$
C. $y = 18.4x + 3$
D. $y = 6.6x + 5.2$

13. McKenzie shades $\frac{1}{5}$ of a piece of paper. Then, she shades an additional area $\frac{1}{5}$ the size of what she just shaded. Next, she shades another area $\frac{1}{5}$ as large as the previous one. As she continues the process to infinity, what is the limit of the shaded fraction of the paper?

A. $\frac{1}{5}$
B. $\frac{1}{4}$
C. $\frac{1}{3}$
D. $\frac{1}{2}$

14. Which of these would best illustrate change over time?
    A. Pie chart
    B. Line graph
    C. Box-and-whisker plot
    D. Venn diagram

Refer to the following for question 15:

The box-and-whisker plot displays a district's standardized test scores by subject.

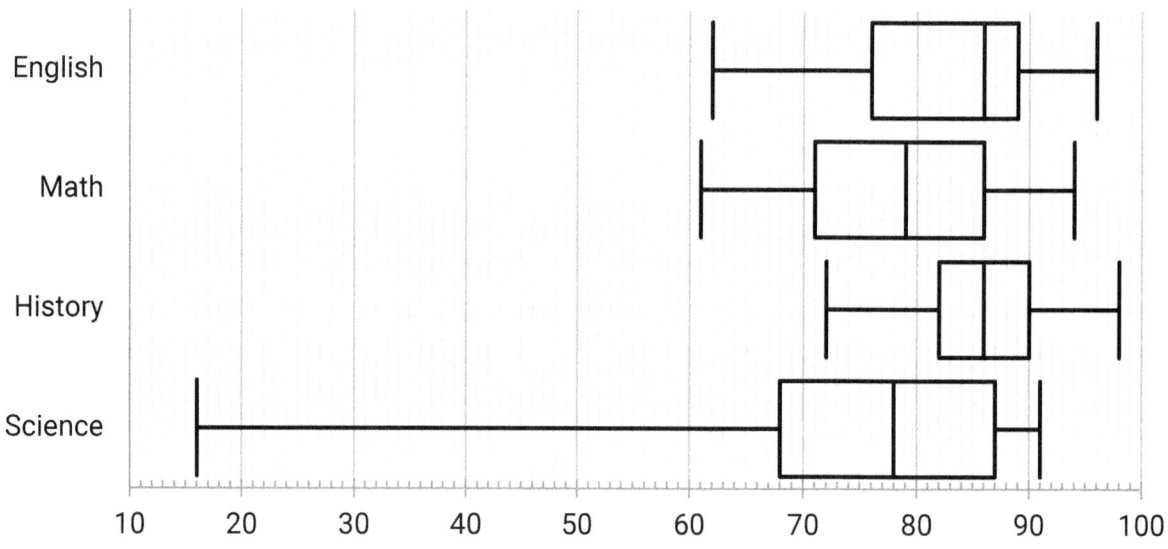

15. Which of the following statements is NOT true of the data?
  A. The median better reflects student performance in Science than the mean.
  B. The mean test score for English and history is the same.
  C. The median of the History scores is the same as the 3rd quartile score for Math.
  D. The median test score is above the mean for English.

16. Mr. Gomez is a sixth-grade teacher presenting a unit on compound probability. He places ten marbles labeled with the digits 0 through 9 in a bowl on his podium. He draws a marble, records the number, and then places the marble back in the bowl. He repeats the process. What is the probability that he drew two 5s in a row?
  A. $\frac{1}{10}$
  B. $\frac{1}{5}$
  C. $\frac{1}{100}$
  D. $\frac{1}{50}$

17. Addison tosses a six-sided die twelve times and records the results in the table below.

Toss	1	2	3	4	5	6	7	8	9	10	11	12
Results	2	5	1	2	3	6	6	2	4	5	4	3

Which of the following statements is true?
  A. The experimental probability of tossing a 6 is greater than the theoretical probability.
  B. The experimental probability of tossing a 3 is greater than the theoretical probability.
  C. The experimental probability of tossing a 1 is greater than the theoretical probability.
  D. The experimental probability of tossing a 2 is greater than the theoretical probability.

18. Quinn deposits $250 from each quarterly paycheck into a savings account. How much will he have deposited in the account after 5 years?
   A. $4,800
   B. $5,000
   C. $5,200
   D. $5,400

19. Mrs. Patterson's classroom has sixteen empty chairs. All the chairs are occupied when every student is present. If $\frac{2}{5}$ of the students are absent, how many students make up her entire class?
   A. 16 students
   B. 24 students
   C. 32 students
   D. 40 students

20. Olivia receives her weekly paycheck and calculates that she will spend $\frac{1}{4}$ of it on groceries. If the groceries cost $120, what is the amount of her paycheck?
   A. $360
   B. $425
   C. $480
   D. $600

Answer Key and Explanations for Test #5

Mathematics

1. D: The original cost may be represented by the equation $45 = x - 0.25x$ or $45 = 0.75x$. Dividing both sides of the equation by 0.75 gives $x = 60$.

2. C: The associative property of multiplication states that when three or more numbers are multiplied, the product is the same regardless of the way in which the numbers are grouped (i.e., where parentheses are inserted or removed). Choice C shows that the product of 2, 3, and 4 is the same with two different groupings of the factors. Choice A demonstrates the distributive property. Choice B shows grouping, but the factors are different. Choice D demonstrates the commutative property of multiplication. Therefore, the correct choice is C.

3. B: The mean is pulled towards the longer tail of a skewed distribution in most cases. It is not pulled towards the area with the higher frequency of scores. When outliers are added to an otherwise symmetric distribution, the mean shifts towards those outliers. For example, if a runner typically finishes a race in about 5 minutes and has one bad day in which she takes 20 minutes, that single outlier could significantly increase her mean time.

4. C: To find the probability of an event, divide the number of favorable outcomes by the total number of outcomes. When there are two events in which the first depends on the second, multiply the first ratio by the second ratio. In the first part of the problem, the probability of choosing a licorice jelly bean is two out of twenty possible outcomes, or $\frac{2}{20}$. Then, because one jelly bean has already been chosen, there are four cinnamon beans out of a total of 19, or $\frac{4}{19}$. By multiplying the two ratios and dividing by a common denominator, one arrives at the final probability of $\frac{2}{95}$.

5. A: In the third line of the problem, the student incorrectly added the 5 and 2 rather than multiplying 2(2). According to the order of operations, the student should multiply before adding.

6. C: The volume of a pyramid may be calculated using the formula $V = \frac{1}{3}Bh$, where B represents the area of the base and h represents the height. Since the base is a square, the area of the base is equal to 6^2, or 36 square inches. Substituting 36 for B and 9 for h gives $V = \frac{1}{3}(36)(9)$, which simplifies to $V = 108$ cubic inches.

7. B: The volume of Natasha's tent can be found by using the volume formula for a square pyramid, $V = \frac{1}{3}Bh = \frac{1}{3}s^2h$, where B is the area of the base, s is the side length of the square base, and h is the height of the pyramid. Therefore, the volume of her tent is $\frac{x^2h}{3}$. If she were to increase the length of each side of the square base by 1 ft, the tent's volume would be $\frac{(x+1)^2h}{3} = \frac{(x^2+2x+1)(h)}{3} = \frac{x^2h+2xh+h}{3} = \frac{x^2h}{3} + \frac{2xh+h}{3}$. Notice this is the volume of Natasha's tent, $\frac{x^2h}{3}$, increased by $\frac{2xh+h}{3}$.

8. C: A reflection across the x-axis will result in a triangle with vertices at $(2, -3)$, $(4, -7)$, and $(6, -3)$. A rotation of 270 degrees counterclockwise is denoted by the following: $(x, y) \rightarrow (y, -x)$. Thus, a rotation of the reflected triangle by 270 degrees will result in a figure with vertices at

$(-3, -2)$, $(-7, -4)$, and $(-3, -6)$. The transformed triangle indeed has these coordinates as its vertices.

9. D: The triangle is a 45-45-90 right triangle. Thus, if each leg is represented by x, the hypotenuse is represented by $x\sqrt{2}$. Thus, the hypotenuse is equal to $8\sqrt{2}$ cm.

10. D: The histogram only shows that there are 8 trees between 70 and 75 feet tall. It does not show the individual heights of the trees, so this information cannot be obtained from the graph.

11. C: If x is a prime number and the greatest common factor of x and y is greater than 1, the greatest common factor of x and y must be x. The least common multiple of two numbers is equal to the product of those numbers divided by their greatest common factor. So, the least common multiple of x and y is $\frac{xy}{x} = y$. Therefore, the two quantities are the same.

12. D: All four answer choices are linear equations in slope-intercept form, $y = mx + b$, where m is the jogger's rate (slope) and b is the jogger's distance from his front door at the beginning of his run (y-intercept). To find the rate, choose any two times (e.g., $x = 0$ and $x = 3$) and divide the change in distance by the change in time: $m = \frac{25.0 - 5.2}{3 - 0} = \frac{19.8}{3} = 6.6$. Therefore, the rate is 6.6 meters per second. The starting distance from the door is the distance at $x = 0$, which is $b = 5.2$ meters. The linear equation that represents this situation is $y = 6.6x + 5.2$.

13. B: The sequence $\frac{1}{5}, \frac{1}{25}, \frac{1}{125}, \frac{1}{625}$ ... may be used to represent the situation. Substituting the initial value of $\frac{1}{5}$ and the common ratio of $\frac{1}{5}$ into the formula $S = \frac{a}{1-r}$:

$$S = \frac{\frac{1}{5}}{1 - \frac{1}{5}} = \frac{\frac{1}{5}}{\frac{4}{5}} = \frac{1}{4}$$

14. B: A line graph is often used to show change over time. A Venn diagram shows the relationships among sets. A box-and-whisker plot displays how numeric data are distributed throughout the range. A pie chart shows the relationship of parts to a whole.

15. B: The line through the center of the box represents the median. The median test score for English and History is the same, not the mean test score, which makes choice B the correct answer. Note that for Science, the median is a better representation of the data than the mean. There is at least one outlier (a point that lies outside of two standard deviations from the mean), which brings down the average test score. In cases such as this, the mean is not the best measure of central tendency, so choice A is not the correct answer. The median of the History scores is 87, and the 3rd quartile scores for Math is also 87, so choice C is not the answer. The median of the English scores is 86, and based on the spread of data, the mean is lower than the median, so choice D is also not correct.

16. C: This is a compound event. Since the marble is replaced after the first draw, the probability of each event is $\frac{1}{10}$. The probability of drawing two 5s in a row is $\frac{1}{10} \times \frac{1}{10} = \frac{1}{100}$.

17. D: The theoretical probability of tossing any particular number is $\frac{1}{6}$. Since she tosses a two $\frac{3}{12}$, or $\frac{1}{4}$ times, the experimental probability of tossing a 2 is greater than the theoretical probability. The experimental probability should grow closer to the experimental probability as she tosses the die more times.

18. B: There are 60 months in 5 years. Since a quarter is 3 months, the following proportion may be written.

$$\frac{250}{3} = \frac{x}{60}$$

We solve by first cross-multiplying.

$$3x = 15{,}000$$

Then, divide both sides of the equation by 3.

$$x = 5{,}000$$

Therefore, Quinn will have deposited $5,000 into the account after 5 years.

19. D: There are 16 empty chairs. This gives $\frac{2}{5}$ of the total enrollment. So, the full class must be:

$$\text{Class} = \frac{5}{2} \times 16 = 40 \text{ students}$$

Another option is to use proportions.

$$\frac{2}{5} = \frac{16}{x}$$

First, cross multiply to get: $2x - 80$. Then, divide each side by 2 to solve for x. So, $x = 40$, which means there are 40 students in the entire class.

20. C: Olivia's paycheck x may be modeled by $\frac{1}{4}x = 120$. Multiplying both sides of the equation by 4 gives $x = 480$. Her paycheck is $480.

TSI Math Practice Test #6

1. In a game of chance, 3 dice are thrown at the same time. What is the probability that all three will land on a 6?

   A. $\frac{1}{6}$
   B. $\frac{1}{18}$
   C. $\frac{1}{30}$
   D. $\frac{1}{216}$

2. Evaluate the expression $(x - 2y)^2$, where $x = 3$ and $y = 2$.

   A. -2
   B. -1
   C. 1
   D. 4

3. The ratio of new car sales to used car sales at the car lot is $3 : 5$. If the total car sales were $287,400 last month, what was the total of the used car sales?

   A. $107,775
   B. $179,625
   C. $192,450
   D. $204,500

4. A function $f(x)$ is defined by $f(x) = 2x^2 + 7$. What is the value of $2f(x) - 3$?

   A. $4x^2 + 11$
   B. $4x^4 + 11$
   C. $x^2 + 11$
   D. $4x^2 + 14$

5. Prizes are to be awarded to the best pupils in each class of an elementary school. The number of students in each grade is shown in the table, and the school principal wants the number of prizes awarded in each grade to be proportional to the number of students. If there are twenty prizes, how many should go to fifth-grade students?

Grade	1	2	3	4	5
Students	35	38	38	33	36

   A. 3
   B. 4
   C. 5
   D. 7

6. What is the surface area of a cube, in square inches, if the length of one side of the cube is 3 inches?

   A. 9 in^2
   B. 21 in^2
   C. 27 in^2
   D. 54 in^2

7. Which of the following represents the solution to the system of linear equations
$\begin{cases} 5x + 9y = -7 \\ 2x - 4y = 20 \end{cases}$?

   A. $x = 3, y = 2$
   B. $x = 4, y = 3$
   C. $x = 4, y = -3$
   D. $x = 3, y = -2$

8. To determine a student's grade, a teacher throws out the lowest grade obtained on 5 tests, averages the remaining grades, and rounds to the nearest integer. If Betty scored 72, 75, 88, 86, and 90 on her tests, what grade will she receive?

   A. 68
   B. 85
   C. 88
   D. 84.8

9. A colony of Escherichia coli is inoculated from a Petri dish into a test tube containing 50 mL of nutrient broth. The test tube is placed in a 37 °C incubator and agitator. After one hour, the number of bacteria in the test tube is determined to be 8×10^6. Given that the doubling time of Escherichia coli is 20 minutes with agitation at 37 °C, approximately how many bacteria should the test tube contain after eight hours of growth?

   A. 2.56×10^8
   B. 2.05×10^9
   C. 1.7×10^{14}
   D. 1.7×10^{13}

10. The ratio of employee wages and benefits to all other operational costs of a business is $2:3$. If a business's total operating expenses are $130,000 per month, how much money does the company spend on employee wages and benefits?

    A. $43,333.33
    B. $86,666.67
    C. $52,000.00
    D. $78,000.00

11. The formula for the volume of a sphere is $V = \frac{4}{3}\pi r^3$. If $r = \frac{3}{2}x$, what is the volume of the sphere in terms of x?

    A. $2\pi x^3$
    B. $\frac{9}{2}\pi x^3$
    C. $\frac{27}{8}\pi x^3$
    D. $\frac{4}{3}\pi x^3$

12. The figure shows an irregular quadrilateral and the lengths of its sides. Which of the following expressions best represents the perimeter of the quadrilateral?

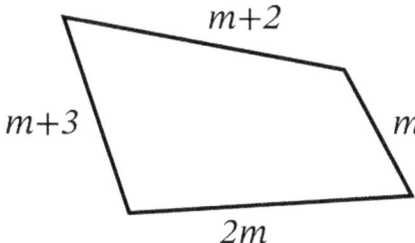

- A. $m^4 + 5$
- B. $2m^4 + 5$
- C. $4m + 5$
- D. $5m + 5$

13. Which of the following represents the graph of $y = (x - 4)^2 + 3$?

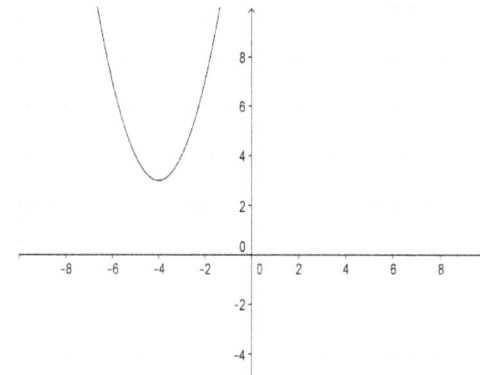

A.

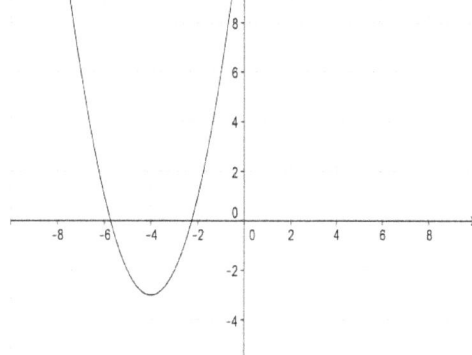

B.

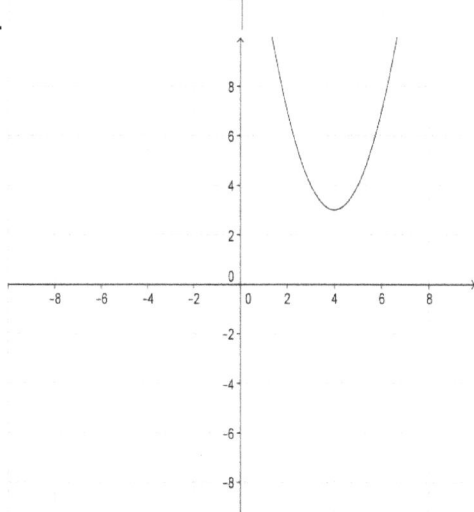

C.

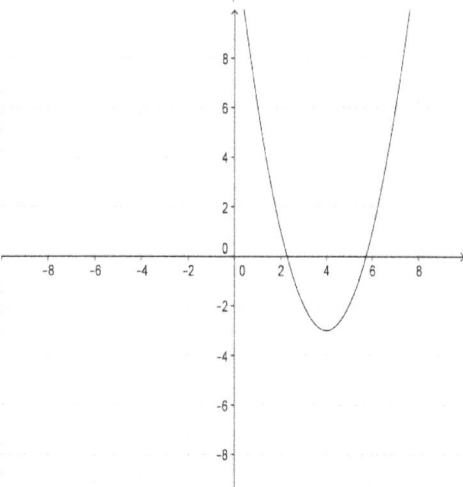

D.

14. A private tutor works with 11 five-year-olds, 8 six-year-olds, 9 seven-year-olds, 14 eight-year-olds, 11 nine-year-olds, and 13 ten-year-olds. If a student is randomly selected for a free session, what is the probability that he or she is no more than eight years old?

   A. $\frac{7}{11}$
   B. $\frac{14}{33}$
   C. $\frac{4}{11}$
   D. $\frac{3}{7}$

15. Andre is traveling at a speed of 65 miles per hour. At this rate, how long will it take Andre to travel 195 miles?

   A. 3 hours
   B. 3.25 hours
   C. 4.5 hours
   D. 585 minutes

16. If $a = 3$ and $b = 4$, simplify the following expression: $6a + b - 7$

   A. 12
   B. 15
   C. 20
   D. 22

17. Solve the system of equations.
$$3x + 4y = 2$$
$$2x + 6y = -2$$

   A. $\left(0, \frac{1}{2}\right)$
   B. $\left(\frac{2}{5}, \frac{1}{5}\right)$
   C. $(2, -1)$
   D. $\left(-1, \frac{5}{4}\right)$

18. Mandy can buy 4 containers of yogurt and 3 boxes of crackers for $9.55. She can buy 2 containers of yogurt and 2 boxes of crackers for $5.90. How much does one box of crackers cost?

   A. $1.75
   B. $2.00
   C. $2.25
   D. $2.50

19. A mathematics test has a 4 : 2 ratio of data analysis problems to algebra problems. If the test has 18 algebra problems, how many data analysis problems are on the test?

   A. 24
   B. 28
   C. 36
   D. 38

20. Kendra uses the pie chart below to represent the allocation of her annual income. Her annual income is $40,000.

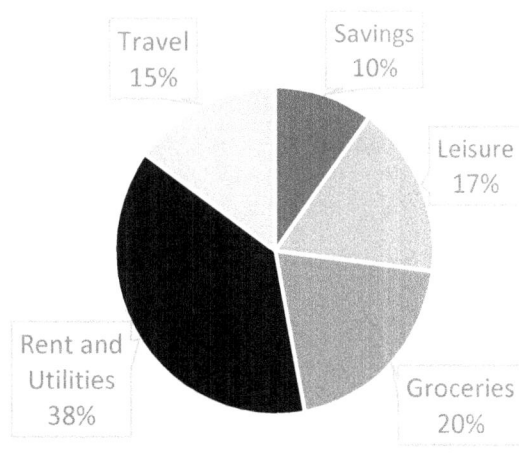

Which of the following statements is true?
   A. The amount of money she spends on travel and savings is more than $11,000.
   B. The amount of money she spends on rent and utilities is approximately $15,000.
   C. The amount of money she spends on groceries and savings is more than $13,000.
   D. The amount of money she spends on leisure is less than $5,000.

Answer Key and Explanations for Test #6

1. D: For each die there is a $\frac{1}{6}$ chance that a 6 will be on top because a die has 6 sides. The probability that a 6 will show for each die is not affected by the results from another roll of the die. In other words, these probabilities are independent. So, the overall probability of throwing 3 sixes is the product of the individual probabilities: $P = \frac{1}{6} \times \frac{1}{6} \times \frac{1}{6} = \frac{1}{6^3} = \frac{1}{216}$. Therefore, the probability that all three dice will land on a 6 is $\frac{1}{216}$.

2. C: To evaluate the expression, start by substituting in the given values.

$$(3 - 2(2))^2$$

Then, use the order of operations to simplify. Start by simplifying the expression inside the parentheses.

$$(3 - 4)^2 = (-1)^2 = 1$$

Therefore, the expression is equal to 1 when $x = 3$ and $y = 2$.

3. B: The ratio of new car sales to used car sales is 3 : 5. This means that the total number of cars sold (both new and used) is $3 + 5 = 8$. The used car sales are $\frac{5}{8}$ of the total sales:

$$\frac{5}{8} \times \$287{,}400 = \$179{,}625$$

4. A: Start by substituting the function $f(x)$ into the expression $2f(x) - 3$.

$$2(2x^2 + 7) - 3$$

From here, simplify the expression using the distributive property.

$$4x^2 + 14 - 3$$

Finally, combine like terms.

$$4x^2 + 11$$

5. B: First, determine the proportion of students in Grade 5. Since the total number of students is 180, this proportion is $\frac{36}{180} = 0.2$, or 20%. Then, determine the same proportion of the total prizes, which is 20% of 20, or $0.2 \times 20 = 4$. Therefore, 4 prizes should go to fifth-grade students.

6. D: The surface area of a cube is obtained by multiplying the area of each face by 6 because there are 6 faces. The area of each face is the square of the length of one edge.

$$A = 6 \times 3^2 = 6 \times 9 = 54$$

Therefore, the surface area of the cube is 54 in^2.

7. C: Using the method of elimination to solve the system of linear equations, multiply each term in the top equation by –2 and each term in the bottom equation 5. Doing so produces two new equations with x-terms that will add to 0.

$$\begin{cases} -10x - 18y = 14 \\ 10x - 20y = 100 \end{cases}$$

The sum of $-10x - 18y = 14$ and $10x - 20y = 100$ may be written as $-38y = 114$. Solve this equation for y.

$$-38y = 114$$
$$y = -3$$

Substitute the y-value of –3 into the top, original equation, and solve for x.

$$5x + 9(-3) = -7$$
$$5x - 27 = -7$$
$$5x = 20$$
$$x = 4$$

Thus, the solution to the system of equations is $x = 4, y = -3$.

8. B: The lowest score, 72, is eliminated. The average of the remaining four grades is:

$$\text{Average} = \frac{75 + 88 + 86 + 90}{4} = 84.75$$

Rounding to the nearest integer gives a final grade of 85.

9. D: Bacterial growth is exponential. Let x be the number of times the population doubles, a be the number of bacteria in the colony originally transferred into the broth, and y be the number of bacteria in the broth after x doubling times. After 1 hour, the population would have doubled three times:

$$a(2)^x = y$$
$$a(2^3) = 8 \times 10^6$$
$$8a = 8 \times 10^6$$
$$a = 10^6$$

So, the number of bacteria originally transferred into the petri dish was 10^6. The equation for determining the number of bacteria is $y = (2^x) \times 10^6$. Since the bacteria double every twenty minutes, they go through three doubling times every hour. So, when the bacteria are allowed to grow for eight hours, they will have gone through $8 \times 3 = 24$ doubling times. When $x = 24$, $y = (2^{24}) \times 10^6 = 16{,}777{,}216 \times 10^6$, which is approximately 1.7×10^{13}.

10. C: When you have a ratio, you can find the fraction that each part of the ratio is of the whole by dividing a part by the sum of the parts. Since the ratio of wages and benefits to other costs is $2:3$, the amount of money spent on wages and benefits is $\frac{2}{2+3} = \frac{2}{5}$ of total operational costs.

$$\frac{2}{5} \times \$130{,}000 = \$52{,}000$$

11. B: To find the volume of the sphere, substitute the given value for r into the original volume formula.

$$V = \frac{4}{3}\pi \left(\frac{3}{2}x\right)^3$$

Now, simplify the expression, starting with the parentheses.

$$V = \frac{4}{3}\pi \left(\frac{27}{8}x^3\right)$$

Now, multiply the fractions.

$$V = \frac{108}{24}\pi x^3$$

Finally, simplify the fractions.

$$V = \frac{9}{2}\pi x^3$$

12. D: The perimeter (P) of the quadrilateral is simply the sum of its sides:

$$P = m + (m+2) + (m+3) + 2m$$

Put together like terms by adding the variables (m-terms) together. Then, add the constants. This gives you $P = 5m + 5$.

In this problem, it seems that some of the variables do not have a number in front of them. However, when there is no coefficient, this means multiplication by 1. So, $m = 1m$, $x = 1x$, and so on.

13. C: This graph is shifted 4 units to the right and 3 units up from that of the parent function, $y = x^2$.

14. A: The probability of an event is the number of possible occurrences of that event divided by the number of all possible outcomes. A student who is eight years old or less can be five, six, seven, or eight years old.

$$\frac{\text{number of 5-, 6-, 7-, and 8- year- old students}}{\text{total number of students}} = \frac{11+8+9+14}{11+8+9+14+11+13} = \frac{42}{66} = \frac{7}{11}$$

Therefore, the probability that he or she is no more than eight years old is $\frac{7}{11}$.

15. A: We can express Andre's speed as the rate 65 miles to 1 hour, or $\frac{65}{1}$. Next, we can set up a proportion to determine how long it will take Andre to travel 195 miles. Since we are comparing miles to hours, our proportion should be $\frac{65}{1} = \frac{195}{x}$. To solve for x, we must determine how much greater 195 is than 65. We can do this using division. $195 \div 65 = 3$, which tells us that 195 is 3 times greater than 65. Now, we must multiply our denominator, 1, by 3 as well to keep our proportion balanced. The product of 1 and 3 is 3, making $x = 3$. It will take Andre 3 hours to travel 195 miles.

16. B: To simplify this expression, start by substituting in the given values.

$$6(3) + (4) - 7$$

From here, use the order of operations to simplify.

$$18 + 4 - 7 = 22 - 7 = 15$$

17. C: A system of linear equations can be solved by using matrices or by using the graphing, substitution, or elimination (also called linear combination) method. The elimination method is shown here:

$$3x + 4y = 2$$
$$2x + 6y = -2$$

In order to eliminate x by linear combination, multiply the top equation by 2 and the bottom equation by –3 so that the coefficients of the x-terms will be additive inverses.

$$2(3x + 4y = 2)$$
$$-3(2x + 6y = -2)$$

Then, add the two equations and solve for y.

$$6x + 8y = 4$$
$$\underline{-6x - 18y = 6}$$
$$-10y = 10$$
$$y = -1$$

Substitute –1 for y in either of the given equations and solve for x.

$$3x + 4y = 2$$
$$3x + 4(-1) = 2$$
$$3x - 4 = 2$$
$$3x = 6$$
$$x = 2$$

The solution to the system of equations is $(2, -1)$.

18. C: The situation may be modeled by this system of equations:

$$\begin{cases} 4y + 3c = 9.55 \\ 2y + 2c = 5.90 \end{cases}$$

Multiplying the bottom equation by −2 gives:

$$\begin{cases} 4y + 3c = 9.55 \\ -4y - 4c = -11.80 \end{cases}$$

Adding the two equations gives $-c = -2.25$, or $c = 2.25$. Thus, one box of crackers costs $2.25.

19. C: The proportion can be written as $\frac{\text{data analysis problems}}{\text{algebra problems}} = \frac{4}{2} = \frac{x}{18}$. Cross multiplying gives $2x = 72$. This can be solved by dividing both sides by 2, which results in $x = 36$. Thus, there are 36 data analysis problems on the test.

20. B: The amount she spends on rent and utilities is equal to 0.38($40,000), or $15,200, which is approximately $15,000.

TSI Math Practice Test #7

Mathematics

1. A dress is marked down by 20% and placed on a clearance rack, under a sign reading "Take an extra 25% off already reduced merchandise." What fraction of the original price is the final sale price of the dress?

   A. $\frac{2}{5}$
   B. $\frac{9}{20}$
   C. $\frac{3}{5}$
   D. $\frac{11}{20}$

2. The variables x and y have a linear relationship. The table below shows a few sample values. Which of the following graphs correctly represents the linear equation relating x and y?

x	y
-2	-11
-1	-8
0	-5
1	-2
2	1

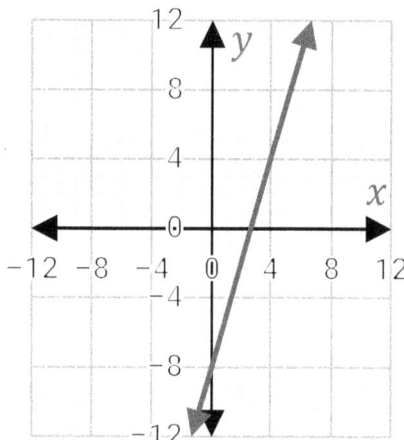

A.

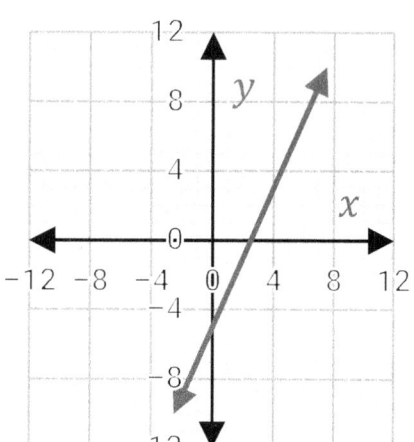

B.

C.

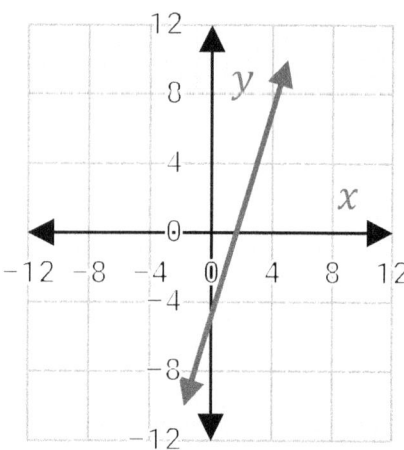

D.

3. Which of these is NOT a net of a cube?

A.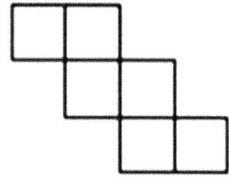

B.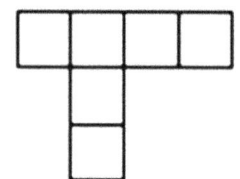

C.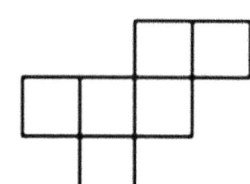

D.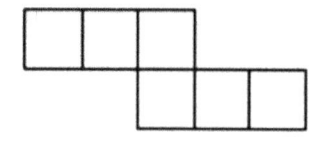

4. Two companies offer monthly cell phone plans, both of which include free text messaging. Company A charges a $25 monthly fee plus five cents per minute of phone conversation, while Company B charges a $50 monthly fee and offers unlimited calling. At what total duration of monthly calls do both companies charge the same amount?
    A. 500 hours
    B. 8 hours and 33 minutes
    C. 8 hours and 20 minutes
    D. 5 hours

5. Kayla rolls a die and tosses a coin. What is the probability she gets an even number and heads?
    A. $\frac{1}{6}$
    B. $\frac{1}{4}$
    C. $\frac{1}{3}$
    D. 1

6. A coin is tossed 300 times. How many of those tosses can you expect to show heads?
    A. 50
    B. 100
    C. 150
    D. 200

7. In order to analyze the real estate market for two different zip codes within the city, a realtor examined the most recent 100 home sales in each zip code. She considered a house which sold within the first month of its listing to have a market time of one month; likewise, she considered a house to have a market time of two months if it sold after having been on the market for more than one month but before the end of the second month. Using this definition of market time, she determined the frequency of sales by the number of months on the market. The results are displayed below. Which of the following is a true statement for these data?

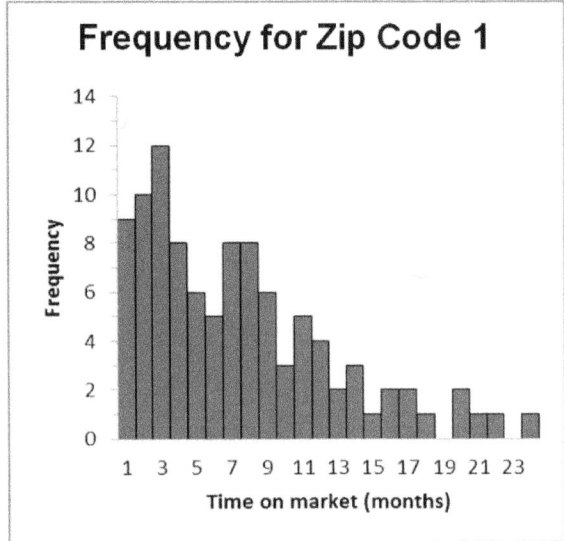
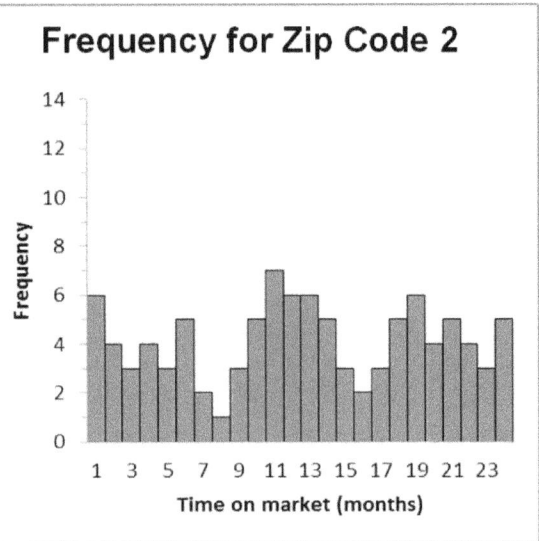

A. The median time a house spent on the market in Zip Code 1 is five months less than Zip Code 2.
B. On average, a house spent seven months longer on the market in Zip Code 2 than in Zip Code 1.
C. The mode time on the market is higher for Zip Code 1 than for Zip Code 2.
D. The median time on the market is less than the mean time on the market for Zip Code 1.

8. Hannah spends at least $16 on 4 packages of coffee. Which of the following expresses this relationship in terms of the cost of a package of coffee, p?

A. $16 \geq 4p$
B. $16 < 4p$
C. $16 > 4p$
D. $16 \leq 4p$

9. Which of the following represents the net of a triangular prism?

A.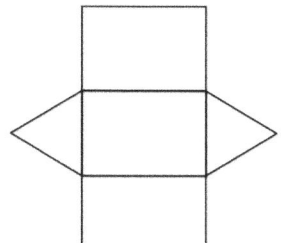

B.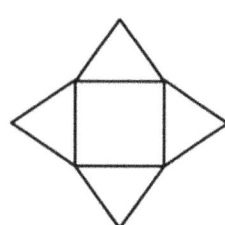

C.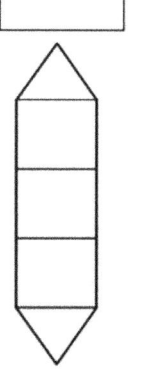

D.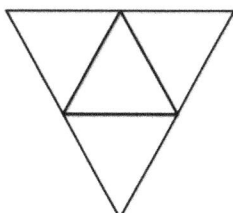

10. Amy saves $450 every 3 months. How much does she save after 3 years?
    A. $4,800
    B. $5,200
    C. $5,400
    D. $5,800

11. Jason decides to donate 1% of his annual salary to a local charity. If his annual salary is $45,000, how much will he donate?
    A. $4.50
    B. $45
    C. $450
    D. $4,500

12. Eli rolls a six-sided die and tosses a coin. What is the probability that he gets a prime number or tails?
    A. $\frac{1}{4}$
    B. $\frac{1}{3}$
    C. $\frac{1}{2}$
    D. $\frac{3}{4}$

13. What linear equation includes the data in the table below?

x	y
−3	1
1	−11
3	−17
5	−23
9	−35

A. $y = -3x - 11$
B. $y = -6x - 8$
C. $y = -3x - 8$
D. $y = -12x - 11$

14. A gift box has a length of 14 inches, a height of 8 inches, and a width of 6 inches. How many square inches of wrapping paper are needed to wrap the box?

A. 56
B. 244
C. 488
D. 672

15. A ball has a diameter of 7 inches. Which of the following best represents the volume?

A. 165.7 in^3
B. 179.6 in^3
C. 184.5 in^3
D. 192.3 in^3

16. What is the distance on a coordinate plane from $(-8, 6)$ to $(4, 3)$?

A. $\sqrt{139}$
B. $\sqrt{147}$
C. $\sqrt{153}$
D. $\sqrt{161}$

17. The table below shows the average amount of rainfall Houston receives during the summer and autumn months.

Month	Rainfall (in inches)
June	5.35
July	3.18
August	3.83
September	4.33
October	4.5
November	4.19

What percentage of rainfall in this timeframe occurs during October?

A. 13.5%
B. 15.1%
C. 16.9%
D. 17.7%

18. What is the midpoint of the line segment below?

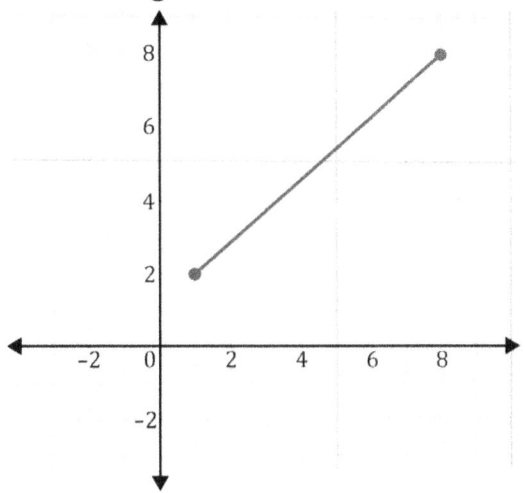

A. (3.5,4)
B. (4,4)
C. (4.5,5)
D. (5,5)

19. Given this stem-and-leaf plot, what are the mean and median values?

Stem	Leaf
1	6 8
2	0 1
3	4
4	5 9

A. Mean = 28 and median = 20
B. Mean = 29 and median = 20
C. Mean = 29 and median = 21
D. Mean = 28 and median = 21

20. Which of the following expressions is equivalent to $-3x(x-2)^2$?

A. $-3x^3 + 6x^2 - 12x$
B. $-3x^3 - 12x^2 + 12x$
C. $-3x^2 + 6x$
D. $-3x^3 + 12x^2 - 12x$

Answer Key and Explanations for Test #7

Mathematics

1. C: When the dress is marked down by 20%, the cost of the dress is 80% of its original price. Since a percentage can be written as a fraction by placing the percentage over 100, the reduced price of the dress can be written as $\frac{80}{100}x$, or $\frac{4}{5}x$, where x is the original price. When discounted an extra 25%, the dress costs 75% of the reduced price. This results in the expression $\frac{75}{100}\left(\frac{4}{5}x\right)$, which can be simplified to $\frac{3}{4}\left(\frac{4}{5}x\right)$, or $\frac{3}{5}x$. So the final price of the dress is three-fifths of the original price.

2. D: We can use the table to find the linear equation in slope-intercept form, $y = mx + b$, where m is the slope and b is the y-intercept. The table shows the y-intercept (the y-value at $x = 0$) to be -5. The slope is the ratio of the change in y-values to the corresponding change in x-values. As the x-value increases by 1, the y-value increases by 3. Thus, the slope is $\frac{3}{1}$, or 3. So the equation is $y = 3x - 5$.

Only the graphs in choices B and D have a y-intercept at -5. Of these two graphs, only choice D has a y-value increase of 3 for each x-value increase of 1, indicating a slope of 3.

3. B: A cube has six square faces. The arrangement of these faces in a two-dimensional figure is a net of a cube if the figure can be folded to form a cube. If choice B is folded, the bottom square in the second column will overlap the fourth square in the top row, so the figure does not represent a net of a cube. The other figures represent three of the eleven possible nets of a cube.

4. C: The expression representing the monthly charge for Company A is $\$25 + \$0.05m$, where m is the time in minutes spent talking on the phone. Set this expression equal to the monthly charge for Company B, which is $50. Solve for m to find the number of minutes the two companies charge the same amount.

$$\$25 + \$0.05m = \$50$$
$$\$0.05m = \$25$$
$$m = 500$$

Notice that the answer choices are given in hours, not in minutes. Since there are 60 minutes in an hour, $m = \frac{500}{60}$ hours $= 8\frac{1}{3}$ hours. One-third of an hour is 20 minutes, so m is 8 hours and 20 minutes.

5. B: The probability may be written as $P(E \text{ and } H) = P(E) \times P(H)$. The probability of rolling an even number on a die is $E = \frac{3}{6} = \frac{1}{2}$. The probability of a coin landing on heads is $H = \frac{1}{2}$. Substituting the probability of each event gives $P(E \text{ and } H) = \frac{1}{2} \times \frac{1}{2} = \frac{1}{4}$.

6. C: The probability of tossing a coin and getting heads is $\frac{1}{2}$. Multiply the probability by the number of coin tosses: $\frac{1}{2} \times 300 = 150$. You would expect to get heads about 150 times.

7. D: Since there are 100 homes' market times represented in each set, the median time a home spends on the market is between the 50th and 51st data point in each set. The 50th and 51st data points for Zip Code 1 are six months and seven months, respectively, so the median time a house in Zip Code 1 spends on the market is between six and seven months (6.5 months), which by the realtor's definition of market time is a seven-month market time. The 50th and 51st data points for Zip Code 2 are both thirteen months, so the median time a house in Zip Code 2 spends on the market is thirteen months. Therefore, there is a six-month difference between the median of Zip Code 1 and the median of Zip Code 2.

To find the mean market time for 100 houses, find the sum of the market times and divide by 100. If the frequency of a one-month market time is 9, the number 1 is added nine times (1×9), if the frequency of a two-month market time is 10, the number 2 is added ten times (2×10), and so on. So, to find the average market time, divide by 100 the sum of the products of each market time and its corresponding frequency. For Zip Code 1, the mean market time is 7.38 months, which, by the realtor's definition of market time, is an eight-month market time. For Zip Code 2, the mean market time is 12.74, which, by the realtor's definition of market time, is a thirteen-month market time. Therefore, the difference between the mean of Zip Code 1 and the mean of Zip Code 2 is 4 months.

The mode market time is the market time for which the frequency is the highest. For Zip Code 1, the mode market time is three months, and for Zip Code 2, the mode market time is eleven months. Therefore, the median time a house spends on the market in Zip Code 1 is less than the mean time a house spends on the market in Zip Code 1.

8. D: Since Hannah spends at least $16, the relation of the cost of a package of coffee to the minimum cost may be written as $4p \geq 16$. Alternatively, the inequality may be written as $16 \leq 4p$.

9. A: The net of a triangular prism has three rectangular faces and two triangular faces, and the rectangular faces must all be able to connect to each other directly. This is shown in choice A.

10. C: There are 36 months in 3 years. Since Amy saves $450 every 3 months, the following proportion can be written to find the amount she saves in 36 months: $\frac{450}{3} = \frac{x}{36}$. Cross multiplying gives you the equation $3x = 16,200$, which can be solved for x. Dividing both sides of the equation by 3 gives $x = 5,400$.

11. C: The amount he donates is equal to 1% of $45,000. To calculate this value, multiply the two numbers. To multiply a percentage by another number, first convert the percentage to a decimal by changing the percentage sign to a decimal point and moving the decimal point two places to the left. Therefore, $1\% = 0.01$. Now the two numbers can be multiplied: $0.01 \times \$45,000 = 1 \times \$450 = \$450$. Thus, he donates $450.

12. D: Let $P(T)$ represent the probability of getting tails on the coin toss. We can see that $P(T) = \frac{1}{2}$. Let $P(P)$ be the chance of getting a prime number on the die. Of the possible outcomes (1 through 6), three are prime (2, 3, and 5), so $P(P) = \frac{3}{6} = \frac{1}{2}$.

Since $P(P)$ and $P(T)$ are not mutually exclusive, $P(P \text{ or } T) = P(P) + P(T) - P(P \text{ and } T)$. Because the events are independent, $P(P \text{ and } T) = P(P) \times P(T)$. Substituting the probability of each event gives $P(P \text{ or } T) = \frac{1}{2} + \frac{1}{2} - \left(\frac{1}{2} \times \frac{1}{2}\right) = \frac{1}{2} + \frac{1}{2} - \frac{1}{4} = \frac{3}{4}$.

13. C: Using the points $(-3, 1)$ and $(1, -11)$, the slope may be written as $m = \frac{-11-1}{1-(-3)}$ or $m = -3$. Substituting the slope of -3 and the x- and y-values from the point $(-3, 1)$, into the slope-intercept form of an equation gives $1 = -3(-3) + b$, which simplifies to $1 = 9 + b$. Subtracting 9 from both sides of the equation gives $b = -8$. Thus, the linear equation that includes the data in the table is $y = -3x - 8$.

14. C: The surface area of a rectangular prism may be calculated using the formula $SA = 2lw + 2wh + 2hl$. Substituting the dimensions of 14 inches, 6 inches, and 8 inches gives $SA = 2(14)(6) + 2(6)(8) + 2(8)(14)$. Thus, the surface area is 488 square inches.

15. B: The volume of a sphere may be calculated using the formula $V = \frac{4}{3}\pi r^3$, where r represents the radius. Substituting 3.5 for r gives $V = \frac{4}{3}\pi(3.5)^3$, which simplifies to $V \approx 179.6$ in^3.

16. C: The distance may be calculated using the distance formula, $d = \sqrt{(x_2 - x_1)^2 + (y_2 - y_1)^2}$. Substitute the given coordinates into the formula.

$$d = \sqrt{(4 - (-8))^2 + (3 - 6)^2}$$
$$d = \sqrt{(12)^2 + (-3)^2}$$
$$d = \sqrt{144 + 9}$$
$$d = \sqrt{153}$$

Therefore, the distance between the two points is $\sqrt{153}$.

17. D: Begin by calculating the total rainfall in the summer and autumn months by adding all the values together. The total rainfall is 25.38 inches. Then, create a ratio comparing the rainfall in October to the total rainfall. The ratio $\frac{4.5}{25.38}$ represents the fraction of rainfall received during October. Convert the ratio to a percentage by dividing the numerator by the denominator and then multiplying by 100: $\frac{4.5}{25.38} \approx 0.177 = 17.7\%$. Therefore, about 17.7% of the rain fell during October.

18. C: A line segment with endpoints (x_1, y_1) and (x_2, y_2) has the midpoint $\left(\frac{x_1+x_2}{2}, \frac{y_1+y_2}{2}\right)$. The line segment shown has endpoints (1,2) and (8,8), so its midpoint is $\left(\frac{1+8}{2}, \frac{2+8}{2}\right)$, or (4.5,5).

19. C: The mean is the average of the data and can be found by dividing the sum of the data by the number of data: $\frac{16+18+20+21+34+45+49}{7} = 29$. The median is the middle data point when the data are ranked numerically. The median is 21.

20. D: The expression $(x - 2)^2$ may be expanded as $x^2 - 4x + 4$. Multiplication of $-3x$ by this expression gives $-3x^3 + 12x^2 - 12x$.

TSI Math Practice Test #8

Mathematics

1. Andrew rolls a die. What is the probability he gets a 4 or an even number?

    A. $\frac{1}{4}$
    B. $\frac{1}{2}$
    C. $\frac{2}{3}$
    D. $\frac{3}{4}$

2. Which of the following is the graph of the equation $y = -4x - 6$?

A.
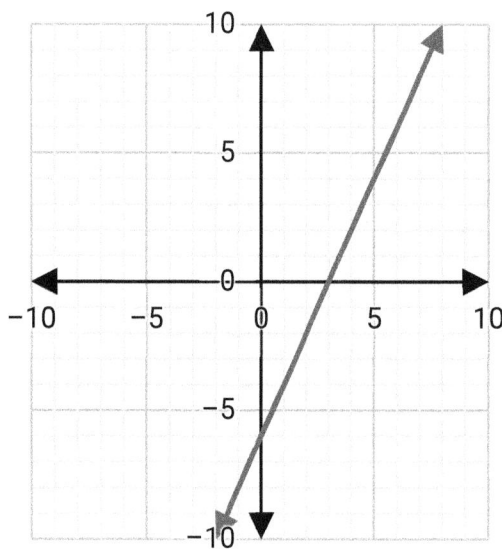

B.
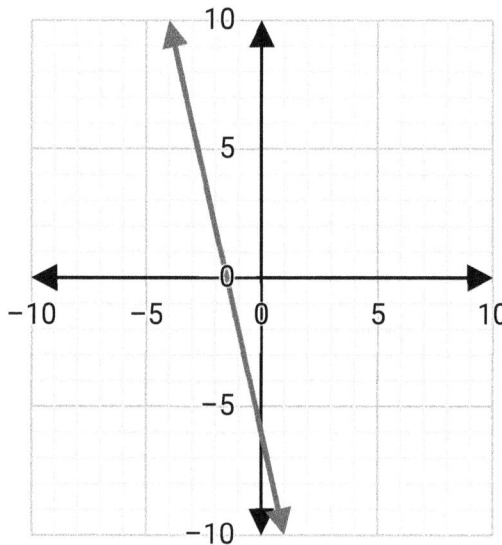

C.
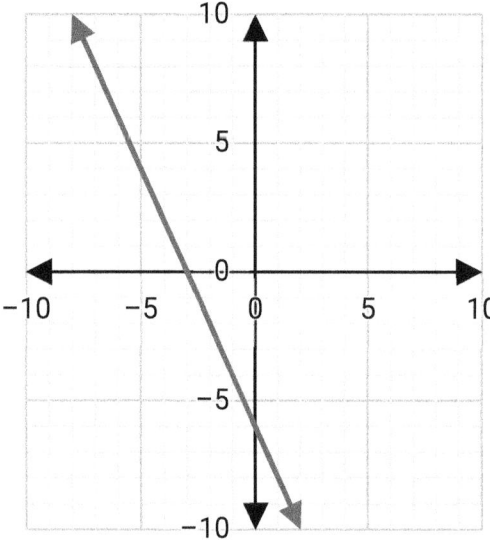

D.
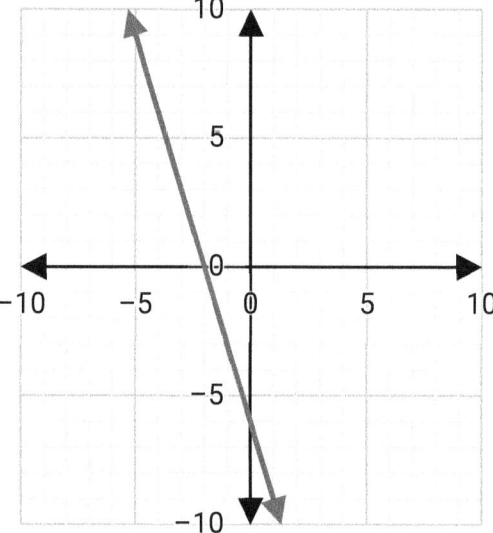

3. Kevin saves $3 during Month 1. During each subsequent month, he plans to save 4 more dollars than he saved during the previous month. Which of the following equations represents the amount he will save during the nth month?

   A. $a_n = 3n - 1$
   B. $a_n = 3n + 4$
   C. $a_n = 4n + 3$
   D. $a_n = 4n - 1$

4. Elijah pays a $30 park entrance fee plus $4 for every ticket he buys. Which of the following equations correctly represents his total cost y in terms of the number of tickets x?

   A. $y = 30x + 4$
   B. $y = 34x$
   C. $y = 4x + 30$
   D. $y = 34x + 30$

5. Claus has $20 to spend at the local fair. The entrance fee is $2.50, and tickets for the booths are $2 each. Which of the following inequalities represents the number of tickets x that Claus can afford with his $20?

   A. $2.50x + 2x \leq 20$
   B. $2.50 + 2x \leq 20$
   C. $2x \leq 20 + 2.50$
   D. $2.50 + 2x \geq 20x$

6. Solve $\frac{x-2}{x-1} = \frac{x-1}{x+1} + \frac{2}{x-1}$.

   A. $x = 2$
   B. $x = -5$
   C. $x = 1$
   D. No solution

7. A can has a radius of 1.5 inches and a height of 3 inches. Which of the following best represents the volume of the can? Use 3.14 for π.

   A. 17.2 in^3
   B. 19.4 in^3
   C. 21.2 in^3
   D. 23.4 in^3

8. In a town of 35,638 people, about a quarter of the population is under the age of 35. Of those, just over a third attend local K–12 schools. If the number of students in each grade is about the same, how many fourth graders likely reside in the town?

   A. Fewer than 100
   B. Between 200 and 300
   C. Between 300 and 400
   D. More than 400

9. Nikki buys a used book that is marked down 35% from the original price. She pays 8.25% sales tax. Her total cost is $9.14. What was the original price of the book?

   A. $11.99
   B. $12.49
   C. $12.99
   D. $13.49

10. A random sample of 90 students at an elementary school were asked these three questions:

   Do you like carrots?
   Do you like broccoli?
   Do you like cauliflower?

The results of the survey are shown below. If these data are representative of the population of students at the school, which of these is most probable?

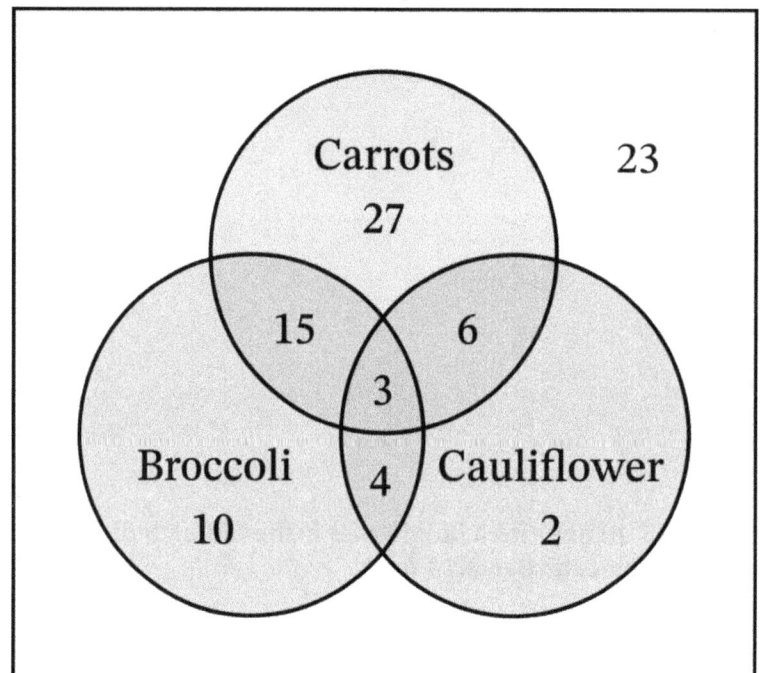

   A. A student chosen at random likes broccoli.
   B. Given a student chosen at random likes carrots, they will also like at least one other vegetable.
   C. Given a student chosen at random likes cauliflower and broccoli, they will also like carrots.
   D. A student chosen at random does not like carrots, broccoli, or cauliflower.

11. Which of the following represents an inversely proportional relationship?

   A. $y = 3x$
   B. $y = \frac{1}{3}x$
   C. $y = \frac{3}{x}$
   D. $y = 3x^2$

12. A tree with a height of 15 feet casts a shadow that is 5 feet in length. A man standing at the base of the shadow formed by the tree is 6 feet tall. How long is the shadow cast by the man?

   A. 1.5 feet
   B. 2 feet
   C. 2.5 feet
   D. 3 feet

13. Eric has a beach ball with a radius of 9 inches. He is planning to wrap the ball with wrapping paper. Which of the following is the best estimate for the number of square feet of wrapping paper he will need? Use 3.14 for π.

   A. 4.08
   B. 5.12
   C. 7.07
   D. 8.14

14. Ms. Elliott asks her fifth-grade students, "Do you prefer chocolate or vanilla ice cream?" If the probability of her students preferring chocolate ice cream is 0.6, what is the probability of her students preferring vanilla ice cream?

   A. 0.6
   B. 0.4
   C. 0.3
   D. 0.5

15. Kayla has a $75 budget to purchase gifts for her colleagues. She wants to buy coffee mugs and note pads. She may purchase a maximum of 30 items. Each coffee mug costs $6 and each note pad costs $3. Which of the following graphs correctly shows the possible combinations of coffee mugs and note pads that she may buy?

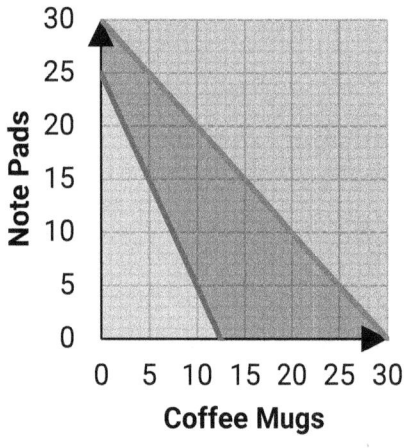
A.

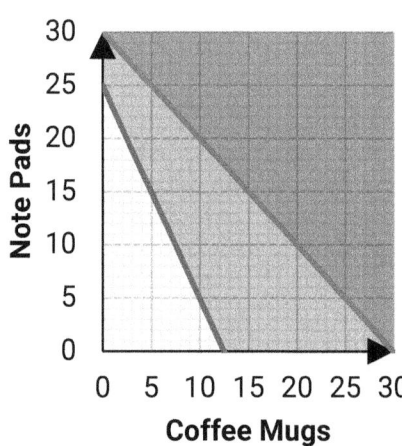
B.

C.

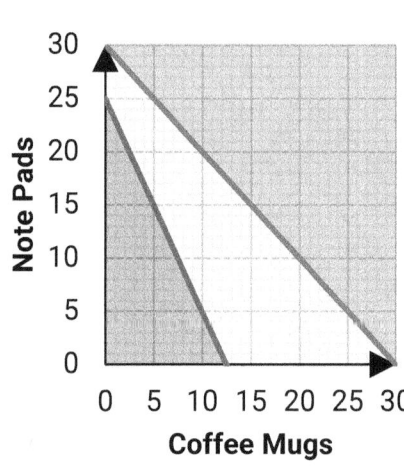
D.

16. For which of these does a rotation of 120° about the center of the polygon map the polygon onto itself?

   A. Square
   B. Regular hexagon
   C. Regular octagon
   D. Regular decagon

17. A man standing on a flat, level surface casts a shadow that is 6.2 ft in length. The man is 5.8 ft tall. Which of the following best represents the distance from the top of his head to the end of the shadow?

   A. 7 ft
   B. 7.5 ft
   C. 8 ft
   D. 8.5 ft

18. Andrea must administer $\frac{1}{12}$ of a medicine bottle to a patient. If the bottle contains $3\frac{4}{10}$ fluid ounces of medicine, how much medicine should be administered?

   A. $\frac{17}{60}$ fluid ounces
   B. $\frac{15}{62}$ fluid ounces
   C. $\frac{3}{19}$ fluid ounces
   D. $\frac{17}{67}$ fluid ounces

19. What is the correct solution for x in the following system of equations?
$$\begin{cases} x - 1 = y \\ y + 3 = 7 \end{cases}$$

   A. $x = 6$
   B. $x = 5$
   C. $x = 4$
   D. $x = 8$

20. What is the approximate area of the shaded region between the circle and the square in the figure shown below? Use 3.14 for π.

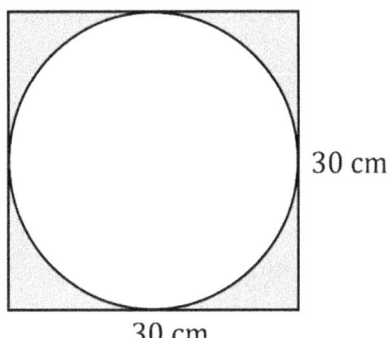

   A. 177 cm²
   B. 181 cm²
   C. 187 cm²
   D. 193 cm²

Answer Key and Explanations for Test #8

Mathematics

1. B: Since they are not mutually exclusive events, $P(4 \text{ or } E) = P(4) + P(E) - P(4 \text{ and } E)$. Substituting the probability of each event gives $P(4 \text{ or } E) = \frac{1}{6} + \frac{1}{2} - \frac{1}{6} = \frac{1}{2}$.

2. B: The equation $y = -4x - 6$ is in slope-intercept form, $y = mx + b$, where m is the slope and b is the y-intercept. All four graphs show the correct y-intercept, -6, but only one shows the correct slope, -4. The slope of a line can be found by picking any two points (x_1, y_1) and (x_2, y_2) on the line and calculating $m = \frac{y_2 - y_1}{x_2 - x_1}$. For choice B, we can choose points $(0, -6)$ and $(-2, 2)$, which gives us $m = \frac{2-(-6)}{-2-0} = -4$. None of the other graphs have a slope of -4.

3. D: This situation may be modeled by an arithmetic sequence, with a common difference of 4 and an initial value of 3. Substituting the common difference and initial value into the formula, $a_n = a_1 + (n-1)d$, gives $a_n = 3 + (n-1)(4)$, which simplifies to $a_n = 4n - 1$.

4. C: Elijah's total cost is $30 plus $4 times the number of tickets. Rewriting this in mathematical notation (using y for total cost and x for the number of tickets) gives $y = 30 + 4x$, which is equivalent to choice C.

5. B: Claus has $20 to spend, so the amount he spends must be less than or equal to ($\leq$) $20. The entrance fee of $2.50 is only charged once, so it should not be multiplied by x. The cost of a ticket multiplied by x represents the cost of buying x tickets. The entrance fee plus the cost of the tickets is Claus's total cost: $2.50 + 2x \leq 20$.

6. B: Notice that $x = 1$ results in a zero in the denominator, so choice C cannot be correct since $x \neq 1$. To solve, subtract $\frac{2}{x-1}$ from both sides, then cross-multiply.

$\frac{x-2}{x-1} = \frac{x-1}{x+1} + \frac{2}{x-1}$	Write out the original equation.
$\frac{x-4}{x-1} = \frac{x-1}{x+1}$	Subtract $\frac{2}{x-1}$ from both sides.
$(x+1)(x-4) = (x-1)(x-1)$	Cross multiply.
$x^2 - 3x - 4 = x^2 - 2x + 1$	Multiply the binomials on both sides.
$-3x - 4 = -2x + 1$	Subtract x^2 from both sides.
$-4 = x + 1$	Add $3x$ to both sides.
$-5 = x$	Subtract 1 from both sides.

7. C: The volume of a cylinder may be calculated using the formula $V = \pi r^2 h$, where r represents the radius of the circular base and h represents the height of the cylinder. Substituting 3.14 for π,

1.5 for r, and 3 for h gives $V = (3.14)(1.5)^2(3) = 21.195$, which rounds to 21.2. Therefore, the volume of the can is approximately 21.2 in^3.

8. B: The population is approximately 36,000, so one-quarter of the population consists of about 9,000 individuals under age 35. A third of 9,000 is 3,000, which is the approximate number of students in grades K–12. Since there are thirteen grades, divide 3,000 by 13. There are about 230 students in each grade. So, the number of fourth graders is between 200 and 300.

9. C: The original price x may be modeled by the equation $(x - 0.35x) \times 1.0825 = 9.14$, which simplifies to $0.703625x = 9.14$. Dividing each side of the equation by the coefficient of x gives $x \approx 12.99$. The book was originally $12.99.

10. B: Determine the probability of each choice.

For choice A, this is the total number of students in the broccoli circle of the Venn diagram divided by the total number of students surveyed:

$$\frac{10 + 4 + 3 + 15}{90} = \frac{32}{90} \approx 35.6\%$$

For choice B, this is the total number of students in the carrots circle and also in at least one other circle divided by the total number in the carrots circle:

$$\frac{15 + 3 + 6}{15 + 3 + 6 + 27} = \frac{24}{51} \approx 47.1\%$$

For choice C, this is the number of students in the intersection of all three circles divided by the total number in the overlap of the broccoli and cauliflower circles:

$$\frac{3}{3 + 4} = \frac{3}{7} \approx 42.9\%$$

For choice D, this is the number of students outside of all the circles divided by the total number of students surveyed:

$$\frac{23}{90} \approx 25.6\%$$

Since choice B has the highest percentage, it is the choice that is most probable.

11. C: An inversely proportional relationship is written in the form $y = \frac{k}{x}$; thus, the equation $y = \frac{3}{x}$ shows that y is inversely proportional to x.

12. B: The following proportion may be written and solved for x: $\frac{15 \text{ ft}}{5 \text{ ft}} = \frac{6 \text{ ft}}{x \text{ ft}}$. Cross multiplying results in $15x = 30$. Dividing by 15 gives $x = 2$. Thus, the shadow cast by the man is 2 feet in length.

13. C: The surface area of a sphere may be calculated using the formula $SA = 4\pi r^2$. Substituting 9 for r and 3.14 for π gives $SA = 4(3.14)(9)^2$, which simplifies to $SA = 1,017.36$. So, the surface area of the ball is approximately 1,017.36 square inches. There are twelve inches in a foot, so there are $12^2 = 144$ square inches in a square foot. In order to convert this measurement to square feet, the following proportion may be written and solved for x: $\frac{1}{144} = \frac{x}{1,017.36}$. So $x = 7.07$. He needs approximately 7.07 square feet of wrapping paper.

14. B: Since the events are mutually exclusive, the sum of their individual probabilities is 1.0. Subtracting 0.6 from 1.0 yields 0.4. Therefore, the correct choice is B.

15. C: The situation may be modeled by the system of inequalities $\begin{cases} 6x + 3y \leq 75 \\ x + y \leq 30 \end{cases}$ where x is the number of coffee mugs and y is the number of note pads. Some algebraic manipulation gives us the inequalities in slope-intercept form: $\begin{cases} y \leq -2x + 25 \\ y \leq -x + 30 \end{cases}$. All four choices graph these lines correctly, but only choice C correctly shades just the region that is below both lines, indicating that both conditions are met.

16. B: All regular polygons have rotational symmetry. The angle of rotation is the smallest angle by which the polygon can be rotated such that it maps onto itself; any multiple of this angle will also map the polygon onto itself. The angle of rotation for a regular polygon is the angle formed between two lines drawn from consecutive vertices to the center of the polygon. Since the vertices of a regular polygon lie on a circle, for a regular polygon with n sides, the angle of rotation measures $\frac{360°}{n}$. Therefore, a square has rotational symmetry about the angle 90° and its multiples. A regular hexagon has rotational symmetry about the angle 60° and its multiples. A regular octagon has rotational symmetry about 45° and its multiples. And a regular decagon has rotational symmetry about 36° and its multiples. Since 120° is a multiple of 60°, the correct answer is a regular hexagon.

17. D: The Pythagorean theorem may be used to find the diagonal distance from the top of his head to the base of the shadow. Using the following equation, we can determine this distance, c: $5.8^2 + 6.2^2 = c^2$. Thus, $c \approx 8.5$. The distance is approximately 8.5 ft.

18. A: The amount to be administered may be written as $\frac{1}{12} \times \frac{34}{10}$, which equals $\frac{17}{60}$. Thus, she should administer $\frac{17}{60}$ fluid ounces of medicine.

19. B: The equation $y + 3 = 7$ is solved by subtracting 3 from both sides to yield $y = 4$. Substituting $y = 4$ into $x - 1 = y$ yields $x - 1 = 4$. Adding 1 to both sides of this equation yields $x = 5$.

20. D: The area of the square is $A = s^2 = (30 \text{ cm})^2 = 900 \text{ cm}^2$. The area of the circle is $A = \pi r^2 = (3.14)(15 \text{ cm})^2 \approx 707 \text{ cm}^2$. The area of the shaded region is equal to the difference between the area of the square and the area of the circle, or $900 \text{ cm}^2 - 707 \text{ cm}^2$, which equals 193 cm².

TSI Math Practice Test #9

Mathematics

1. Sophia is at the market buying fruit for her family of four. Kiwifruit is only sold in packages of three. If Sophia would like each family member to have the same number of kiwifruits, which of the following approaches can Sophia use to determine the fewest number of kiwifruits she should buy?

   A. Sophia needs to determine the greatest common multiple of 3 and 4.
   B. Sophia needs to determine the least common multiple of 3 and 4.
   C. Sophia needs to determine the least common divisor of 3 and 4.
   D. Sophia needs to determine the greatest common divisor of 3 and 4.

2. A crane raises one end of a 3,300-pound steel beam. The other end rests upon the ground. If the crane supports 30% of the beam's weight, how many pounds does it support?

   A. 330 lb
   B. 700 lb
   C. 990 lb
   D. 1,100 lb

3. Ms. Chen is instructing her students on divisibility rules. Which of the following rules can be used to determine if a number is divisible by 6?

   A. The last digit of the number is divisible by 2 or 3.
   B. The number ends in 6.
   C. The number is divisible by 2 and 3.
   D. The last two digits of the number are divisible by 6.

Refer to the following for question 4:

The box-and-whisker plot displays student test scores by class period.

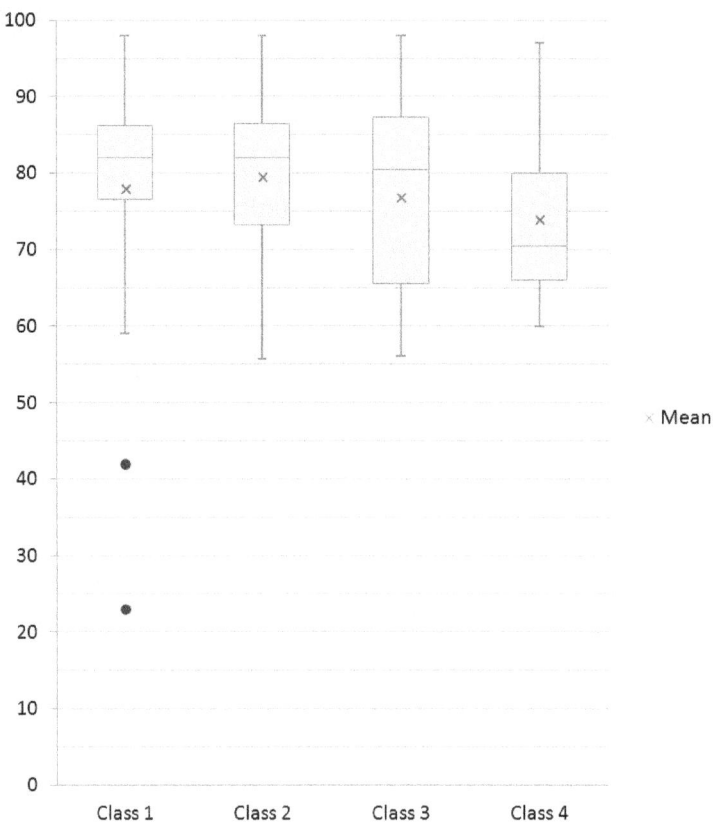

4. **Which of the following statements is true of the data?**
   A. The mean better reflects student performance in class 1 than the median.
   B. The mean test score for class 1 and 2 is the same.
   C. The median test score for class 1 and 2 is the same.
   D. The median test score is above the mean for class 4.

5. **Adam rolls a standard six-sided die. What is the probability he rolls a number greater than or equal to 5?**
   A. $\frac{1}{6}$
   B. $\frac{1}{5}$
   C. $\frac{1}{4}$
   D. $\frac{1}{3}$

6. Miss Wise asks her students to work in pairs to construct Venn diagrams which classify rational numbers, irrational numbers, real numbers, and integers. As she walks around the room to observe their progress, which of the following criterion could she use to assess the students' understanding of these sets of numbers?

   A. The set of integers should include the other three sets.
   B. The set of rational numbers should include the other three sets.
   C. The set of irrational numbers should include the other three sets.
   D. The set of real numbers should include the other three sets.

7. Carlos spends $\frac{1}{8}$ of his monthly salary on utility bills. If his utility bills total $320, what is his monthly salary?

   A. $2,440
   B. $2,520
   C. $2,560
   D. $2,600

8. Which of the following options represents equivalency between mathematical expressions?

   A. $3 + x + 3x + 3 + x = 5x + 6$
   B. $7x - 2x = 9x$
   C. $2y + 2y + 2y = 6y^3$
   D. $2.5(x + 2) = 2.5x + 2$

9. If $f(x) = \frac{x^3 - 2x + 1}{3x}$, what is $f(2)$?

   A. $\frac{1}{3}$
   B. $\frac{1}{2}$
   C. $\frac{5}{6}$
   D. $\frac{5}{2}$

10. Identify the cross-section polygon formed by a plane containing the given points on the cube.

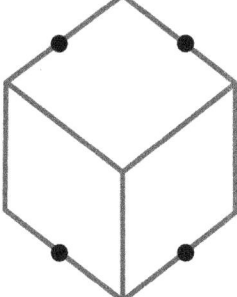

   A. Rectangle
   B. Trapezoid
   C. Pentagon
   D. Hexagon

183

11. A 6th grade math teacher is introducing the concept of positive and negative numbers to a group of students. Which of the following models would be the most effective when introducing this concept?
   A. Fraction strips
   B. Venn diagrams
   C. Shaded regions
   D. Number lines

12. Coach Weybright's 6th-grade basketball team has played 36 games this season. The ratio of wins to losses is 2 : 1. If x represents the number of wins, which of the following proportions can be used to determine the number of wins?
   A. $\frac{x}{36} = \frac{2}{1}$
   B. $\frac{x}{2} = \frac{1}{36}$
   C. $\frac{x}{3} = \frac{36}{2}$
   D. $\frac{x}{36} = \frac{2}{3}$

13. A dartboard consists of two concentric circles with radii of 3 inches and 6 inches. If a dart is thrown onto the board, what is the probability the dart will land in the inner circle?
   A. $\frac{1}{4}$
   B. $\frac{1}{2}$
   C. $\frac{1}{3}$
   D. $\frac{1}{5}$

14. Attending a summer camp are 12 six-year-olds, 15 seven-year-olds, 14 eight-year-olds, 12 nine-year-olds, and 10 ten-year-olds. If a camper is randomly selected to participate in a special event, what is the probability that he or she is at least eight years old?
   A. $\frac{2}{9}$
   B. $\frac{22}{63}$
   C. $\frac{4}{7}$
   D. $\frac{3}{7}$

15. Which of these tables properly displays the measures of central tendency that can be used for nominal, interval, and ordinal data?

a.

	Mean	Median	Mode
Nominal			x
Interval	x	x	x
Ordinal		x	x

b.

	Mean	Median	Mode
Nominal			x
Interval	x	x	x
Ordinal	x	x	x

c.

	Mean	Median	Mode
Nominal	x	x	x
Interval	x	x	x
Ordinal	x	x	x

d.

	Mean	Median	Mode
Nominal			x
Interval	x	x	
Ordinal	x	x	x

16. Kim's current monthly rent is $800. She is moving to another apartment complex, where the monthly rent will be $1,100. What is the percent increase in her monthly rent amount?

   A. 25.5%
   B. 27%
   C. 35%
   D. 37.5%

17. You wish to determine the area of a regular pentagon, and all you know is the length of one side. What additional information is sufficient for you to be able to compute the area?

   A. The length of all the other sides
   B. The width of the pentagon
   C. The length of the apothem
   D. No other information needed

18. How many diagonals are in a dodecagon?

   A. 12
   B. 24
   C. 54
   D. 108

19. On a floor plan drawn at a scale of 1 : 100, the area of a rectangular room is 30 cm². What is the actual area of the room?

   A. 30,000 cm²
   B. 300 m²
   C. 3,000 m²
   D. 30 m²

20. Ben's current monthly rent is $750. He is moving to another apartment complex, where the monthly rent will be $900. What is the percent increase in his monthly rent amount?

   A. 15%
   B. 17.5%
   C. 19.25%
   D. 20%

Answer Key and Explanations for Test #9

Mathematics

1. B: Sophia needs to find multiples of 3 (3, 6, 9, 12, 15, ...) and multiples of 4 (4, 8, 12, 16, ...) and find the least common multiple between them, which is 12. The greatest common divisor of 3 and 4 is 1. The least common divisor between two numbers is always 1. The greatest common multiple can never be determined. Therefore, the correct answer is choice B.

2. C: It is helpful to recall that percentages can be converted to decimals. 30% of 3,300 is $0.3 \times 3,300 = 990$. Therefore, the crane supports 990 pounds.

3. C: A number that is divisible by 6 is divisible by 2 and 3. A number is divisible by 2 if it is even, and it is divisible by 3 if the sum of the digits is divisible by 3. For example, the number 12 is divisible by 2 and 3, so it is also divisible by 6.

4. C: The line through the center of the box represents the median. The median test score for classes 1 and 2 is 82.

Note that for class 1, the median is a better representation of the data than the mean. There are two low outliers, points which lie outside of two standard deviations from the mean, which bring down the average test score. In cases such as this, the mean is not the best measure of central tendency.

5. D: The number of outcomes in the event is 2 (rolling a 5 or 6), and the sample space is 6 (numbers 1 to 6). Thus, the probability may be written as $\frac{2}{6}$, which simplifies to $\frac{1}{3}$.

6. D: Real numbers include all rational and irrational numbers. Rational numbers include all integers. The set of real numbers include the other three sets.

7. C: His monthly salary may be modeled as $\frac{1}{8}x = 320$. Multiplying both sides of the equation by 8 gives $x = 2,560$.

8. A: $3 + x + 3x + 3 + x = 5x + 6$ correctly shows how the combination of like terms on the left side of the equation results in the expression on the right side of the equation. $7x - 2x = 9x$ incorrectly combines like terms by adding the coefficients rather than subtracting them. $2y + 2y + 2y = 6y^3$ incorrectly adds the exponents of like terms instead of just adding the coefficients of like terms. $2.5(x + 2) = 2.5x + 2$ incorrectly distributes the 2.5 across the parentheses by neglecting to multiply the 2.5 with the last term in the expression.

9. C: Substitute 2 for each x and simplify.

$$f(2) = \frac{(2)^3 - 2(2) + 1}{3(2)} = \frac{8 - 4 + 1}{6} = \frac{5}{6}$$

10. D: The cross-section is a hexagon.

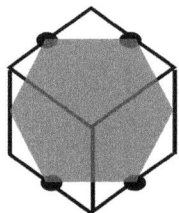

11. D: Number lines can help students understand the concepts of positive and negative numbers. Fraction strips are most commonly used with fractions. Venn diagrams are commonly used when comparing groups. Shaded regions are commonly used with fractions or percentages.

12. D: This problem can be represented using the proportion $\frac{number\ of\ wins}{total\ games} = \frac{number\ of\ wins}{total\ games}$. If the ratio of wins to losses is 2 : 1, then the ratio of wins to total games is 2 : 3. The proportion to determine the number of wins is $\frac{x}{36} = \frac{2}{3}$.

13. A: The probability that the dart will land in the inner circle is equal to the ratio of the area of inner circle to the area of the outer circle, or $\frac{\pi(3)^2}{\pi(6)^2}$. This reduces to $\frac{1}{4}$.

14. C: If all possible outcomes are equally likely, then the probability of an event is the number of outcomes in which that event occurs, divided by the number of possible outcomes. A camper who is at least eight years old can be eight, nine, or ten years old, so the probability of randomly selecting a camper at least eight years old is:

$$\frac{\text{number of eight-, nine-, and ten-year-old campers}}{\text{total number of campers}} = \frac{14 + 12 + 10}{12 + 15 + 14 + 12 + 10} = \frac{36}{63} = \frac{4}{7}$$

15. A: Nominal data are data that are collected which have no intrinsic quantity or order. For instance, a survey might ask the respondent to identify his or her gender. While it is possible to compare the relative frequency of each response (for example, "most of the respondents are women"), it is not possible to calculate the mean, which requires data to be numeric, or median, which requires data to be ordered. Interval data are both numeric and ordered, so mean and median can be determined, as can the mode, the interval within which there are the most data. Ordinal data has an inherent order, but there is not a set interval between two points. For example, a survey might ask the respondents whether they were very dissatisfied, dissatisfied, neutral, satisfied, or very satisfied with the customer service received. Since the data are not numeric, the mean cannot be calculated, but since ordering the data is possible, the median has context.

16. D: This problem can be solved using the percent change formula: $\%\ change = \frac{new - old}{old} \times 100\%$. Thus, the percentage increase is represented as $\%\ change = \frac{1,100 - 800}{800} \times 100\% = 37.5\%$.

17. D: Since the pentagon is regular, all the sides are equal, and the shape is convex. Because of this, there are enough constraints to determine the area as a function of the side length of the pentagon.

18. C: To find the number of diagonals in a polygon, use the formula $\frac{n(n-3)}{2}$, where n is the number of sides on the polygon. A dodecagon has 12 sides, so substitute 12 for n and simplify.

$$\frac{12(12-3)}{2} = \frac{12(9)}{2} = \frac{108}{2} = 54$$

Therefore, a dodecagon has 54 diagonals.

19. D: Since there are 100 cm in a meter, on a 1 : 100 scale drawing, each centimeter represents one meter. Therefore, an area of one square centimeter on the drawing represents one square meter in actuality. Since the area of the room in the scale drawing is 30 cm², the room's actual area is 30 m².

Another way to determine the area of the room is to write and solve an equation, such as this one: $\frac{l}{100} \times \frac{w}{100} = 30 \text{ cm}^2$, where l and w are the dimensions of the actual room.

$$\frac{lw}{10{,}000} = 30 \text{ cm}^2$$
$$\text{Area} = 300{,}000 \text{ cm}^2$$

Since this is not one of the answer choices, convert cm² to m².

$$300{,}000 \text{ cm}^2 \times \frac{1 \text{ m}}{100 \text{ cm}} \times \frac{1 \text{ m}}{100 \text{ cm}} = 30 \text{ m}^2$$

20. D: The percent change can be found using the following formula.

$$\% \text{ Change} = \frac{\text{new} - \text{old}}{\text{old}} \times 100$$

The old value is his current rent (750), and the new value is his new monthly rent (900).

$$\% \text{ Change} = \frac{900 - 750}{750} \times 100$$
$$\% \text{ Change} = \frac{150}{750} \times 100$$
$$\% \text{ Change} = \frac{1}{5} \times 100$$
$$\% \text{ Change} = 20$$

Since the percent change is positive, this represents a percent increase of 20%.

TSI Math Practice Test #10

Mathematics

1. A dress is marked down 45%. The cost, after taxes, is $39.95. If the tax rate is 8.75%, what was the original price of the dress?

A. $45.74
B. $58.61
C. $66.79
D. $72.31

2. What is the value of the expression $-3 \times 5^2 + 2(4 - 18) + 33$?

A. −130
B. −70
C. −20
D. 74

3. Aaron goes on a run every morning down the straight country road that he lives on. The graph below shows Aaron's distance from home at times throughout his morning run. Which of the following statements is (are) true?

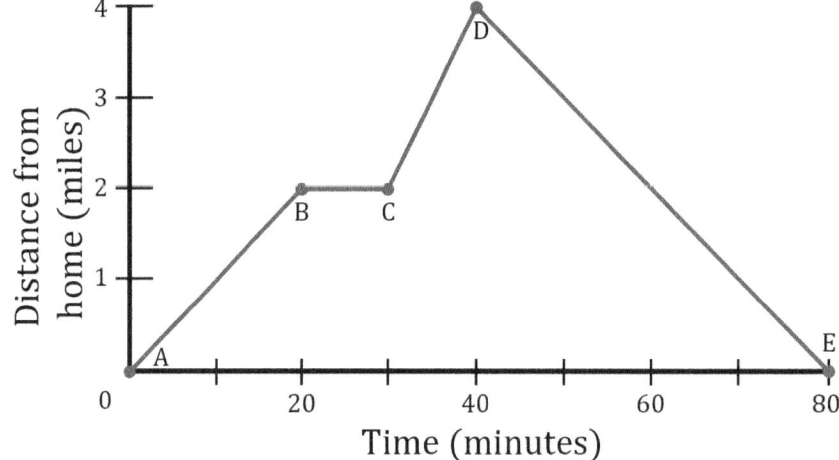

I. Aaron's average running speed was 6 mph.
II. Aaron's running speed from A to B was the same as from D to E.
III. Aaron ran a total distance of four miles.

A. I only
B. II only
C. I and II
D. I, II, and III

4. If a, b, and c are even integers and $3a^2 + 9b^3 = c$, which of these is the largest number which must be factor of c?

   A. 2
   B. 3
   C. 6
   D. 12

5. Tom needs to buy ink cartridges and printer paper. Each ink cartridge costs $30. Each ream of paper costs $5. He has $100 to spend. Which of the following inequalities may be used to find the combinations of ink cartridges and printer paper that he may purchase?

   A. $30c + 5p \leq 100$
   B. $30c + 5p < 100$
   C. $30c + 5p > 100$
   D. $30c + 5p \geq 100$

6. Marcus is mowing yards and doing odd jobs to earn money for a new video game system that costs $325. Marcus only charges $6.50 per hour. Which of the following equations represents the number of hours Marcus needs to work to earn $325?

   A. $6.50x = 325$
   B. $6.50 + x = 325$
   C. $325x = 6.50$
   D. $6.50x + 325 = x$

7. What is the constant of proportionality represented by the table below?

x	y
2	-8
5	-20
7	-28
10	-40
11	-44

   A. -12
   B. -8
   C. -6
   D. -4

8. Jeni buys a phone charger for $28. If it had been marked down 30%, what was the original cost?

   A. $30
   B. $32
   C. $35
   D. $40

9. Mrs. Vories, a fifth-grade teacher, asks her class to use compatible numbers to help her determine approximately how many chicken nuggets she needs to buy for a school-wide party. The school has 589 students and each student will be served nine nuggets. Which student correctly applied the concept of compatible numbers?

  A. Madison estimates: $500 \times 10 = 5{,}000$ nuggets
  B. Audrey estimates: $600 \times 5 = 3{,}000$ nuggets
  C. Ian estimates: $600 \times 10 = 6{,}000$ nuggets
  D. Andrew estimates: $500 \times 5 = 2{,}500$ nuggets

10. In how many distinguishable ways can a family of five be seated at a circular table with five chairs if Tasha and Mac must be kept separated by at least one chair?

  A. 6
  B. 12
  C. 24
  D. 60

11. Which number comes next in the sequence?

$$16, 24, 34, 46, 60$$

  A. 56
  B. 72
  C. 74
  D. 76

12. If the midpoint of a line segment graphed on the xy-coordinate plane is $(3, -1)$ and the slope of the line segment is -2, which of these is a possible endpoint of the line segment?

  A. $(-1, 1)$
  B. $(0, -5)$
  C. $(7, 1)$
  D. $(5, -5)$

13. The two prisms shown below are similar. What is the measurement of x?

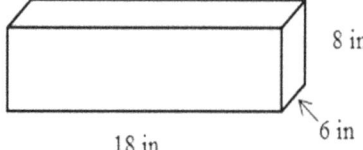
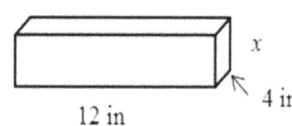

  A. $4\frac{3}{4}$ in
  B. $5\frac{1}{3}$ in
  C. $5\frac{2}{3}$ in
  D. $5\frac{3}{4}$ in

14. A developer decides to build a fence around a neighborhood park, which is positioned on a rectangular lot. Rather than fencing along the lot line, he fences x feet from each of the lot's boundaries. By fencing a rectangular space 141 yd² smaller than the lot, the developer saves $432 in fencing materials, which cost $12 per linear foot. How much does he spend?

    A. $160
    B. $456
    C. $3,168
    D. The answer cannot be determined from the given information.

15. Which of the following is the best representation of 30,490 in scientific notation?

    A. 3.049×10^{-4}
    B. 3.049×10^{3}
    C. 30.490×10^{3}
    D. 3.049×10^{4}

16. Zeke drove from his house to a furniture store in Atlanta and then back home along the same route. It took Zeke three hours to drive to the store. By driving an average of 20 mph faster on his return trip, Zeke was able to save an hour of driving time. What was Zeke's average driving speed on his round trip?

    A. 24 mph
    B. 48 mph
    C. 50 mph
    D. 60 mph

17. Ann must walk from Point A to Point B and then to Point C. Finally, she will walk back to Point A. If each unit represents 5 miles, which of the following BEST represents the total distance she will have walked?

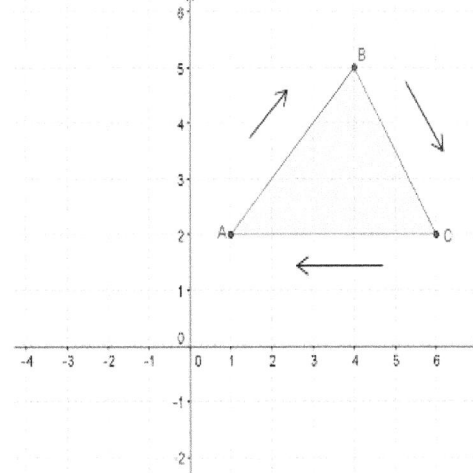

    A. 42 miles
    B. 48 miles
    C. 56 miles
    D. 64 miles

18. What is the perimeter of the trapezoid graphed below?

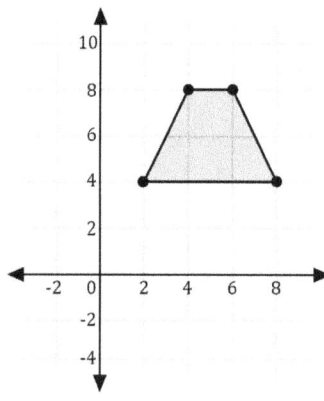

- A. $4 + \sqrt{10}$
- B. $8 + 4\sqrt{5}$
- C. $4 + 2\sqrt{5}$
- D. $8 + 2\sqrt{22}$

19. Which of the following transformations has been applied to $\triangle ABC$?

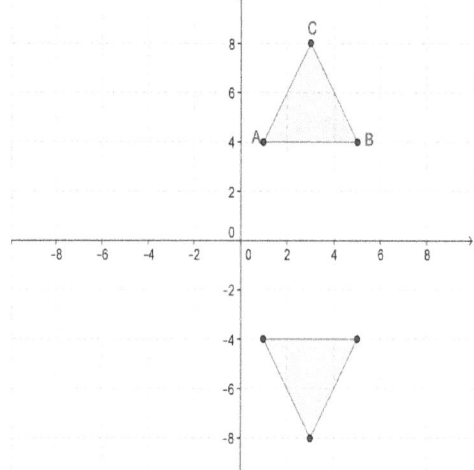

- A. Translation
- B. Rotation of 90 degrees
- C. Reflection
- D. Dilation

20. Mr. Mancelli teaches fifth-grade math. He is making prize bags for the winners of a math game. If he has eight candy bars and twelve packages of gum, what is the largest number of identical prize bags he can make without having any left-over candy bars or packages of gum?

- A. 2
- B. 4
- C. 6
- D. 8

Answer Key and Explanations for Test #1

Mathematics

1. C. The original price may be modeled by the equation:

$$(x - 0.45x) + 0.0875(x - 0.45x) = \$39.95$$

This simplifies to $0.598125x = \$39.95$. Dividing each side of the equation by the coefficient of x gives $x \approx \$66.79$.

2. B: Use the order of operations to find the value for this expression. The order of operations is: parentheses, exponents, multiplication and division, addition and subtraction.

$$-3 \times 5^2 + 2(4 - 18) + 33$$
$$= -3 \times 5^2 + 2(-14) + 33$$
$$= -3 \times 25 + 2(-14) + 33$$
$$= -75 + (-28) + 33$$
$$= -70$$

The value of the expression is −70.

3. C: Aaron ran four miles from home and then back again, so he ran a total of eight miles. Therefore, statement III is false. Statements I and II, however, are both true. Since Aaron ran eight miles in eighty minutes, he ran an average of 1 mile every 10 minutes, or 6 miles every 60 minutes, which is 6 mph. He ran two miles from point (A) to (B) in 20 minutes, which is a rate of 1 mile per 10 minutes, and four miles from (D) to (E) in 40 minutes, which is also a rate of 1 mile per 10 minutes, so his running speed between both sets of points was the same.

4. D: Since a and b are even integers, each can be expressed as the product of 2 and an integer. So, if we let $a = 2x$ and $b = 2y$, then $3(2x)^2 + 9(2y)^3 = c$.

$$3(4x^2) + 9(8y^3) = c$$
$$12x^2 + 72y^3 = c$$
$$12(x^2 + 6y^3) = c$$

Since c is the product of 12 and some other integer, 12 must be a factor of c. Incidentally, the numbers 2, 3, and 6 must also be factors of c since each is also a factor of 12.

5. A: The inequality will be less than or equal to, since he may spend $100 or less on his purchase.

6. A: Marcus needs $325 for the new gaming system. If he earns $6.50 an hour, the number of hours he needs to work can be determined by dividing $325 by $6.50 which is written as $\frac{325}{6.50} = x$. Multiplying both sides of the equation by 6.50 yields $6.50x = 325$.

7. D: The constant of proportionality is equal to the slope. Using the points, $(2, -8)$ and $(5, -20)$, the slope may be written as $\frac{-20-(-8)}{5-2}$, which equals −4.

8. D: The original cost may be represented by the equation $28 = x - 0.3x$ or $28 = 0.7x$. Dividing both sides of the equation by 0.7 gives $x = 40$.

9. C: The number 589 can be estimated to be 600. The number 9 can be estimated to be 10. The number of chicken nuggets is approximately 600×10, which is 6,000 nuggets. Therefore, the correct choice is (C).

10. B: One way to approach this problem is to first consider the number of arrangements of the five members of the family if Tasha (T) and Mac (M) must sit together. Treat them as a unit seated in a fixed location at the table; then arrange the other three family members (A, B, and C):

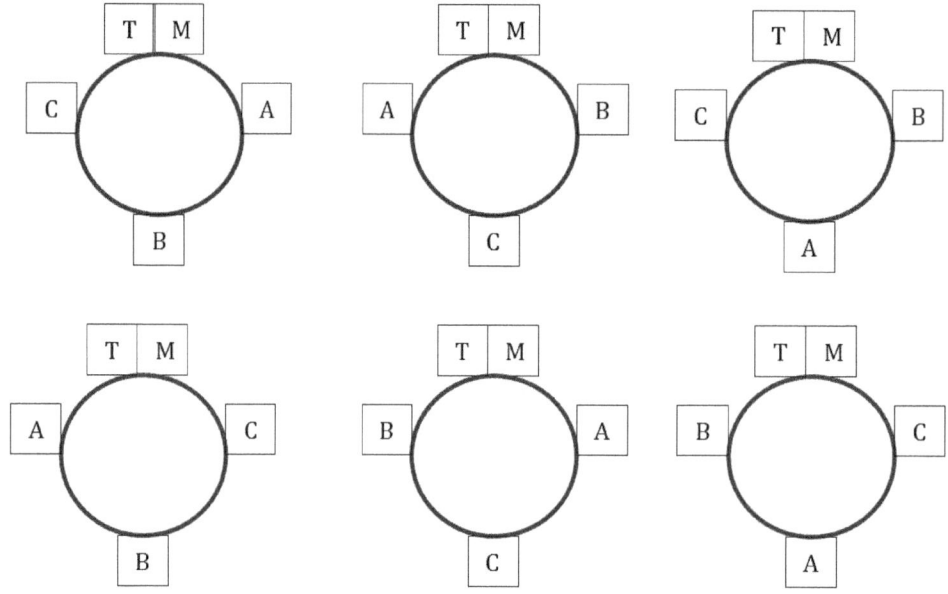

There are six ways to arrange four units around a circle as shown. Any other arrangement would be a rotation in which the elements are in the same order and would therefore not be a unique arrangement. Of course, Mac and Tasha are not actually a single unit. They would still be sitting beside each other if they were to trade seats, so there are 12 arrangements in which the two are seated next to one another. In all other arrangements of the five family members, they are separated. Therefore, to find the number of arrangements in which Tasha and Mac are *not* sitting together, subtract 12 from the possible arrangement of five units around a circle. There are $(n - 1)!$ ways to arrange n units around a circle for $n > 1$. So, $(5 - 1)! - 12 = 24 - 12 = 12$.

11. D: The numbers in this sequence progress according to a pattern. Each progressing number can be expressed by the equation $x + 2 = n$, where x is the difference between the previous two numbers and n is the number added to the previous number, to yield the progressing number. For instance, the difference in 24 and 16 is 8. By adding 2 to 8, you know that you must add 10 to 24 in order to yield 34. In the next part of the sequence, $x = 10$ and $n = 12$. $34 + 12 = 46$, the next number in the sequence. Therefore, by following this pattern, you would add 16 to 60, which results in 76.

12. D: The point $(5, -5)$ lies on the line segment that has a slope of –2 and passes through $(3, -1)$. If $(5, -5)$ is one of the endpoints of the line segment, then the other would be $(1,3)$.

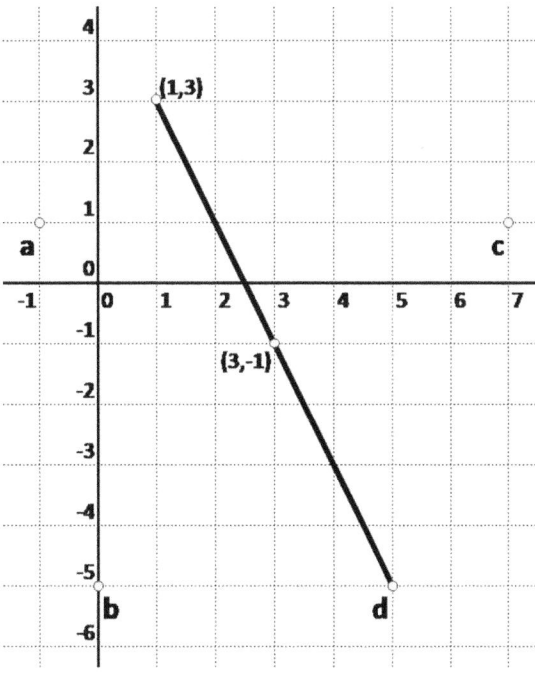

13. B: Since the figures are similar, the following proportion may be written and solved for x.

$$\frac{6}{4} = \frac{8}{x}$$
$$6x = 4 \times 8$$
$$6x = 32$$
$$x = \frac{32}{6} = 5\frac{2}{6} = 5\frac{1}{3}$$

Therefore, the measure of x is $5\frac{1}{3}$ in.

14. C: If l and w represent the length and width of the enclosed area, its perimeter is equal to $2l + 2w$; since the fence is positioned x feet from the lot's edges on each side, the perimeter of the lot is $2(l + 2x) + 2(w + 2x)$. Since the amount of money saved by fencing the smaller area is $432, and since the fencing material costs $12 per linear foot, 36 fewer feet of material are used to fence around the playground than would have been used to fence around the lot. This can be expressed as the following equation.

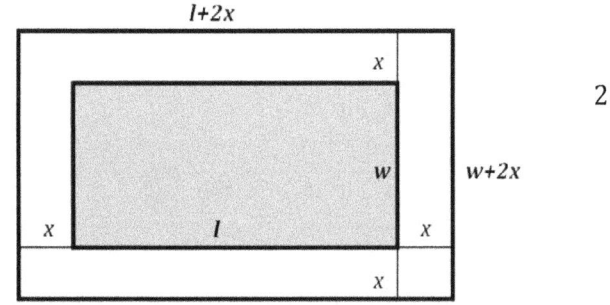

$$2(l + 2x) + 2(w + 2x) - (2l + 2w) = 36$$
$$2l + 4x + 2w + 4x - 2l - 2w = 36$$
$$8x = 36$$
$$x = 4.5 \text{ ft}$$

The difference in the area of the lot and the enclosed space is 141 yd², which is the same as 1,269 ft². So, $(l + 2x)(w + 2x) - lw = 1{,}269$. Substituting 4.5 for x, we get the following equation that we can solve for $l + w$.

$$(l + 9)(w + 9) - lw = 1{,}269$$
$$lw + 9l + 9w + 81 - lw = 1{,}269$$
$$9l + 9w = 1{,}188$$
$$9(l + w) = 1{,}188$$
$$l + w = 132 \text{ ft}$$

Therefore, the perimeter of the enclosed space, $2(l + w)$, is $2(132) = 264$ ft. The cost of 264 ft of fencing is $264 \times \$12 = \$3{,}168$.

15. D: In scientific notation, only one digit should remain to the left of the decimal. In the original number, the decimal point is four places to the right of the first digit, 3. Therefore, $30{,}490 = 3.049 \times 10^4$ is the correct answer. Choice C, 30.490×10^3 is equal to the correct value, but it incorrectly places two digits to the left of the decimal point.

16. B: Rate in miles per hour can be expressed as, $\text{mph} = \frac{\text{distance in miles}}{\text{time in hours}}$. So, Zeke's driving speed on the way to Atlanta and home from Atlanta in mph can be expressed as $\frac{d}{3}$ and $\frac{d}{2}$, respectively, where d is the distance between Zeke's house and his destination. Since Zeke drove 20 mph faster on his way home, (speed home) − (speed to store) = 20. Substitute Zeke's speeds and solve for d.

$$\frac{d}{2} - \frac{d}{3} = 20$$

$$6\left(\frac{d}{2} - \frac{d}{3} = 20\right)$$
$$3d - 2d = 120$$
$$d = 120$$

Since the distance between Zeke's house and the store in Atlanta is 120 miles, Zeke drove a total distance of 240 miles in five hours. Therefore, his average speed was $\frac{240 \text{ miles}}{5 \text{ hours}} = 48$ mph.

17. D: The perimeter of the triangle is equal to the sum of the side lengths. The length of the longer diagonal side may be represented as $d = \sqrt{(4-1)^2 + (5-2)^2}$, which simplifies to $d = \sqrt{18}$. The length of the shorter diagonal side may be represented as $d = \sqrt{(6-4)^2 + (2-5)^2}$, which simplifies to $d = \sqrt{13}$. The base length is 5 units. Thus, the perimeter is equal to $5 + \sqrt{18} + \sqrt{13}$, which is approximately 12.85 units. Since each unit represents 5 miles, the total distance she will have walked is equal to the product of 12.85 and 5, or approximately 64 miles.

18. B: The perimeter is equal to the sum of the lengths of the two bases, 2 and 6 units, and the diagonal distances of the other two sides. Using the distance formula, each side length may be represented as $d = \sqrt{20} = 2\sqrt{5}$. Thus, the sum of the two sides is equal to $2\sqrt{20}$, or $4\sqrt{5}$. The whole perimeter is equal to $8 + 4\sqrt{5}$.

19. C: The original triangle was reflected across the x-axis. When reflecting across the x-axis, the x-values of each point remain the same, but the y-values of the points will be opposites.

$$(1,4) \rightarrow (1,-4) \quad (5,4) \rightarrow (5,-4) \quad (3,8) \rightarrow (3,-8)$$

20. B: Since Mr. Mancelli has eight candy bars, he can make at most eight identical bags, each containing a single candy bar and a single package of gum; in this case, however, he will have four packages of gum remaining. To determine the greatest number of prize bags he can make so that no candy bars or packages of gum remain, he needs to find the largest number of groups that both 8 and 12 can be split into. In other words, he must find the greatest common divisor (or greatest common factor) of 8 and 12. The factors of 8 are 1, 2, 4, and 8. The factors of 12 are 1, 2, 3, 4, 6, and 12. The greatest common divisor of 8 and 12 is 4. He can make four prize bags, each of which contains two candy bars and three packages of gum. Therefore, the correct choice is B.

How to Overcome Test Anxiety

Just the thought of taking a test is enough to make most people a little nervous. A test is an important event that can have a long-term impact on your future, so it's important to take it seriously and it's natural to feel anxious about performing well. But just because anxiety is normal, that doesn't mean that it's helpful in test taking, or that you should simply accept it as part of your life. Anxiety can have a variety of effects. These effects can be mild, like making you feel slightly nervous, or severe, like blocking your ability to focus or remember even a simple detail.

If you experience test anxiety—whether severe or mild—it's important to know how to beat it. To discover this, first you need to understand what causes test anxiety.

Causes of Test Anxiety

While we often think of anxiety as an uncontrollable emotional state, it can actually be caused by simple, practical things. One of the most common causes of test anxiety is that a person does not feel adequately prepared for their test. This feeling can be the result of many different issues such as poor study habits or lack of organization, but the most common culprit is time management. Starting to study too late, failing to organize your study time to cover all of the material, or being distracted while you study will mean that you're not well prepared for the test. This may lead to cramming the night before, which will cause you to be physically and mentally exhausted for the test. Poor time management also contributes to feelings of stress, fear, and hopelessness as you realize you are not well prepared but don't know what to do about it.

Other times, test anxiety is not related to your preparation for the test but comes from unresolved fear. This may be a past failure on a test, or poor performance on tests in general. It may come from comparing yourself to others who seem to be performing better or from the stress of living up to expectations. Anxiety may be driven by fears of the future—how failure on this test would affect your educational and career goals. These fears are often completely irrational, but they can still negatively impact your test performance.

Elements of Test Anxiety

As mentioned earlier, test anxiety is considered to be an emotional state, but it has physical and mental components as well. Sometimes you may not even realize that you are suffering from test anxiety until you notice the physical symptoms. These can include trembling hands, rapid heartbeat, sweating, nausea, and tense muscles. Extreme anxiety may lead to fainting or vomiting. Obviously, any of these symptoms can have a negative impact on testing. It is important to recognize them as soon as they begin to occur so that you can address the problem before it damages your performance.

The mental components of test anxiety include trouble focusing and inability to remember learned information. During a test, your mind is on high alert, which can help you recall information and stay focused for an extended period of time. However, anxiety interferes with your mind's natural processes, causing you to blank out, even on the questions you know well. The strain of testing during anxiety makes it difficult to stay focused, especially on a test that may take several hours. Extreme anxiety can take a huge mental toll, making it difficult not only to recall test information but even to understand the test questions or pull your thoughts together.

Effects of Test Anxiety

Test anxiety is like a disease—if left untreated, it will get progressively worse. Anxiety leads to poor performance, and this reinforces the feelings of fear and failure, which in turn lead to poor performances on subsequent tests. It can grow from a mild nervousness to a crippling condition. If allowed to progress, test anxiety can have a big impact on your schooling, and consequently on your future.

Test anxiety can spread to other parts of your life. Anxiety on tests can become anxiety in any stressful situation, and blanking on a test can turn into panicking in a job situation. But fortunately, you don't have to let anxiety rule your testing and determine your grades. There are a number of relatively simple steps you can take to move past anxiety and function normally on a test and in the rest of life.

Physical Steps for Beating Test Anxiety

While test anxiety is a serious problem, the good news is that it can be overcome. It doesn't have to control your ability to think and remember information. While it may take time, you can begin taking steps today to beat anxiety.

Just as your first hint that you may be struggling with anxiety comes from the physical symptoms, the first step to treating it is also physical. Rest is crucial for having a clear, strong mind. If you are tired, it is much easier to give in to anxiety. But if you establish good sleep habits, your body and mind will be ready to perform optimally, without the strain of exhaustion. Additionally, sleeping well helps you to retain information better, so you're more likely to recall the answers when you see the test questions.

Getting good sleep means more than going to bed on time. It's important to allow your brain time to relax. Take study breaks from time to time so it doesn't get overworked, and don't study right before bed. Take time to rest your mind before trying to rest your body, or you may find it difficult to fall asleep.

Along with sleep, other aspects of physical health are important in preparing for a test. Good nutrition is vital for good brain function. Sugary foods and drinks may give a burst of energy but this burst is followed by a crash, both physically and emotionally. Instead, fuel your body with protein and vitamin-rich foods.

Also, drink plenty of water. Dehydration can lead to headaches and exhaustion, especially if your brain is already under stress from the rigors of the test. Particularly if your test is a long one, drink water during the breaks. And if possible, take an energy-boosting snack to eat between sections.

Along with sleep and diet, a third important part of physical health is exercise. Maintaining a steady workout schedule is helpful, but even taking 5-minute study breaks to walk can help get your blood pumping faster and clear your head. Exercise also releases endorphins, which contribute to a positive feeling and can help combat test anxiety.

When you nurture your physical health, you are also contributing to your mental health. If your body is healthy, your mind is much more likely to be healthy as well. So take time to rest, nourish your body with healthy food and water, and get moving as much as possible. Taking these physical steps will make you stronger and more able to take the mental steps necessary to overcome test anxiety.

Mental Steps for Beating Test Anxiety

Working on the mental side of test anxiety can be more challenging, but as with the physical side, there are clear steps you can take to overcome it. As mentioned earlier, test anxiety often stems from lack of preparation, so the obvious solution is to prepare for the test. Effective studying may be the most important weapon you have for beating test anxiety, but you can and should employ several other mental tools to combat fear.

First, boost your confidence by reminding yourself of past success—tests or projects that you aced. If you're putting as much effort into preparing for this test as you did for those, there's no reason you should expect to fail here. Work hard to prepare; then trust your preparation.

Second, surround yourself with encouraging people. It can be helpful to find a study group, but be sure that the people you're around will encourage a positive attitude. If you spend time with others who are anxious or cynical, this will only contribute to your own anxiety. Look for others who are motivated to study hard from a desire to succeed, not from a fear of failure.

Third, reward yourself. A test is physically and mentally tiring, even without anxiety, and it can be helpful to have something to look forward to. Plan an activity following the test, regardless of the outcome, such as going to a movie or getting ice cream.

When you are taking the test, if you find yourself beginning to feel anxious, remind yourself that you know the material. Visualize successfully completing the test. Then take a few deep, relaxing breaths and return to it. Work through the questions carefully but with confidence, knowing that you are capable of succeeding.

Developing a healthy mental approach to test taking will also aid in other areas of life. Test anxiety affects more than just the actual test—it can be damaging to your mental health and even contribute to depression. It's important to beat test anxiety before it becomes a problem for more than testing.

Study Strategy

Being prepared for the test is necessary to combat anxiety, but what does being prepared look like? You may study for hours on end and still not feel prepared. What you need is a strategy for test prep. The next few pages outline our recommended steps to help you plan out and conquer the challenge of preparation.

STEP 1: SCOPE OUT THE TEST

Learn everything you can about the format (multiple choice, essay, etc.) and what will be on the test. Gather any study materials, course outlines, or sample exams that may be available. Not only will this help you to prepare, but knowing what to expect can help to alleviate test anxiety.

STEP 2: MAP OUT THE MATERIAL

Look through the textbook or study guide and make note of how many chapters or sections it has. Then divide these over the time you have. For example, if a book has 15 chapters and you have five days to study, you need to cover three chapters each day. Even better, if you have the time, leave an extra day at the end for overall review after you have gone through the material in depth.

If time is limited, you may need to prioritize the material. Look through it and make note of which sections you think you already have a good grasp on, and which need review. While you are studying, skim quickly through the familiar sections and take more time on the challenging parts.

Write out your plan so you don't get lost as you go. Having a written plan also helps you feel more in control of the study, so anxiety is less likely to arise from feeling overwhelmed at the amount to cover.

STEP 3: GATHER YOUR TOOLS

Decide what study method works best for you. Do you prefer to highlight in the book as you study and then go back over the highlighted portions? Or do you type out notes of the important information? Or is it helpful to make flashcards that you can carry with you? Assemble the pens, index cards, highlighters, post-it notes, and any other materials you may need so you won't be distracted by getting up to find things while you study.

If you're having a hard time retaining the information or organizing your notes, experiment with different methods. For example, try color-coding by subject with colored pens, highlighters, or post-it notes. If you learn better by hearing, try recording yourself reading your notes so you can listen while in the car, working out, or simply sitting at your desk. Ask a friend to quiz you from your flashcards, or try teaching someone the material to solidify it in your mind.

STEP 4: CREATE YOUR ENVIRONMENT

It's important to avoid distractions while you study. This includes both the obvious distractions like visitors and the subtle distractions like an uncomfortable chair (or a too-comfortable couch that makes you want to fall asleep). Set up the best study environment possible: good lighting and a comfortable work area. If background music helps you focus, you may want to turn it on, but otherwise keep the room quiet. If you are using a computer to take notes, be sure you don't have any other windows open, especially applications like social media, games, or anything else that could distract you. Silence your phone and turn off notifications. Be sure to keep water close by so you stay hydrated while you study (but avoid unhealthy drinks and snacks).

Also, take into account the best time of day to study. Are you freshest first thing in the morning? Try to set aside some time then to work through the material. Is your mind clearer in the afternoon or evening? Schedule your study session then. Another method is to study at the same time of day that you will take the test, so that your brain gets used to working on the material at that time and will be ready to focus at test time.

STEP 5: STUDY!

Once you have done all the study preparation, it's time to settle into the actual studying. Sit down, take a few moments to settle your mind so you can focus, and begin to follow your study plan. Don't give in to distractions or let yourself procrastinate. This is your time to prepare so you'll be ready to fearlessly approach the test. Make the most of the time and stay focused.

Of course, you don't want to burn out. If you study too long you may find that you're not retaining the information very well. Take regular study breaks. For example, taking five minutes out of every hour to walk briskly, breathing deeply and swinging your arms, can help your mind stay fresh.

As you get to the end of each chapter or section, it's a good idea to do a quick review. Remind yourself of what you learned and work on any difficult parts. When you feel that you've mastered the material, move on to the next part. At the end of your study session, briefly skim through your notes again.

But while review is helpful, cramming last minute is NOT. If at all possible, work ahead so that you won't need to fit all your study into the last day. Cramming overloads your brain with more information than it can process and retain, and your tired mind may struggle to recall even previously learned information when it is overwhelmed with last-minute study. Also, the urgent nature of cramming and the stress placed on your brain contribute to anxiety. You'll be more likely to go to the test feeling unprepared and having trouble thinking clearly.

So don't cram, and don't stay up late before the test, even just to review your notes at a leisurely pace. Your brain needs rest more than it needs to go over the information again. In fact, plan to finish your studies by noon or early afternoon the day before the test. Give your brain the rest of the day to relax or focus on other things, and get a good night's sleep. Then you will be fresh for the test and better able to recall what you've studied.

STEP 6: TAKE A PRACTICE TEST

Many courses offer sample tests, either online or in the study materials. This is an excellent resource to check whether you have mastered the material, as well as to prepare for the test format and environment.

Check the test format ahead of time: the number of questions, the type (multiple choice, free response, etc.), and the time limit. Then create a plan for working through them. For example, if you have 30 minutes to take a 60-question test, your limit is 30 seconds per question. Spend less time on the questions you know well so that you can take more time on the difficult ones.

If you have time to take several practice tests, take the first one open book, with no time limit. Work through the questions at your own pace and make sure you fully understand them. Gradually work up to taking a test under test conditions: sit at a desk with all study materials put away and set a timer. Pace yourself to make sure you finish the test with time to spare and go back to check your answers if you have time.

After each test, check your answers. On the questions you missed, be sure you understand why you missed them. Did you misread the question (tests can use tricky wording)? Did you forget the information? Or was it something you hadn't learned? Go back and study any shaky areas that the practice tests reveal.

Taking these tests not only helps with your grade, but also aids in combating test anxiety. If you're already used to the test conditions, you're less likely to worry about it, and working through tests until you're scoring well gives you a confidence boost. Go through the practice tests until you feel comfortable, and then you can go into the test knowing that you're ready for it.

Test Tips

On test day, you should be confident, knowing that you've prepared well and are ready to answer the questions. But aside from preparation, there are several test day strategies you can employ to maximize your performance.

First, as stated before, get a good night's sleep the night before the test (and for several nights before that, if possible). Go into the test with a fresh, alert mind rather than staying up late to study.

Try not to change too much about your normal routine on the day of the test. It's important to eat a nutritious breakfast, but if you normally don't eat breakfast at all, consider eating just a protein bar. If you're a coffee drinker, go ahead and have your normal coffee. Just make sure you time it so that the caffeine doesn't wear off right in the middle of your test. Avoid sugary beverages, and drink enough water to stay hydrated but not so much that you need a restroom break 10 minutes into the test. If your test isn't first thing in the morning, consider going for a walk or doing a light workout before the test to get your blood flowing.

Allow yourself enough time to get ready, and leave for the test with plenty of time to spare so you won't have the anxiety of scrambling to arrive in time. Another reason to be early is to select a good seat. It's helpful to sit away from doors and windows, which can be distracting. Find a good seat, get out your supplies, and settle your mind before the test begins.

When the test begins, start by going over the instructions carefully, even if you already know what to expect. Make sure you avoid any careless mistakes by following the directions.

Then begin working through the questions, pacing yourself as you've practiced. If you're not sure on an answer, don't spend too much time on it, and don't let it shake your confidence. Either skip it and come back later, or eliminate as many wrong answers as possible and guess among the remaining ones. Don't dwell on these questions as you continue—put them out of your mind and focus on what lies ahead.

Be sure to read all of the answer choices, even if you're sure the first one is the right answer. Sometimes you'll find a better one if you keep reading. But don't second-guess yourself if you do immediately know the answer. Your gut instinct is usually right. Don't let test anxiety rob you of the information you know.

If you have time at the end of the test (and if the test format allows), go back and review your answers. Be cautious about changing any, since your first instinct tends to be correct, but make sure you didn't misread any of the questions or accidentally mark the wrong answer choice. Look over any you skipped and make an educated guess.

At the end, leave the test feeling confident. You've done your best, so don't waste time worrying about your performance or wishing you could change anything. Instead, celebrate the successful completion of this test. And finally, use this test to learn how to deal with anxiety even better next time.

> **Review Video: Test Anxiety**
> Visit mometrix.com/academy and enter code: 100340

Important Qualification

Not all anxiety is created equal. If your test anxiety is causing major issues in your life beyond the classroom or testing center, or if you are experiencing troubling physical symptoms related to your anxiety, it may be a sign of a serious physiological or psychological condition. If this sounds like your situation, we strongly encourage you to seek professional help.

Online Resources

Due to our efforts to try to keep this book to a manageable length, we've created a link that will give you access to all of your online resources:

mometrix.com/resources719/tsimath-27346

www.ingramcontent.com/pod-product-compliance
Lightning Source LLC
Chambersburg PA
CBHW060512300426
44112CB00017B/2633